Protecting Your Wealth
in Good Times and Bad

Also by Richard A. Ferri
All About Index Funds (McGraw-Hill, 2002)

Protecting Your Wealth
in Good Times and Bad

Richard A. Ferri

McGraw-Hill

New York Chicago San Francisco Lisbon London
Madrid Mexico City Milan New Delhi San Juan
Seoul Singapore Sydney Toronto

This publication is designed to provide accurate and authoritative information in regard to the subject matter covered. It is sold with the understanding that neither the author nor the publisher is engaged in rendering legal, accounting, or other professional service. If legal advice or other expert assistance is required, the services of a competent professional person should be sought.
        —*From a Declaration of Principles jointly adopted by a Committee of the American Bar Association and a Committee of Publishers*

McGraw-Hill books are available at special quantity discounts to use as premiums and sales promotions, or for use in corporate training programs. For more information, please write to the Director of Special Sales, McGraw-Hill, 2 Penn Plaza, New York, NY 10128. Or contact your local bookstore.

 This book is printed on recycled, acid-free paper containing a minimum of 50% recycled de-inked fiber.

Contents

Contents

Preface

*P*ROTECTING YOUR WEALTH IN GOOD TIMES AND BAD is an essential guidebook to a secure saving and investing strategy. Step by step, this book walks you through the process of developing and implementing a sound lifelong plan to grow and protect your hard-earned assets. Understanding how the accumulation and distribution of money will take place during the course of your life is critical to forming a financial plan. Equally as important is the use of proper investing principles during all stages of wealth accumulation and throughout retirement. This process can be applied from the first day you start your first full-time job, until late in retirement, when family members may be called upon to assist you in financial matters. The very essence of this book is to help you build and maintain wealth so you can enjoy your Golden Years without financial worry.

Whether you are a doctor, business professional, skilled worker, or someplace in between, *Protecting Your Wealth in Good Times and Bad* will teach you how to develop and maintain a savings and investment plan that is easy to understand, low risk, low cost, and practical. I suggest reading this book in its entirety, and then creating a simple strategy based on the concepts you have learned.

Now More than Ever

The research for *Protecting Your Wealth in Good Times and Bad* was started several years ago, but the book could only be published now. As data was being compiled in the mid-1990s, we were in a major bull market. At the time, few people thought about reducing the risk in their portfolios. In fact, it was in vogue to take more risk. The stock market was booming and the media went crazy over the number of 20-something-year-old technology wizards who were becoming billionaires overnight. The typical investor wanted a piece of the action and people felt secure getting deeper into the market despite rising prices. It was common to hear young people talk about getting the "money thing" over with by the time they were 40 years old, so they could enjoy the rest of their life without the burden of mandatory labor. On the same note, a large group of middle-aged pre-retirees increased their exposure to stocks in an effort to push their savings "over the hump" and get out of the rat race a couple of years early.

It is amazing how a couple of bad years can change things. A bear market started in March of 2000 and has turned into the worst downturn since the Great Depression of 1929 to 1932. By the fall of 2002, the S&P 500 was off by more than 40% from its high and the tech-heavy NASDAQ market had fallen more than 80%. The swift action wiped the smiles off the faces of countless would-be 40-year-old millionaires and placed an unprecedented number of pre-retirees and retirees in a financial bind. For many, gone were the dreams of a secure retirement. Now a large number of Americans faced the real possibility of working until they are no longer able to work and many current retirees are being forced to cut back on their spending or go back to work.

Last year, horror stories about losing wealth were becoming a favorite of the mass media—"55-Year-Old Enron Employee Loses Everything," "More Retirees on Food Stamps Due to Market Woes," and so on. Granted, those stories are extreme, but they are real and they hint at retirement problems that are just beginning to unfold in America. Social Security benefits have been cut twice in the last 30 years and will be cut again in the future. In addition, the number of workers eligible for employer-funded retirement plans has dwindled as employers shift the burden of retirement savings to their employees. In the meantime, individuals are not accumulating enough money outside of work-related savings to make up the shortfall. Less government benefits, less employer benefits, and less personal savings all add up to a lower standard of living in retirement.

The shortfall in retirement funds is likely to get worse in the coming years as more baby boomers reach age 60. The worker-to-retiree ratio is starting to fall and the government cannot raise taxes on fewer workers to pay for more retirees. Part-time work may be one answer, but Wal-Mart cannot afford to hire 30 million store greeters and McDonald's can hire only a limited number of people to wipe tables. Unless there is vast improvement in the way we save and invest for retirement, large numbers of future retirees will wither away in their Golden Years mopping floors under the Golden Arches.

The idea of having to work in retirement is not a vision that people embrace. Nevertheless, it is clear that most retirees will have to do some type of work to make ends meet. Ironically, the Social Security system discourages retirees from working part-time by taxing more of their benefits. This is especially so for early retirees. If you retire at age 62, file to collect Social Security, and then take a part-time job working 20 hours per week for $15 per hour, the government will cut your Social Security benefit by about $5,000 per year—and then tax a portion of the remaining benefit as ordinary income. It makes no sense for the government to discourage productive retirees from working, but that is the way our Social Security system operates.

Protect Your Wealth!

America needs a solution. *Protecting Your Wealth in Good Times and Bad* is one step in the right direction. It is the goal of this book to educate people on how to accumulate more wealth through saving and investing. Hopefully, if you follow the advice in this book, your retirement woes will be greatly reduced.

In addition, *Protecting Your Wealth in Good Times and Bad* touches on a wide range of topics, including tax issues, home ownership, estate planning, withdrawal rates in retirement, health and life insurance, and Social Security. Not all of these issues are discussed in detail, so you will need to do more research and read many more books. If you are an experienced retiree, the material in this book will help prepare your family to make financial decisions on your behalf when you are no longer able to.

Protecting Your Wealth in Good Times and Bad is a combination of book research and years of personal experience helping and talking with concerned people every day about these issues. To make the material relevant to all readers, this book differentiates people into four categories: Early Savers, Midlife Accumulators, Pre-Retirees, and Retirees, and Experienced Retirees. The chapter for last category, Experienced Retirees, is mixed with helpful information for older individuals and for their adult children who are acting on their behalf.

All the people I meet and talk with professionally are different, but their financial needs are essentially the same. Their first concern is accumulating enough wealth so that the income generated during retirement will cover all expenses. The second concern has to do with not outliving their money. The third concern is staying healthy enough to enjoy it. While I cannot do anything about the third concern, the ideas of this book will help you manage your wealth so that you can take care of the first two. In pursuit of these objectives, the book is divided into three parts.

Part One: Saving, Investing, and the Mistakes We Make (Chapters 1-6)

The first part of the wealth accumulation puzzle is about saving. As a nation, we do not save enough. Despite numerous tax-advantaged retirement savings accounts set up by Congress, only about 50% of us are participating to any degree. Perhaps we have a false sense of security because we believe government programs are going to take care of us in our old age. Or perhaps a winning lottery ticket is in everyone's future. From a practical standpoint, a regular savings program is essential to building a nest egg—and the earlier you start to save, the better off you will be.

The second piece of the secure retirement puzzle is investing the money we save. Unfortunately, as a nation, we are not doing a good job investing our personal wealth. When investing money, people tend to make three basic mistakes. First, we think there are ways to predict when to buy and when to sell. The recent bull-and-bear market has proven this idea to be fallacy. The markets look the best and attract the most suitors at the time they are the most dangerous. The second mistake we make is chasing hot investment fads. People tend to go for glitzy and invest where the returns have recently been high. If an investment has already made a lot of money, it is usually time to sell, not to buy. Finally, people tend to pay much too much for advice, especially since most advice is mediocre at best. There are high-cost ways to invest and low-cost ways. Every dollar you save in commissions and fees expenses goes right to your bottom line.

Are people to blame for these and other investment mistakes? Yes and no. Many bad ideas originate from mediocre investment advisors. There are several reasons why bad advice has proliferated on Wall Street. One is the lack of training, which is a chronic problem with most stockbrokers and financial advisors. Most commission-oriented financial firms do a poor job of educating their salespeople about the basics of investment management, and these brokers have little encouragement or incentive from their firms to educate themselves. The second reason for all the mediocre advice coming out of financial advisors is the large number of conflicts of interest that exist in the industry. For example, stockbrokers are paid larger fees to recommend high-commission mutual funds over low-cost substitutes, many financial planners steer clients into costly insurance products that they may not need, and financial publications get paid large advertising dollars to write articles expounding the merits of second-rate investment products. In the financial services industry, it is very hard to discern how much pushback advisors get for recommending one strategy over another. One of the best ways to improve your investment performance is by being very selective about where you get your advice and knowing how your advisor is getting paid and how much.

Part Two: Building Blocks to Success (Chapters 7-12)

Part Two covers the fundamentals of accumulating wealth, focusing on how to save and invest. Before investing your savings, you must decide where to invest. Perhaps you work for an employer that has a 401(k) or similar savings plan. This will allow you to automatically save and invest pre-tax. Ideally, your employer may have a match, meaning they will put in a certain amount of money for every $1 that you invest, up to a maximum amount. A match is wonderful because it is free money. Other types of savings plans do not include an employer match, but the tax benefits are just as generous.

After a savings account has been funded, then you need to make the investment selection. Typically, the investment choices include several stock and bond mutual funds. The selection process can be intimidating and confusing, but the information in Part Two covers the basics. The most important feature to look for when selecting a stock or bond mutual fund is a low fee. That is why the book is a big advocate of *index mutual funds*. These market-matching investments have the lowest fees in the fund industry. In addition to stocks and bonds, other retirement investments are covered in a chapter discussing homes, real estate, small business, and stock compensation.

Once you decide which investments have potential, you need to put a portfolio together based on the concept of *asset allocation*. There is an entire chapter covering asset allocation and how it works. Finally, you will want to know what your expected return on your new portfolio should be. This is never an easy question to answer, but I take a stab at it in the chapter on forecasting market returns.

Part Three: A Lifelong Saving and Investing Guide (Chapters 13-16)

Saving and investing during your lifetime can be separated into four distinct phases of life. Each one of these four phases has a chapter devoted to it in Part Three. The four phases are Early Savers, Midlife Accumulators, Pre-Retirees and Retirees, and Experienced Retirees.

Early Savers are young people who are just getting established in their careers and in their lives. Their vision of retirement is vague at best, so the tools used to assist them in saving and investing must be very flexible. A consistent savings program is the key in the Early Saver years.

Midlife Accumulators are well into their careers and their lifestyles. In addition to saving for retirement, they are buying braces for their children, larger homes, and second and third automobiles and trying to put a little away for a child's education. The bills are piling up, but savings cannot be neglected. Retirement plans begin to form at this stage, which means greater detail can be added to the long-term financial plan. The tools used in this phase are more powerful and more precise than in the Early Saver years.

Pre-retirement starts about five years prior to calling it quits. At this point, detailed financial plans are needed to map out expected income and outflows during retirement. This part of the book explains how to adjust a portfolio to create the income needed to replace a missing paycheck. It is also a time of practicing *risk avoidance* in a portfolio, which means reducing the amount of equity in retirement accounts as soon as possible. Once in retirement, retirees will deal with issues involving Social Security benefits, Medicare, Medigap insurance, the possible sale of a home, etc. This chapter is enlightening for those not yet retired, but thinking about it.

The last chapter of *Protecting Your Wealth in Good Times and Bad* is very special because it deals with Experienced Retirees. The issues discussed in this chapter concern getting an estate in order and asking an adult child for help managing affairs. Elderly retirees need assistance with their money matters and it is beneficial to select the right person to assist well in advance. Typically, that person is a son or daughter, but it can also be a relative or professional trustee. *Protect Your Wealth* offers an investment guide for these trustees to ensure the investment portfolios continue to be handled properly and to ensure the estate is ready to pass to the next generation.

Two Ways to Read This Book

This is my third book on personal financial management and, in my opinion, it is my most important contribution so far to the field. Naturally, I would like you to read this entire book from cover to cover. That way you get the complete message. But, I am not naive. About 90% of readers will get less than halfway through the book and then put it on the shelf with their other dozen or so half-read investment books.

If you are in the 10% who will read the book through, then start with Part I and read through to Part III. However, if you one of the 90% who will get halfway through the book, start reading Part Three first and then use Parts One and Two as reference material. Just to make sure this message comes across clear, here it is again:

If you have time to read only part of this book, read Part Three.

While reading this book, please remember two important points. First, there is no perfect plan for saving and investing. This book is intended as a guide so that you can discover for yourself the best plan of action that fits your needs. A good plan put into action is better than a perfect plan that is never developed. Action speaks louder than words. Second, *Protecting Your Wealth in Good Times and Bad* is one book among several that you should read about managing your money. It is one course in a lifelong self-study program where the diploma is financial security. Appendix C has a partial list of other great books that I encourage you to read, understand, and incorporate in your personal plan of action.

Acknowledgments

Hundreds of people directly and indirectly helped with this book. I would first like to thank all of my fine clients, who will remain nameless, for giving me the priceless insight into their lives that was needed to put experience onto paper. In addition, thank-you to all the dedicated people who manage and monitor the Morningstar conversation boards, especially Taylor, Mel, Adrian, Jared, Alex, and the other fine folks who are regulars on the Vanguard Diehards site, www.diehards.org.

In addition, thanks to John Bogle, for reviewing the manuscript and for being a role model by tirelessly promoting business ethics in an industry that has trouble differentiating between right and wrong. Thanks to Larry Swedroe, Bill Bernstein, Michael LeBoeuf, and Bill Schultheis, whose ideas and writings always impress and inspire. Karen Norman, CPA, a member of The Garrett Planning Network, provided expertise on several financial planning issues. Thank you, Catherine Dassopoulos of McGraw-Hill, for pushing the deadline back three times. Thanks to Dennis and Barb of Greaney Photography, Inc. for their excellent work. Many thanks to my business partner, Scott Salaske, for his tireless proofreading efforts. Finally, a special thanks to my wife, Daria, for her unending support and for not being too upset when the power cord to my laptop melted the cigarette lighter in our new car. Well, we didn't need that lighter anyway.

Dedication
To my loving wife. Daria, for turning dreams into realities.

Part One

Saving, Investing, and the Mistakes We Make

Chapter 1

A National
Savings Dilemma

*One day in 1984 my wife, Claudia, told me, "The government gets
a third and we can spend a third, but we need to save a third."
That's the smartest advice anyone ever gave me. We're rich now.*
—Lee Trevino, golf great

RETIREMENT. Most people who are in it seem to enjoy it and
those who are not think about it often. If you ask a working person
what separates him or her from retirement, the first thing that
comes to mind is *money*—or rather the lack of it. Technically, people
can retire when they have accumulated enough sources of
income from pensions, investments, and eventually Social
Security so they do not have to work any longer. Financial security
means having enough income to pay the household bills, travel,
buy gifts, take care of medical concerns, and enjoy the rest of
your life without running out of money.

Retirement becomes an option when you attain financial security.
That's what this book is all about. It lays the ground rules for
accumulating and investing money prior to retirement and explains
how to conserve and distribute your wealth during your retirement

years. The main objective in *Protecting Your Wealth in Good Times and Bad* is to reach a point in life when you work only if you want to and, if you stop working, when you do not fear outliving your money.

Retirees are living longer and healthier, traveling more, enjoy better housing, better automobiles, better communications, and generally spending more money than prior generations. As life expectancy extends and lifestyles rise, future retirees will need more income and will rely more on their personal savings for that income than past generations. Traditional sources of retirement income— Social Security and employer pension plans—are on the decline. As a result, the nest egg people accumulate during their working years will dictate their quality of life in retirement. That is why it is important for you to protect your wealth from simple, yet costly mistakes. Every penny counts. Through proper planning, prudence, and perseverance, you can accumulate the wealth you need to enjoy your Golden Years.

The State of Retirement Savings

A secure retirement means having enough sources of income to maintain your standard of living after a regular paycheck stops. Unfortunately, traditional sources of retirement income from an employer pension and Social Security have diminished and will continue to fall in the future. At the same time the cost of retirement will continue to rise. This will be a dilemma for many people. Neither employers nor the government are as generous as they used to be. Most employers are cutting back benefits for retirees. The Social Security system will not survive in its current form when 50 million baby boomers retire over the next 25 years.

Several large companies have already dropped employer-funded defined benefit pension plans (DB plans) in favor of employee-funded 401(k) and other types of defined contribution plans (DC plans). (See Figure 1-1 for details.) By shifting the responsibility for retirement savings to an employee-funded plan, employers can save a significant amount of money and reduce their incredibly large regulatory burden. Several large employers continue to fund retirement plans, but have shifted to the more liberal cash balance plans, in

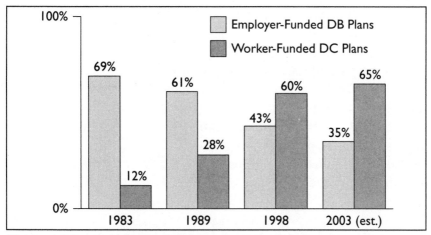

Figure 1-1. Percent of households in a company plan
Source: Study by Edward Wolff, New York University, from *Federal Reserve Survey of Consumer Finances*

which retirement benefits vary with market conditions and there is no liability on the employer to make up the difference. In addition to changes at large firms, hundreds of thousands of small businesses offer no retirement plan at all to their employees. Consequently, millions of workers must set up their own individual retirement accounts and fund them on a regular basis.

The reduction in the number of employer-funded DB plans is occurring for several reasons. First, since a DB plan guarantees monthly retirement checks for all eligible employees and since the rate of return on the investments in a pension account is uncertain, the plan can become very expensive to the company in the years ahead if there is not enough money in the fund to pay benefits. Second, DB plans are expensive to administer and maintain. The record-keeping cost and regulatory burden increase as the plan grows. Third, DB plans do not work well for employees in today's dynamic business environment, where people shift jobs and careers more frequently than in the past.

Due to legal uncertainties and escalating costs, several companies have converted defined benefit plans into cash balance plans. A cash balance plan is a hybrid of a defined benefit and a defined contribution plan (such as a 401(k) plan). Like DB plans, employers make contributions to cash balance plans based on a percentage of a worker's pay and monthly benefits are guaranteed at retirement. However, unlike a DB plan, the benefit amount at retirement is unknown while a person is still employed. The amount of monthly pay at retirement will be ultimately determined by an employee's account balance at retirement, rather than by a preset formula based on pay grade. This protects the employer from escalating pension costs and adverse market conditions.

There are benefits to the changes in workplace retirement plans. Working in America today means changing careers at least once during your lifetime, either by choice or by circumstance. Technological innovation and employer cost control programs have reduced job security. In addition, mergers, acquisitions, and bankruptcies lead directly to cutbacks in the labor force. The dynamics of the workplace have made it difficult for most people to accumulate large retirement benefits from one employer and expensive for employers to track benefits for former workers. As a result, employers have opted to fund "portable" plans. That means cash balance plans and worker-funded plans that people can take with them when they leave. With such plans, when an employee is released or retires, he or she simply takes the retirement money. The employer is no longer liable for the assets or responsible for administering the assets throughout that person's life. The former employee is no longer tied to the fate of the employer. It is a much simpler approach.

Sources of Retirement Income

President George W. Bush forecast a steep reduction in Social Security benefits during a speech at the National Summit on Retirement Savings in 2002. He acknowledged that future retirees could expect Social Security benefits of less than 30% of what they earned before retirement. This is well below the current figure, near 50%. President Bush acknowledged the expected shortfall in Social Security income must be replaced by a combination of personal savings and part-time work.

Financial planners estimate that retirees need, on average, 75% of their pre-tax working income to maintain the same standard of living in retirement. Current retirees derive about 70% of their income from Social Security and traditional employer pension plans, according to the 2002 Retirement Confidence Survey results in Table 1-1. As President Bush explained, that number will change dramatically in the future. While baby boomers should expect only about 30% of their retirement income to come from Social Security and an employer pension, younger workers should expect less than 20%.

	Ages 20-39	Ages 40-59	Retirees
Savings in an employer plan	42%	34%	8%
Savings outside employer	18%	13%	9%
Employer DB pension plan	12%	15%	22%
Social Security	7%	16%	48%
Part-time employment	10%	9%	1%
Sale of house or business	4%	6%	5%
Other sources	7%	7%	7%

Table 1-1. How people expect to pay for retirement
Source: 2002 Retirement Confidence Survey, sponsored by Employee Benefit Research Institute and American Savings Education Council, January 2002

Several Savings Plans Available

Saving for retirement is in the national interest and a priority on Capitol Hill. The more Americans save today, the healthier the country's economy will be in the future. Government and corporate leaders have implemented many retirement programs that offer citizens the opportunity to save on a tax-advantaged basis. This means money that goes into a retirement account grows without being taxed on an annual basis and the contribution is either a tax deduction from current income or tax-free when withdrawn.

According to the Department of Labor, nearly 400,000 employers offer employees a 401(k) tax-deferred savings plan and tens of thousands of nonprofit and government employers offer plans to hospital workers, teachers, and government workers. In addition, small businesses also have their own version of employee-funded retirement plans. Contributions to these plans are made through regular payroll deductions and many employers match a portion of those savings each year. There are about 71 million people eligible for retirement savings plans where they work and over 80% of workers participate. All totaled, these plans held over $1.6 trillion in assets by the end of 2001.

While the number of people participating in employer-sponsored retirement savings plans is impressive, about 50% of American workers are not offered any kind of retirement plan at work. Those people must save for retirement on their own, which is often very difficult because many of those people are working in low-paying jobs (see Figure 1-2).

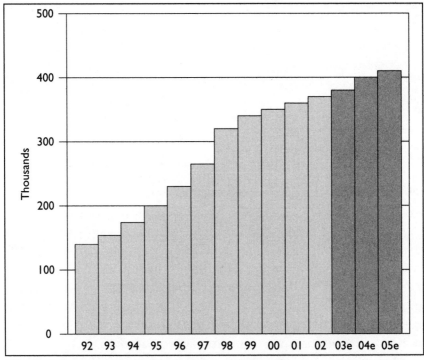

Figure 1-2. Growth in 401(k) plans (e = estimated)
Source: U.S. Department of Labor, Employee Benefits Security Administration

A second popular savings vehicle set up by Congress is the Individual Retirement Account (IRA). There are several types of IRAs to choose from, including traditional IRAs, Roth IRAs, and educational IRAs. One popular type of IRA account is a "rollover." When a person leaves an employer, he or she can transfer his or her portion of the pension plan into an IRA rollover account and avoid paying income tax on that money until it is withdrawn during retirement. The increase in job turnover has resulted in tens of millions of IRA rollover accounts. Some people have four, five, or more IRA rollovers scattered everywhere. All totaled, there are over 200 million IRAs of all types across the nation. These holdings account for over $2.6 trillion in investors' assets.

A third way to save for retirement is in insurance-related products. Many investors place their after-tax dollars in fixed and variable annuities, whole-life insurance, and other tax-deferred insurance policies. The money invested in insurance products grows tax-free until a withdrawal is made from the policy.

Most financial planners agree that investing in insurance products is not the best way to save for retirement. The costs in these products are generally high compared with the alternatives. As a result, the added expense wipes out any tax advantage. Nevertheless, through marketing, the insurance industry has done a good job of educating people about their responsibility to save for retirement and, as a result, the insurance industry has gathered over a trillion dollars in retirement assets. For more information, see Chapter 7, Types of Retirement Accounts.

Not Nearly Enough

Social Security benefits have already been cut twice, once in 1977 and again in 1983. The program will likely be sliced severely over the next 20 years as members of the baby boomer generation retire. If it is not fixed, there will be no money left for those born after 1960.

The answer to the Social Security problem is twofold. The retirement age must be raised and the amount of benefits must be cut. Neither solution is politically correct, so little is done to fix the problem. Nevertheless, to get the system in line with the life expectancy of the typical baby boomer, the retirement age for full Social Security benefits should be age 70 and overall benefits should be cut by about 30%. If this is done, the program has a chance of remaining in the black.

Some people claim that the Social Security trust fund should be turned over to participants so they can invest in private IRA-type accounts. I believe this is a bad idea for two reasons.

First, there is no money to turn over. The government takes all the money out of the Social Security Trust Fund and issues IOUs. These IOUs are special bonds purchased from the Treasury Department. The money from those bonds is then used by the government for day-to-day operations, which makes the federal deficit look smaller than it actually is. In a few years, the government will have to start paying back those bonds and our federal deficit will swell.

The second problem with turning Social Security funds over to individuals is investment mismanagement. After reading Chapters 2 through 6, you will agree that the average person has done a poor job of managing his or her retirement money. Few individual investors educate themselves about the markets by reading books and by attending relevant and unbiased investment classes.

Another problem facing the workforce is that private employers are cutting retirement benefits, including contributions to 401(k) plans. As the economy slows and regulations increase, the practice of matching employee contributions to employee finance savings has slowed. After the Enron bankruptcy in 2002, there was a congressional investigation into the amount of Enron stock employees held in 401(k) accounts. This led to more restrictions on the use of company stock in retirement plans, which increased the cost to employers of funding the plans and gave employers more reasons to question the wisdom of having retirement plans. In addition to regulatory issues, there are increasing legal concerns. Trustees of pension plans are finding themselves the targets of employee lawsuits over investment decisions, lawsuits that increase insurance costs for the employer. While Congress strongly encourages employers to set up retirement plans for employees, more business owners will opt out in the future, due to increased costs, regulatory burden, and legal concerns.

The decline in traditional sources of retirement income means that people must save more in personal accounts. Unfortunately, there is not much evidence that personal savings rise as employer benefits drop. The average 42-year-old 401(k) participant puts just 6.5% of his or her compensation into the plan and lower-paid par-

	Ages 20-39	Ages 40-59	Retirees
$0	22%	13%	11%
$1-24,999	36%	17%	25%
$25,000-49,999	9%	9%	4%
$50,000-74,999	7%	7%	4%
$75,000-99,999	3%	7%	5%
$100,000-249,999	5%	14%	8%
Over $250,000	2%	9%	9%
No Answer/Don't Know	16%	24%	34%

Table 1-2. Retirement savings amounts in 2001
Source: January 2002 Retirement Confidence Survey sponsored by Employee
Benefit Research Institute and American Education Council

ticipants tend to select the default contribution rate of 2%-3%. This savings rate is much too low and it will not lead to a secure retirement. Table 1-2 shows the results of historically low savings rates across the broad population.

Close to 40% of middle-aged workers have saved less than $50,000 for retirement. If you add to that category half of the people who did not answer the question or did not know, then about 50% of middle-aged workers have saved less than $50,000. The average amount saved by a middle-aged worker should be double that amount. Some people say that having $100,000 at age 50 is an unrealistic target. I disagree. If a 22-year-old started saving $50 per week and generated a 7% return on that money, he or she would have $93,690 by age 40.

The lack of savings at an early age can place people well below the amount they should have accumulated by middle age, a deficit that is nearly impossible to make up. Let's look at an example. Using a benchmark of 75% of pre-retirement income, a 50-year-old worker who makes $43,000 per year will need approximately $32,000 per year at retirement at age 65 in order to live the lifestyle he or she has grown accustomed to. About $12,000 will likely come from Social Security, so the other $20,000 must come from savings and part-time work. To avoid the necessity for working part time by withdrawing

$20,000 per year from savings at age 65, the 50-year-old would need about 20 times $20,000 in a retirement nest egg. That is $400,000 in savings—before factoring in inflation.

According to Table 1-2, the amount a typical 50-year-old has saved is $50,000. That means the typical 50-year-old will have to save about $10,000 per year and earn a 7% rate of return on that money to get near the $400,000 target by age 65. Let's face the facts. Saving $10,000 per year for someone making $43,000 is very difficult and earning 7% per year is not easy either, considering the mistakes people make investing their money. In addition, the $400,000 target does not even take into consideration the inflation rate over the next 15 years.

We have a big problem in America. Unless we start saving more money for retirement, and investing that money wisely, most workers will be required to work full or part time well beyond age 65, and well beyond the age at which their parents retired. The popular visions of travel, relaxation, and recreation during retirement will be only for those who have saved enough. Most retirees will not have the resources or the time. The numbers do not add up any other way.

Where Do You Start?

Saving for retirement is difficult. If you are like most Americans, after paying house bills, putting gas in the car, taking care of the family, and going out to dinner and a movie once in a while, there is nothing left to save. So, what is the answer?

The best way to save for retirement is to do it before the money gets into your pocket. Over 50 million people are covered under a salary reduction employer savings plan of some sort. People should strive to save 10% of their pre-tax salary in an employer plan, if available. That way, saving increases and you get a tax break on those savings. If your employer does not have a savings plan, then have money automatically withdrawn from your checking account each month and transferred to a personal retirement savings account such as an Individual Retirement Account (IRA). Chapter 7 explains various types of employer and personal savings accounts in more detail.

If you cannot afford to give up a full 10% of your pre-tax paycheck, then start by putting what you can into an account. Increase the percentage every time you get a raise or a bonus. Keep increasing the percentage of savings until it reaches 10%. If you are behind on saving for retirement, try to put away 15%. The more you save now, the better off you will be later in life.

The second step is self-education. *Protecting Your Wealth in Good Times and Bad* is just one book in a series of books you should read and learn from. John Hancock Financial conducted a survey of 801 participants in various 401(k) plans. One of the questions asked in the survey was how many hours each person devoted to investment research. Half of all Americans spend less than six hours each year reading about investment topics. Compare that with the amount of time spent watching television. On average, adults watch more than three hours of television per day, or 1380 hours per year. The best investment books on the market this year may sell 10,000 copies each, but the top romance novels will sell millions of copies. I am absolutely convinced that the average American would greatly increase his or her personal wealth remarkably by devoting just a small amount of television watching time or romance novel reading time to learning about personal finance.

Saving Is One Piece of the Puzzle

Accumulating and maintaining a nest egg for retirement takes time and patience. There are lots of pieces to the puzzle that you need to fit together. You'll get a good idea of the complexity of the puzzle by asking yourself a few questions. Depending on your age, you may not be able to answer all of the questions. For example, a 60-year-old should be able to answer most of the questions, but a 24-year-old does not yet know how much he or she will need each year in retirement or will want to leave to heirs. Nevertheless, it is a good idea to think about these questions, because they will help you decide when you have enough to retire and how well you will live in retirement:

1. How much have you already saved for retirement?
2. How much will you save each year while working?
3. How many years until you retire?
4. What reasonable rate of return are you forecasting on your savings?
5. At what rate will you withdraw from savings in retirement?
6. How much are you planning to leave to your heirs?

Depending on your age, this book will help you answer each of those questions. Let's go over them in a little more detail now. More precise information on these issues will be discussed in Part Three, A Lifelong Saving and Investing Guide.

1. *How much have you already saved?* This one is easy. Simply gather all your statements from your bank, brokers, mutual fund companies, and work-related plans.
2. *How much will you save each year while working?* Hopefully, you are able to set aside 10% of your income or more each year. Take full advantage of tax-sheltered employer 401(k) plans and other tax-advantaged retirement accounts.
3. *How many years until you retire?* A better question may be "How many years until you *can* retire?" That depends on your age, health, and wealth accumulation. Social Security starts paying full benefits between ages 65 and 67, depending on when you were born.
4. *What rate of return will you earn on your savings?* The high returns of the 1980s and 1990s were an anomaly and may never happen again in your lifetime. Expect no more than a 7% rate of return on your investments; conservative investors should expect less. Why 7%? See Chapter 11, Realistic Market Expectations.
5. *At what rate will you withdraw from savings in retirement?* Take no more than 5% of your savings as annual income at retirement; conservative investors should use 4% as a maximum This withdrawal rate should still allow the account to grow nominally over time, counteracting inflation to some extent.
6. *How much are you planning to leave to your heirs?* That is an easy question for many people. The kids deserve nothing! Realistically, this is not what will happen. We all leave money behind. Later in life, the question becomes whether to gift the money while you are alive or leave it as an inheritance. The amount you give while you are alive should not lower your standard of living.

The number-one financial concern that most people have is to not run out of money while retired. As a result, the amount you can safely withdraw from a retirement account will be driven by the size of your account. That means saving and investing properly during all stages of adulthood.

Chapter Summary

People are living longer and spending more in retirement. At the same time, the traditional sources of retirement income from Social Security and employer-funded pensions are diminishing. Retirees in the future will rely more on their personal savings than in past generations. This creates a problem, since there is a large shortfall in retirement savings accounts across America.

The level of personal retirement savings is no higher today than it was 20 years ago, despite several new tax-advantaged retirement programs offered in and out of the workplace. The new programs simply shifted money from one type of savings plan to another without adding to the pot. As a nation, we need to save more for retirement and we need to invest our retirement savings more effectively to close this gap.

Few people have taken the time to figure out how much they should save for retirement and how to best invest those savings while accumulating money prior to retirement. *Protecting Your Wealth in Good Times and Bad* is a guidebook designed to help you make those critical decisions.

Key Points

1. As a nation, we are not saving enough in retirement accounts to make up for diminishing Social Security benefits and other traditional sources of income.
2. Future retirees should create and follow a disciplined savings plan. A 10% target on pre-tax income is good for most people.
3. Education is a critical first step toward building and maintaining a secure nest egg.

Chapter 2

Investment Return Shortfalls

There was a time when a fool and his money were soon parted, but now it happens to everybody.

—Adlai Stevenson

B UILDING AND MAINTAINING WEALTH can be divided into two tasks. The first task, covered in Chapter 1, is saving money, which includes dutifully depositing small amounts into savings each month while working full-time. The second task is investing those savings properly, from the day your first dollar goes into a savings account until the last day you remain among the living, and in some cases even into the hereafter.

As your wealth grows, the rate of return on that money becomes increasingly important. Given the declining level of retirement income from guaranteed employer pensions and Social Security and the lower returns expected from the financial markets in the future, people cannot afford to make too many investment mistakes. Retirement accounts need to be managed according to a well-tailored, low-cost investment plan that is designed using modern financial planning tools. If managed correctly, a nest egg can grow to the point where it will meet retirement income needs without excessive risk and you will not fear outliving your money.

Unfortunately, the facts show that we do not do a very good job of saving and investing. Several studies on the rate of return in self-directed retirement accounts show that an overwhelming majority of people earn far less than they should be earning. How low are the returns of individual investors?

The Nebraska Retirement System 401(k) plan is one of the oldest 401(k) type plans in existence and has performance data going back several decades. Figure 2-1 illustrates the average performance for workers who participated in the plan from 1970 to 1999. The bar on the right is the annual return that the average worker earned on personal savings in the self-managed portion of the 401(k) plan. The middle bar represents the annual return of professional money managers hired by the Nebraska Retirement System to manage the state's defined benefit plan. The bar on the left is the annual return of a static mix of 45% in the S&P 500 stock index, 45% in a five-year

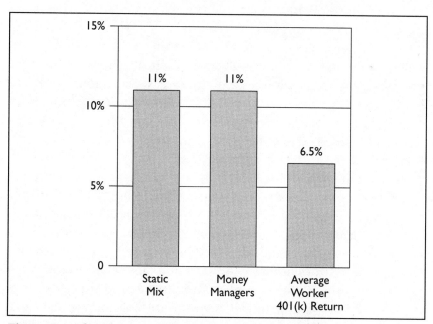

Figure2-1. Nebraska retirement system, 30 years ending 1999
Source: Nebraska Retirement System

Treasury note, and 10% in a Treasury bills. The mix would be considered a conservative, balanced account.

As a group, the professional money managers who control a portion of the state's pension assets matched the performance of the static mix of 45% stocks, 45% bonds, and 10% cash. Looking at the bar to the right in Figure 2-1, we see the average worker earned significantly less than the managers or the static mix. Why? Were the employees misinformed? Did they have poor mutual funds to invest in? The fact is that workers were given a substantial amount of written information covering the fine investment choices in their plan as well as diversification guidelines. They were also allowed to take paid time off during the workweek to attend free investment seminars on investment principles. Nonetheless, the fliers, booklets, and seminars did not help the typical employee.

In 2001, the National Center for Policy Analysis published a study of 401(k)s by benefits attorney Brooks Hamilton and financial columnist Scott Burns, *Reinventing Retirement Income in America*. The study examined the investment returns of hundreds of 401(k) retirement plans and thousands of accounts for the years 1990 through 1995. The authors concluded emphatically that workers underachieved the market's performance in their 401(k) accounts. This was especially true of lower-paid employees. Hamilton and Burns constructed a second database of 500,000 investment returns from 401(k) participants for the year 1998. That year the average 401(k) account returned 8%, whereas a static mix of 45% stocks, 45% bonds, and 10% in T-bills returned 18%.

Further analysis of the Hamilton and Burns database found that a high percentage of low-wage earners held almost two-thirds of their savings in low-yielding fixed-income type investments such as money market funds. One explanation for the concentration in money funds was the "default selection" in many 401k documents. If an employee does not choose to invest in any other option when signing up for a 401(k) type plan, then 100% of his or her savings default to a low-yielding money market fund. For many individuals, the process of selecting investments for a retirement account is too confusing or intimidating. Those employees tend to place their savings in the safest, yet lowest-yielding investments and miss out on the superior long-term gains from stocks and bonds.

The Nebraska Retirement System realized there was a problem and decided to do something about it. With this new information, Nebraska decided to move in an opposite direction from where most other employers were going. Instead of requiring employees to manage their own accounts, the state now offers a new option to current employees. The participants can select a pooled investment account that is professionally managed by state-selected investment firms and be guaranteed a minimum benefit at retirement by the state. All new hires were placed in the new plan starting in 2002.

The pendulum is swinging back to a guaranteed benefit plan in Nebraska. That is a good sign, but the only one so far. Most other government and corporate employers continue to push in the direction of self-management, which implies lower retirement benefits for employees. As of July 1, 2002, Florida started allowing state employees to move their funds out of the state-guaranteed defined benefit plan and into a new self-directed plan. This means employees who move are giving up a guaranteed paycheck at retirement for the hope of growing a larger benefit for themselves by investing their own account. The state will continue to fund both plans, but the retirement income of those employees who switch to the self-directed option will no longer be set according to a standard formula. It will depend on the employees' investment skills. If you are a Florida state employee, I would not recommend switching to the self-directed plan unless you are very confident about your investment knowledge—and then I would think twice.

The country is torn by the question of who should manage retirement plans. Some employees want complete control of their investments and others do not. The challenge is to give control to those who want it and protect those who do not want it, while decreasing administrative costs and the legal liability of the employer. Currently, over 50% of households in America are covered under some type of employee self-managed and self-funded retirement plan where they work, such as a 401(k) plan, while less than 40% of households are still under an employer-funded and employer-managed defined benefit plan, which provides guaranteed income at retirement. Among employers that still fund defined pension benefits are federal, state, and local governments, as well as large corporations that are heavily unionized. However, each year the number of workers responsible for managing their own retirement savings is going up and the number of employers offering monthly pension checks is going down. It is not likely that employers will follow Nebraska's lead and shift back to guaranteed retirement benefits. That would be too costly and carry too much regulatory burden.

Evaluating Poor Performance

There is every indication that the aggregate return of self-managed retirement accounts will continue to be significantly lower than the aggregate return of employer-managed plans. If you have an understanding of why the performance of individually managed accounts has been below average in the past, it will help you correct problems in your own retirement savings for the future.

Basically, there are five main reasons for the poor performance in individual retirement accounts. Four of them apply to all individuals and one of them applies only to employees in companies that have publicly traded stock:

1. A large number of people choose low-yielding investments for a significant portion of their plan, such as money market funds and guaranteed fixed-rate annuities. These investments are simple to understand, and do not require knowledge of the stock market, bond market, or diversification techniques. These investors could earn a higher return on their savings by taking a small amount of risk, but choose not to.

2. On the other end of the spectrum are investors who trade their retirement accounts frequently. These people tend to follow the financial markets closely and attempt to get into or out of investments at the right time. Generally, individuals who trade their accounts frequently receive the lowest returns. This was the conclusion of several studies conducted by University of California professors Brad Barber and Terrance Odean.[1]

3. There are a lot of people who fall in the middle. They do not know what to do, but know they must do something in their account. These investors tend to be casual observers of the markets, but not overly interested in the day-to-day activity. They may listen occasionally to the media chatter about the markets and are aware of the performance of a few mutual funds they own, but they do not react to every market move. When they make a move, the change typically needs to be validated by friends, relatives, coworkers, or media. Basically, most investors follow trends. They tend to do what others do and buy what others buy. This investment strategy nearly always results in performance below a basic buy-and-hold, static stock-and-bond mix.

4. The fourth category of poor performance applies only to people who work for companies that are public and have stock that trades on the stock market. Some employees of these companies put their faith, trust, and money behind their employers by investing a large portion of their retirement savings in their own companies' stocks. Strangely, surveys indicate that employees believe that there is less risk in owning company stock than a diversified portfolio of several stocks. In reality, there is significantly more risk to owning just one stock, even if that is the company you work for. This strategy swings both ways. A heavy concentration of company stock worked well for the early employees of Microsoft, but it did not work for employees of Enron or WorldCom.

5. The final reason for poor performance does not have anything to do with investment behavior; it is all about costs. Investment fees and expenses reduce the performance of every investment account, even large institutional pension plans. However, individuals pay a lot more per dollar invested than large institutions. Depending on the investments owned, a person can give up 2% or more each year to pay for management fees, commissions, and administrative costs. Expenses are a major reason why self-managed retirement accounts do not perform anywhere close to the markets they invest in, although all the risk is still there.

Investment advice found in the mass media and sale ads paid for by Wall Street firms make investing sound so easy. You are told to buy this and sell that, which will put you on the road to riches. The problem is, next month it is a different set of investments, and the month after that yet another. If making money were as easy as following popular advice, why did so many people lose so much money in their retirement accounts between 2000 and 2002?

Here is an unfortunate but true story of a 70-year-old barber in my hometown, whom I will call Ed. In early 1998, Ed had accumulated a $700,000 nest egg by diligently saving for almost 50 years. He was hoping to get his account up to $1 million over the next five years and then retire. Ed was a conservative investor. Most of his money was in bank certificates of deposit, earning a competitive yield, and a small portion was in a diversified stock mutual fund, which was doing quite well. It was a simple portfolio, yet a practical investment approach for his level of expertise.

Every day during the growth stock boom, Ed's customers would talk about investing in technology stocks, especially the red-hot Internet sector. Although his intuition told him to stay away from picking stocks, Ed wondered if he should give it a try. If a few of those stocks worked out, then he could retire earlier. So, during 1999, Ed bought his first technology stock on the advice of a stockbroker customer.

After some surprising success, along with a lot of backslapping from his new best friend the stockbroker, Ed decided that the CD rates he was getting at the bank were no longer attractive and he started rolling out of CDs and putting more money into tech stocks. Over the next six months, Ed traded all kinds of stocks that were recommended to him. He learned all the stock-trading buzzwords and even installed a computer in the office so that he could check quotes and trade stocks during breaks. At night, Ed started analyzing price charts, looking for ones that were "breaking out." He also discovered Internet chat rooms and monitored the conversations to ensure his stocks were well represented.

By early 2000, Ed was a day-trading maniac. He traded in the morning, between customers, during breaks, and at night and he studied stocks all weekend long. Ed believed his stock selection method was refined, that there was little risk of loss. About the time technology stocks were peaking, Ed kept me in his barber chair for nearly an hour explaining in great detail how his system worked and why. He even mentioned that I should consider using his method to invest my clients' money and he generously offered to supply me with his recent picks.

As you may have guessed, Ed arrived a little too late to the party. He almost made it to $1 million before losing over 60% of his retirement savings during the next 30 months. After that, Ed was in no position to retire early. In fact, he was in no position to retire at all.

Despite his near ruin, Ed still feels he was fully justified in his actions. "All of the good stock picks were mine, and all of the lousy ones were my broker's!" he claimed. "My mistake was not firing that broker a long time ago."

What was Ed's real mistake? The real mistake was that Ed did not follow through with the sensible investment plan that he started years ago. If Ed had simply continued to buy bank CDs and put money in the stock fund, he would be hanging up his hair dryer today. Instead, he no longer plans to retire. He cannot afford to.

Behavioral Finance

When you get down to the basics, we are our own worst enemy. We are prone to have warped perceptions of our ability that cause us to act irrationally. Investors look at stock charts and see trends that do not exist and they turn wishful thinking fiction into investment facts. Behavioral finance is the study of how psychology affects investment decision-making, which ultimately affects portfolio performance. This field of study is not new, but it has taken on new meaning over the last 10 years.

Richard H. Thaler, a professor of behavioral science and economics at the University of Chicago, has been studying behavioral finance for over 20 years. His research has shed light on behaviors covering everything from buying lottery tickets to investing retirement money in speculative Internet ventures.

Thaler believes most investors suffer from overconfidence. The average person thinks he or she is above average in many ways.

Numerous surveys have shown that people tend to believe they are better-than-average drivers, better-than-average-looking, better-than-average managers, and are less likely to lose their jobs than their coworkers. In their article, "Aspects of Investor Psychology" (*Journal of Portfolio Management*, Summer 1998), Daniel Kahneman, a psychology professor at Princeton University, and Mark W. Riepe, a senior vice president and research chief at Charles Schwab & Co., wrote:

> The combination of overconfidence and optimism is a potent brew, which causes people to overestimate their knowledge, underestimate risks, and exaggerate their ability to control events.

Overconfidence is a key factor in people's tendency to concentrate their investment holdings in one particular asset class, market sector, or company, according to Thaler. "That's certainly the case when it comes to company stock," he said. "People think they have some sort of inside information, and everyone thinks the company they work for is above-average. That second point can't possibly be the case, and there's no evidence whatsoever to support the first point."[2]

A grand illustration of overconfidence occurred between 1998 and 2001, when technology stocks went from boom to bust. While they were booming, everyone was an expert, but when they collapsed, no one would admit to being a bad stock picker, especially the analysts on Wall Street. Most individual investors I talk with blame somebody else for their loss: a broker, a relative, a coworker, or a TV stock analyst. Ironically, these same investors now say they *knew* the market was high and that the bubble had to burst. Isn't it amazing how our minds distort the truth to protect our egos?

Another area Thaler studied was false pattern recognition. Human beings like patterns. Many people believe that randomness is the exception rather than the rule. Surveys have shown that in a coin-toss experiment many people believe that a sequence of heads-tails-heads-tails-heads is more likely to occur than all heads, all tails, or some other order. In fact, the probability of any of these results is the same. You can see false pattern recognition behavior all over Las

Vegas. Some people who play roulette and baccarat keep meticulous notes of the numbers that come up during the game under the illusion that tracking past random numbers gives some indication of future random numbers. I am amazed to watch these people because when they win, they believe it is skill, but when they lose it is bad luck.

Our fondness for patterns sometimes leads us to assume that investments that have done well in the past will continue to do well in the future and those that have performed poorly will continue to do poorly. Interestingly, people tend to overreact when they think a trend has developed. Once we're convinced that a trend is there, we act as though it will continue indefinitely.

In addition to Thaler's findings, behavioral researchers have learned that children who inherit stocks and stock mutual funds from their parents are less likely to sell those securities than other investments. The reason they give for not selling is that if Dad or Mom bought the securities, then they must be good. I have seen heirs lose millions of dollars holding stocks that they should have diversified away a long time ago.

All of the behavioral research studies can be cumulated into one observation. Investors have only a vague idea of how well they are managing their investments. Most people believe they are doing much better than is actually the case. One study measured the difference between how investors perceived their returns and the actual returns. The research found that that the average difference between perceived returns and actual returns was about 3% per year.[3] In addition, that gap grew larger as the time frame expanded.

The Beardstown Ladies Investment Club of Beardstown, Illinois is a classic example of how wide the gap can grow between perceived investment results and actual results. The women in this legendary investment club rose to prominence in the mid-1990s after they proclaimed fantastic returns for their club investment account. For 10 years ending 1993, the club reported a compounded return of 23.4%, versus a return of 14.9% in the S&P 500. How did they do it? By purchasing stocks like Coke, McDonald's, and other household names. Their complete methodology was published in 1996 in a best-selling book, *Beardstown Ladies' Common-Sense Investment Guide*, which sold over 800,000 copies. The women went on to write four more books—before an error was discovered in their investment calculation.

In late 1997, the managing editor of *Chicago* magazine noticed something peculiar about the investment results published in the *Common-Sense Investment Guide* and concluded that a gross error had been made. The mistake was so large that the accounting firm of Price Waterhouse was called in to clear the air. In the final analysis, the club's worst fears were realized: their return was actually only 9.1% over the period, far below 23.4%, and well below the S&P 500. An embarrassed club treasurer blamed the error on her misunderstanding of the computer program.[4]

What is ironic about the Beardstown Ladies is they were putting themselves out as investment experts, yet no one in the club was expert enough to notice that their reported portfolio returns were exceedingly high in relation to the return of the stocks they purchased. I do not believe these women were trying to deceive anyone. I truly believe they thought they were beating the market.

If you enjoyed reading this section on behavioral finance, I highly recommend reading Larry Swedroe's book, *Rational Investing in Irrational Times* (New York: St. Martin's Press, 2002). It highlights 52 investment common mistakes most people make, referencing all the published literature on the subject.

> *The easiest thing of all is to deceive one's self; for what a man wishes, he generally believes to be true.*
> —Demosthenes

Chapter Summary

There are two sides to a personal retirement savings program. One side is a dedicated savings program and the other involves investing those savings properly. There currently is a shortfall on both sides.

The below-average performance of self-directed accounts can be attributed to two factors: bad behavior by investors and high investment expenses.

Investors behave badly in a number of ways. Some people simply choose to keep their retirement savings in a low-yield money market fund. Others play the markets excessively, which inevitably leads to below-average returns. A third group meanders around, not knowing what to do. Finally, there is a group of corporate employees who load up their retirement accounts with their company stock, believing it is safer than a diversified portfolio of stocks.

In addition to human behavior, a second detriment to performance is high investment costs. This includes expenses relating to trading commissions, management fees, and the internal costs of investment products like mutual funds and variable annuities. On average, investors spend much more than they should to invest their retirement savings.

There is a vast difference between perception and reality in the financial markets. We rank our investment ability at a much higher level than it is. Evidence of this fact is found in our belief that our past investment returns are much higher than they really are. We selectively remember the good investments while discarding the bad ones. We tend to overestimate future returns and underestimate the risks. Awareness of common investment errors outlined in this chapter is a big step toward correcting them.

Key Points

1. As a nation, we are not earning a fair rate of return on self-directed retirement accounts.
2. Lack of investment knowledge and misperceptions about our investment skills are the leading causes of poor results.
3. High fees and expenses contribute to below-average returns.
4. Awareness of these common mistakes is a big step toward correcting them.

Notes

1. Brad M. Barber and Terrance Odean, "Trading Is Hazardous to Your Wealth: The Common Stock Investment Performance of Individual Investors," *Journal of Finance*, Vol. 55, No. 2, April 2000, pp. 773-806.
2. The Vanguard Group, "For Investment Success, Be on Your Best Behavior," *In The Vanguard*, Spring 2002.

3. William. N. Goetzmann and Nadav Peles, "Cognitive Dissonance and Mutual Fund Investors," *Journal of Financial Research*, 20:2, Summer 1997, pp. 145-158. One group of investors consisted of people who were members of an investment club and the other group consisted of people who were less informed participants in a small retirement plan. The informed group had no better record of guessing their performance than the less informed group.

4. Shane Tritsch, "Bull Marketing," *Chicago* magazine, March 1998; Calmetta Y. Coleman, "Beardstown Ladies 'Fess Up to Big Goof," *The Wall Street Journal*, March 18, 1998, p. C1.

Chapter 3

Bear Markets and Bad Investor Behavior

History shows that the biggest risk is not being in the market when it drops, but being out when it rises.

—*Jim Jorgensen*

INVESTING FOR RETIREMENT usually means placing at least a portion of your money in the stock market. The reason is that, over long periods of time, it is highly probable that the returns from stocks will exceed the returns from most other asset classes, such as bonds and money market funds. In addition, stocks provide a hedge against the erosion of principal caused by inflation and taxes.

The extra gain expected from stocks is not without extra risk. There have been several periods when the market fell 20% or more in a short time and other periods when stocks did not outperform bonds or money market funds for a long time. When a deep bear market rolls around, it is often a brutal test of an investor's nerves. Bear markets can be painful emotionally and financially.

Individual investors have no control over the direction of the market. The only decision is to be in or out. When you are in and the stocks fall, you lose money. When you are out and stocks rally, you miss an opportunity. But losing money is only one of the issues. Bear markets can cause anxiety, frustration, sleepless nights, a feeling of hopelessness, and all kinds of uncomfortable side effects.

Due to all the bad stuff a bear market can cause, wouldn't it be wise to find a market expert who will magically get you out of bad markets and into good ones? That is a nice dream, but it is not reality. Market timing does not work. No one can predict the direction of the stock market with enough accuracy to make any money—and if they could, why should they sell their alchemy services to you?

Instead of trying to predict bear markets, investors should simply be prepared for them. Successful investing hinges on the development of a diversified portfolio using an appropriate mix of low-cost mutual funds. This portfolio should include U.S. stock funds, foreign stock funds, bond funds, and real estate funds. A diversified portfolio significantly reduces the impact of a bear market on your portfolio, saving you money and makings you feel better as well. This chapter provides a brief overview of diversification techniques; more detailed information can be found in the Chapter 12, Asset Allocation Explained.

Bear markets should only be a minor nuisance in your life and should have no effect on your retirement savings plan or your ability to sleep at night. They occur as a normal part of the economic cycle in every free-market economy and are a natural part of economic growth. If you live to be in your 80s or older, there is a good chance you will be involved in at least two lengthy bear markets during your life and many more short-term market corrections.

Bear Markets Occur More Often than We Think

When the stock market falls a lot, the mass media tends to talk about the decline like it is the end of the capitalistic system in America. Nearly every newspaper in the country prints a picture of some humbled trader on the floor of the stock exchange, hands holding his head, in complete, utter shock. The caption below the picture reads, "Sell, Sell, Sell!" or "Market Breaks Support" or "Panic on Wall Street."

(I think it is funny to note that most newspaper editors cannot tell the difference between a trader on the floor of the stock exchange and a trader in the commodity pits in Chicago. When they pick a file photo of a "depressed stock trader" for the newspapers, many times it is actually a picture of a commodities trader who has had a bad day trading pork bellies.)

News about movement in the markets is so editorialized that, depending on which news show you watch or which newspaper you read, the reasons given for the market decline could be vastly different. A Los Angeles newspaper may report the market is down due to higher interest rates while a Chicago paper reports the market is down due to profit taking and a Boston paper reports the market is down due to poor earnings. Who is right? Who is wrong? Who knows?

The fact is that the market is down because there were more sellers than buyers, at least on that day. One day in July 2001, *The Wall Street Journal* actually reported, "With many traders on vacation, the market barely budged." It is amazing what passes for news.

A market decline of 10% to 20% is known as a *correction*. Since Wall Street is paid to be bullish on stocks, the word "correction" is a nice replacement for the words "lost money." When Wall Street firms say the market is "in a correction," it is supposed to make you feel better about losing money because it implies the market is setting up for bigger gains in the future. Corrections occur on average every two years and generally coincide with some potentially harmful economic or global event, like Russia defaulting on its debts in 1998.

A *bear market* is a correction of 20% or more. It is widely believed that bear markets coincide with economic recessions. This means lower sales at retail stores and higher unemployment. The truth is, sometimes a bear market forecasts a recession and sometimes it does not. It did not in 1987, but it did in 2000. Economic data is always behind actual economic conditions, so we never know if the market is telling the truth. A standing joke on Wall Street is that the stock market forecast eight out of the last three recessions.

The following tables provide some interesting stock market data on negative years, market corrections, and bear markets in the U.S. The lesson to learn from this data is that bad market conditions occur more frequently than we think.

100 Years of Rolling U.S. Large Stock Returns, 1903 -2002

Criteria, 1903-2002	Number
One year	32
Two years in a row	10
Three years in a row	6
Four years in a row	1
Five years in a row	0

Table 3-1. Number of times the stock market has been negative

Criteria, 1903-2002	Number
Negative over a five-year period	14
Negative over a 10-year period	2
Negative over a 15-year period	0

Table 3-2. Number of rolling periods stocks have been negative

Rolling Periods, 1903-2002	Number
One year	42
Over a five-year period	19
Over a 10-year period	10
Over a 15-year period	2
Over a 20-year period	0

Table 3-3. Number of years stock returns have been lower than T-Bills

Interesting Statistics
- Number of years the stock market was down more than 10%: 16
- Number of years the stock market was down more than 20%: 8
- Longest time for the stock market to recover to its previous high: 14 years.
- Longest time for stock returns to be lower than T-bill returns: 15 years

This Time It's Different

Bull markets dim the memories of bear markets over time. During long bull markets, people gradually forget that investing is risky and instead begin to feel "this time it's different." At the end of the long bull market from 1982 to 1999, some hot stocks began to look like free ATMs, spitting out money month after month, with few interruptions. During this period, the investing public battled for position in line to buy these risky stocks and the mutual funds that held them. This behavior was highly encouraged by Wall Street firms that make a lot more money when people buy stocks instead of bonds. Mutual fund companies, insurance companies, financial magazines, financial television shows, and every other industry segment that benefited from more public participation in the market also cheered as the market moved higher.

In early 2000, about the time a majority of investors started to pin their worldly happiness on the daily close of the NASDAQ, the floor dropped out. In disbelief, many investors reacted by purchasing more shares of stocks that lost money, thus increasing their equity exposure. This was perfectly logical at the time. A popular mantra that worked well during the bull market was "buy the dips," so that is what people did. A few unfortunate investors even took equity out of their homes to increase their exposure, believing that now was their big chance to get in. All of this buying was not without Wall Street urging. Experts called the pullback a "technical correction" and assured the country that a rally would soon take the markets to new heights.

Well, the market did not recover as the experts predicted. There was a small rally in prices, and then a fizzle, and then another small rally, and then a big fizzle. At that point, there was doubt and confusion; smart money started selling. But analysts on Wall Street continued to pound the table, insisting that a rally was near. Alas, no rally developed; prices only went lower. Soon, more selling, as institutional traders rushed for the exit. Many small investors got trampled in the stampede, especially less experienced people who had never seen a bear market.

During a bear market, stocks usually decline much faster than they advance during a bull market. As a result, investors lose money very quickly, which tends to lead to a loss of confidence in the system. Depending on how much damage was done to a personal portfolio during a bear market, an investor could decide to stay out of stocks for a long, long time—and in some cases for life. The two worst bear markets in the twentieth century caused two generations of investors to shun stocks for decades. A large number of investors who borrowed money to buy stocks in the Roaring 20s got caught in the Crash of 1929 and never committed to the stock market again. Years later, many investors who were pelted in the brutal 1973-1974 bear market stayed out for years, despite a quick recovery in prices. The latest bear market has caused many people to cut stock exposure significantly and some people have vowed never to trust Wall Street again.

In Search of a Crystal Ball

You cannot predict the next bear market. Nevertheless, human beings want to believe that somehow they can find a way to know when to get in and when to get out. Vast amounts of time and money are spent looking for undiscovered information or unique trading strategies that have predictive value. But, so far there are no winners.

The people looking for a crystal ball are no dummies. The list of Nobel Laureates who lost money trying to find a mathematical solution is quite long. John Nash, Robert Merton, and Myron Scholes are three who come to mind. Nash tried to develop market-timing systems using mathematical models based on game theory, for which he won the Nobel Prize. He did not succeed. Merton and Scholes were the architects of intrinsic formulas that mathematically predicted the risk and return in hundreds of markets. Those models eventually led to the 1998 collapse of Long-Term Capital Management (LTCM). The failure of LTCM was so potentially devastating to the global economy that the Federal Reserve had to orchestrate a bailout by several Wall Street firms. So, is there a crystal ball that can predict the market? If Nobel Laureates cannot find one that works, then there is no point for us to try.

If I have noticed anything over these 60 years on Wall Street, it is that people do not succeed in forecasting what's going to happen to the stock market.

—*Benjamin Graham*

Investor Beliefs About Trends

Despite overwhelming evidence that the market is not predictable, most investors cling to the belief. It has even become common in our everyday speech. After the market goes up, we routinely say it is *going* up, and after it goes down, we routinely say it is *going* down. In truth, we only know where the market has been, not where it is going.

The simplest form of market prediction is trend following and, by nature, we are all trend followers. This means we believe that past price trends will continue into the future. If the stock market goes up, most people think it will continue to go up; if the market goes down, most people think it will continue to go down.

In early 2002, John Hancock Financial Services conducted a random survey of 801 people who invest in 401(k) and other retirement plans. When asked what they believed the return of the stock market was going to be over the next 20 years, the average answer was an annualized gain of 15%. Where did the respondents get that number? Ironically, for the preceding 20-year period ending in December 2001, the annualized return for the stock market was 15%. Respondents unconsciously extrapolated past returns into the future.

The media reflects popular opinion in news stories. In 1979, after several dismal years in the stock market, most magazines were predicting 10 more dismal years. The August 1979 issue of *BusinessWeek* ran a cover story titled "The Death of Equities." The article recommended that investors abandon the stock market and buy bonds linked to the price of gold, which had soared to $600 per ounce. Ironically, the story ran very close to the bottom of the market for stocks and the top of the market for gold.

It is very hard for people to fight the urge to follow trends. But it is necessary to resist the temptation if you want to be a successful investor. I am not recommending betting against a trend, but this book advocates cutting back on those markets that make gains, following a continuous rebalancing strategy. You will read more about rebalancing in Parts II and III.

Our Life and the Life Cycles of Markets

Most people will participate in two or three large bull and bear market cycles during their lifetime. A complete market cycle seems to run between 15 and 30 years. The total gain during the bull phase averages between five and 10 times its starting price and the loss during the bear phase averages about one-third to one-half the price at the market peak. From start to finish, the total return of a cycle has averaged about 10% per year compounded, depending on the rate of inflation during the period. The average, inflation-adjusted return of the market during a complete cycle is about 6% per year compounded.

Over the last 80 years, there have been three secular (long-term) market cycles. The first began in 1921 and ended in about 1942. The second started in 1943 and ended in 1974. The third cycle started in 1975 and hopefully ended in 2003, although I am speculating on the end date. In each period, as the market went higher, more people jumped on the bandwagon, especially in the final years. This trend-following behavior led to the demise of considerably more investors at the end than had been in at the start. The net result of the "market timing" of sorts was a significant loss in capital for many investors and a loss in the public's faith in Wall Street.

The stock market boomed in the 1920s, fueled by growth prospects after WW I and easy credit from banks. As a result, over 10% of the working population bought common stocks through brokers.[1] In 1929 the crash began. The market downturn was slow at first. Then, as the Federal Reserve tightened credit and Congress enacted a new tariff on imports, the stock market collapsed. Over the next three years, prices dropped 82% from their highs and many people could not pay their banks for loans used to buy stocks. As a result, many major banks became illiquid and closed their doors. The banking crisis sent the economy into a tailspin and threw the country into a period of despair.

The experience of 1929-32 stayed on the minds of Americans for two decades. Despite the fact that the absolute market bottom in stock prices was in 1932, public ownership in stocks continued to decline to a low of 4% in 1951. A turnaround in investor sentiment came at the end of the Korean War, in 1952, when a new generation of investors was emerging. As a new bull market pushed stock prices higher in the 1950s, more investors become enchanted. Many of these new investors were not in the stock market during the Crash of '29, so they were less influenced by events gone by. Also during this period, new telephone technology allowed brokerage firms to expand their reach to every city and town in America. Brokers even went door-to-door selling individual stocks and a new product called "mutual funds."

Renewed vigor fueled the market until the late 1960s. Then, the U.S. became more involved in the Vietnam War, draining the country of precious resources. This caused a peak in prices in 1968, although people kept buying the dips. Stocks as a percent of household financial assets hit a high of 38% in 1969. By that time over 16% of the adult population owned stocks, more than any other time in the economic history of the U.S.

Unfortunately, as a result of continued deficit spending during the war, the U.S. dollar was weakening. One unintended consequence of the decline in the value of the dollar was an unprecedented outflow of gold from the U.S. reserves. In 1973, growing political pressure to curb the outflow of gold forced President Nixon to take the country off the gold standard, which pegged the value of the dollar to the price of gold. This major shift in monetary policy resulted in the collapse of the U.S. dollar and a surge in inflation. Since oil trades on the U.S. dollar, price of oil skyrocketed, which caused an Arab oil embargo, which created long lines at the gas pumps, a severe energy shortage, and ultimately, a deep recession. Between 1973 and 1974, blue-chip stocks fell over 40% and small stocks fell more than 50%. The rapid decline in prices and poor economic outlook drove many investors permanently out of the stock market for the second time in the century.

The bear market bottomed in 1974. Then, from 1975 to 1992, the S&P 500 compounded at a 15.6% annual return, beating the return of bank CDs by 7%. Nevertheless, during this period, experienced investors preferred the safety of FDIC-insured bank deposits. Stock ownership fell back to the 10% level.

Finally, in the early 1990s, a third generation of investors ventured into the stock market. The baby boomers started to become an investment force on Wall Street. Improved information and communications, along with a growing lineup of new and exciting mutual funds, fueled the rise in stock prices. By early 2000, there were significantly more stock investors as a percent of the adult population than ever before. According to Federal Reserve data, the number of households owning equities or equity mutual funds increased from 33% in 1989 to 52% by 2001. This increase was a direct result of more people participating in employer self-directed retirements accounts such as the 401(k).

As the number of investors participating in the stock market rose, the amount of their participation also exploded in the 1990s. Stocks grew from 18% of median household financial assets in 1991 to a historically high rate of 45% by 1999. As you can see in Figure 3-1, when the bear market rolled around in 2000, significantly more households had more exposure to equities than at any other time in history.

Figure 3-1 puts a lot of this information in graphic form. The 52-year chart compares the rolling three-year return of the S&P 500 with the percentage of household financial assets in individual stocks and stock mutual funds. For the entire period, the median household held 25% of its financial assets in stocks. The range was from a low of 12% in 1982 to a high of almost 50% in 2000.

Using the data in Figure 3-1, I estimated the cost of long-term market timing decisions on a generation of investors. The median amount of household financial assets in stocks during the entire 52-year period was about 25%. However, as a group, households moved in and out of the market based on prior period returns. Had the public maintained a constant 25% in stocks during the entire period, instead of changing the asset mix based on past market action, the total return of the static 25% portfolio would have been 3,554% versus a total return of only 2,967% from the trend-following strategy that the public followed.

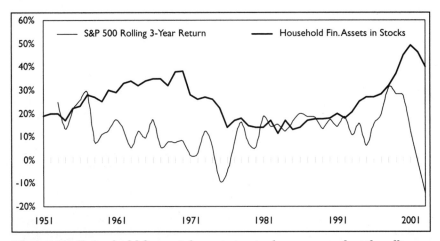

Figure 3-1. Household financial assets in stocks compared with rolling three-year S&P 500 returns

Source: *Federal Reserve Board Bulletin,* January 2002, 50-59.9 percentile of income

Market timing is not helpful to investors over their lifetime. You have nothing to gain by trying to increase stock allocations in a bull market and decrease stocks prior to a bear market. A better alternative is to decide on a static percentage of stocks and bonds that fits your needs and then maintain that allocation for a long, long time. More information on investment planning can be found in Part Three of this book.

TIAA-CREF Study

For a more detailed look at how investors reacted to the final years of the recent bull market, we turn to an in-depth study on retirement saving habits by mutual fund giant and retirement plan provider Teachers Insurance and Annuity Association-College Retirement Equities Fund (TIAA-CREF, New York, NY).[2] TIAA-CREF is a major provider of self-directed retirement plans to public service entities. These include schools, hospitals, universities, and state and local governments. The source for the TIAA-CREF study was the company's own vast database of retirement savers. By analyzing their own client data, the researchers tracked changes in equity allocations as people aged. Also present in the data is the effect of the bull market on asset allocations.

From 1987 to 1994, investors with TIAA-CREF showed an increase in their acceptance of equity risk (Figure 3-2). The average 44-year-old in 1987 gradually increased his or her weighting to stocks from 42% to about 44% by 1994. Then, starting around 1995, investors in all age groups accelerated their allocation to equity, both with invested money and new contributions. By 1999, the now 56-year-olds had increased their retirement holdings to about 57% in equity, a 15% jump from when they were 12 years younger.

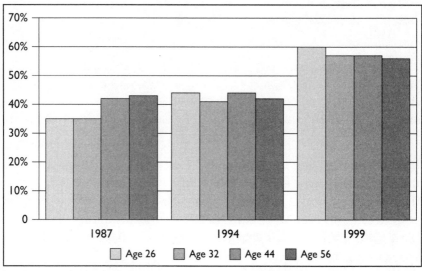

Figure 3-2. TIAA-CREF participant assets in equity based on age
Source: TIAA-CREF

At first glance, you may conclude that the increase in the equity exposure from 1987 to 1999 may be a direct result of the bull market, and some of it was. However, a closer examination reveals an interesting series of events. From 1988 to 1994, the cumulative return of the S&P 500 was 133%, yet the equity allocations for investors in the 40- to 50-year age group did not move very much. That was because a majority of those investors were putting new contributions into safer investments, such as fixed income annuities. This kept the stock percentage fairly stable. In addition, a small number of middle-aged investors were actively reallocating assets out of stocks as the market went up, which was proper action to take in a well-balanced investment plan.

Perhaps the "crash" of 1987 and the market sell-off leading up to the Gulf War in 1991 instilled some caution in investors for a while, but the picture changed again from 1995 to 1999. During that period, the cumulative return of the S&P 500 was an astonishing 251%, which seemed to result in a significant shift in thinking across all age groups in the TIAA-CREF data, particularly among participants in their 40s and 50s. The conservative strategies exhibited earlier by some investors were no longer identifiable.

Figure 3-3 illustrates a gradual increase in new cash contributions allocated to stocks over a 10-year period. In 1989, few investors were placing a large percentage of their new contributions into equities. By 1998, more than half the investors were placing more than 50% of new money into equities—and half of those people were investing 100% in equities.

The significant increase in equity exposure occurred for two reasons. In all age groups, people shifted allocations of new contribu-

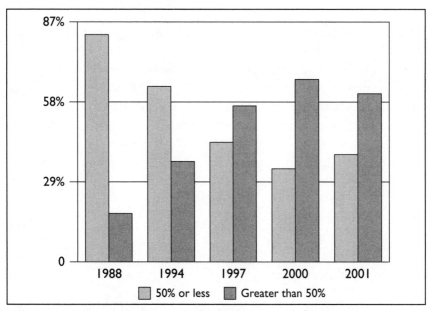

Figure 3-3. TIAA-CREF new contributions to equity funds
Source: TIAA-CREF

tions away from safe investments into equities and they let equity gains ride without rebalancing their portfolio. Clearly, people believed that the past gains in the stock market were going to continue. Perhaps this shift in strategy was a result of greed, or perhaps it was a result hope, or perhaps peer pressure had something to do with the increase in risk. Regardless of the motivation, the shift to greater equity exposure as U.S. stock prices climbed to the highest relative value in history proved to be a costly mistake.

The Calm Before the Storm

Stock prices have reached a permanently high plateau.
—*Irving Fisher, August 1929*

We are in a new paradigm of stock pricing. Old models no longer work.
—*Popular Wall Street saying, 1999*

The four most expensive words in the English language are "This time it's different."
—*Sir John Templeton*

There are a signs when the stock market may be getting a little overvalued. For example, nearly everyone is bullish. Even longtime Wall Street bears become bulls, or at least they stay quiet to avoid a public whipping. Trying to make a case for lower stock prices is about as popular as screaming anti-American slogans during a Veterans Day parade. Second, stock prices go up for any reason and on any news. Even bad news is good news. For example, if a report comes out that predicts lower interest rates, stocks go up on the prospects for an increase in economic activity. On the other hand, if the report predicts higher interest rates, the market still goes up because that means inflation will stay in check, which is good for the growth of corporate earnings.

Another sign that the market may be getting expensive is that absolute nobodies reporting financial news become huge celebrities. These people host financial TV shows and radio shows and write investment books that say nothing of value. Worse, the general public actually pays good money to buy these books and hear these people speak at investment seminars. Finally, and most important, the public is sold on the idea that this bull market is different. That means forget everything we ever learned about relative value of assets or risk avoidance principles and blindly jump into the market because it's going up!

It is interesting to observe that stock prices tend to decrease in price volatility during the final phase of a bull market, which tends to reinforce the false belief that stocks are now somehow safer and that this bull market is different. As you can see from Figures 3-4 and 3-5, stock prices surged in 1996 while the volatility of day-to-day price changes dropped to historically low rates. Prices just kept going up and up and up. It was a self-fulfilling event, for a while.

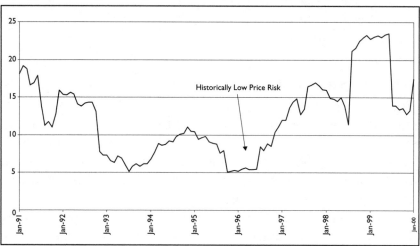

Figure 3-4. 12-month S&P 500 price volatility, 1991-1999
Source: Bloomberg

Volatility picked up in late 1998 after Russia defaulted on its debts and the U.S. markets shuddered. But the increase in volatility did not persist. Within a few months, the market was hitting new highs day after day and volatility was falling again. This again reinforced the belief that the market was in a new paradigm and that we were in a new economic era. By this time it was hard to find any naysayers. Most people were convinced that our economy and the stock market were poised for unprecedented acceleration in the new century.

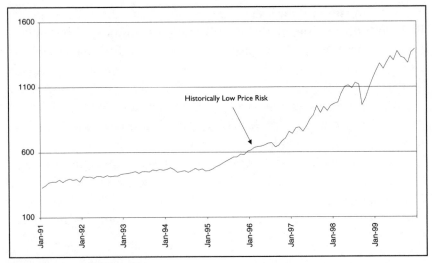

Figure 3-5. S&P 500 prices, 1991-1999
Source: Bloomberg

After the Shakeout

From the beginning of 2000 to the summer of 2002, millions of retirement savers lost huge amounts of money from the portion of their investment accounts invested in the stock market directly or through mutual funds. In addition, large numbers of people lost their jobs as large numbers of new-era companies collapsed and hundreds of technology start-up companies disappeared. Many employees with these companies had their entire net worth riding on company stock options and stock incentive programs. For them, the idea of retiring early in life was replaced by the need to file for unemployment compensation.

A national cry for fairness swept the nation as investors looked to place blame for their misfortunes. Legal claims against Wall Street firms hit a historic high. Thousands of people sued their brokers for unsuitable investment advice. Congress, the Securities and Exchange Commission, and several state attorneys general launched independent investigations. Many corporate executives were indicted and charged with fraud. Investment bankers fired thousands of employees as new business dried up and profits slumped. Mutual fund companies closed or merged hundreds of aggressive growth funds in an effort to bury the performance numbers of the disasters they had on the books. The added regulations and new changes in the securities industry were on par with the massive regulatory changes that took place in the post-depression era in the 1930s.

Individual investors also pulled in their horns and changed the way they invested. People had heard of investing at their risk tolerance level, but never really knew what that meant until they lost a lot of money and panicked. On the plus side, young people were no longer quitting good-paying jobs to become day traders, because day traders were broke and looking for traditional jobs themselves. For most investors, it was their first taste of a real bear market, and they did not know how to act because they did not know what was going wrong with their portfolio or how to fix it.

If anything good came of the experience, it was that many investors finally realized they needed to develop a viable investment plan for retirement, one that could last through a complete market cycle. They also learned that the money made in the late 1990s was a result of luck and not investment skill—and maybe that means they will not believe the Wall Street hype about how they can beat the market. This press release from Boston-based research firm DALBAR, Inc. gives us some indication of hope:

> Boston, MA—June 4, 2001. In a national survey of 1,450 households with incomes of $50,000 or more, DALBAR'S "Turmoil 2001" report found that the downturn in the equity market during 2000 and 2001 has been sufficiently extensive to cause consumers to make changes in their investing preferences. This is in direct contrast to DALBAR'S "Turmoil 1998" report, a study of 1998's extreme but brief volatility, in which investors remained relatively unshaken by short-term market fluctuations. Among the changes identified in this updated report are:
>
> - A general shift to more conservative investment products, but no overall decrease in total saving;
> - Movement away from individual securities and single-sector funds towards products with greater diversification; and,

> • Investors have a better understanding of both the need for financial planning and the risk they can accept.

Bear Markets in Other Asset Classes

So far in this chapter we have talked about bear markets only as they pertain to stocks. However, bear markets occur in the bond market also. When interest rates go up due to a surge in inflation, bond prices can drop almost as fast as stock prices. Since 1926, there have been 21 negative years in the long-term government bond market. Two of the worst returning years for long-term government bonds were 1994, down 7.8%, and 1999, down 9.0%. In addition, since 1926, there have been six five-year periods when bonds were negative, most recently from 1977 to 1981, down 1.1% annually.

The market for gold and precious metals peaked over 20 years ago and has been in a multi-decade bear market ever since. The price of gold touched its record high of $850 per ounce on January 21, 1980 and is currently trading at one-third that price.

The 1980s were the decade of the Rising Sun. Japan's resurgence in manufacturing and banking turned that country's stock market into a global powerhouse. The Nikkei average was so powerful, it was the first market to fully recover from the 1987 global market crash. By early 1990, the Nikkei was trading above the unprecedented level of 30,000. But that was the last time that market traded over 30,000. Boom typically leads to bust, and for the next 10 years the Nikkei slid backwards, losing nearly two-thirds of its value. Over the last few years the Nikkei has bounced along in the mid-teen range.

There is always a bear market occurring somewhere in the world. There is nothing unusual about a bear market in a free market economy. It is a natural phenomenon. Even though our government and business leaders try to mitigate the damage during a downturn, there are no easy solutions or quick fixes. Market pessimism has to run its course. Sometimes a bear market can last a long time, especially if that market went very high during the late bull phase due to extreme optimism. This was the case with the price of gold in the late 1970s, the Nikkei in the 1980s, and possibly our own stock market in the late 1990s. The only cure for a bear market is time. Business economics need time to catch up with prices.

The lesson for investors is to be well diversified and rebalance the mix when needed. Having several different types of investments in a portfolio means that while one is up, the other is down, and that means selling a little of the one that went up and buying some of the one that went down. This rebalancing method runs against the trend-following nature that we all feel, but it is the proper way to manage a retirement portfolio and protect it from the ensuing bear market.

Chapter Summary

Bear markets can be very painful to people saving for retirement, especially those taking too much risk in their portfolios. Since it is impossible to know when the next downturn in the market will occur, wise investors should be prepared. This means having a long-term investment plan, which includes broad diversification, and sticking to that plan during all market conditions.

Bear markets themselves are not the biggest threat to investors; it is the events leading up to a bear market that get people into trouble. Investors tend to become overly optimistic about prospects during the last phase of a bull market, when prices are already high. The euphoria of easy money tempts us to abandon the logic of a well-diversified portfolio and put more money into risky assets. Investors allow their stock winnings to grow, while committing even more capital. No appeal to reason will stop some people from risking much more than they should.

When the bubble bursts and the market collapses, overly committed investors are shocked and bewildered. They cannot believe that the future has turned against them. There is a natural tendency to get mad at the market and at their brokerage firm or mutual fund company. Sometimes the bewilderment leads to very poor, emotional decision-making, such as increasing risk further to "catch up faster" or deciding to get out of the market "when the time is right." A wise investor would never put himself or herself in that situation, and you shouldn't either.

The instinct to follow a market trend, as wrong as it might be for investors, is very difficult to overcome. The only way to mitigate the urge to dive into a bull market or jump out of a bear market is to create an investment plan that fits your needs, implement that plan, and then stick to it through thick and thin.

Key Points

1. Bear markets occur frequently and are normal part of the economic cycle.
2. Contrary to good business sense, the typical investor tends to buy more stocks after the market goes up and sells stocks after it goes down.
3. Trying to time market movements is futile. A better plan is to decide on an appropriate amount of stocks to own and keep that allocation during all market conditions.

Notes

1. Charles R. Geisst, *Wall Street: A History*, New York: Oxford University Press, 1997.
2. *How Do Household Portfolio Shares Vary with Age?* John Ameriks, Columbia University and TIAA-CREF Institute, and Stephen P. Zeldes, Columbia University and National Bureau of Economic Research. September 25, 2000.

Chapter 4

Getting Trampled
by the Herd

Most investors try various markets, lose money, and finally acquire some knowledge through bitter experience. This is roughly analogous to learning how to drive by having a series of accidents.

—Samuel Case

WHEN PEOPLE BEGIN to share the same beliefs about a particular style of investing, a herding effect can occur in the markets. At first, a small crowd starts moving into one segment of the market and, as it moves, prices rise, which causes other investors to be attracted and Wall Street analysts to start commenting. If prices continue to rise, the crowd grows and becomes a larger movement. Soon, the crowd takes on mob-like qualities, meaning that investor IQs drop to the lowest common denominator, bullish rumors and opinions are elevated to important facts, and doubters are ridiculed. By this point, every brokerage firm and popular investment magazine is talking about the wonderful gains being made in that sector and the fantastic prospects for more gains in the future. At the same time, mutual fund companies flood the market with dozens of new funds designed to capture investors chasing the trend. At the peak in prices, no reasonable person will publicly question the wisdom of investing in the sector—and it is the time when individual investors are about to get hurt very badly.

Typically, the early arrivers into a hot segment do well. But, by the time the herd of individual investors gets to the feeding ground, there is nothing left to eat except dirt. Unfortunately, individual investors eat a lot of dirt.

This chapter is an in-depth study of herding behavior and how that behavior lowers investor returns. It shows why people would be wise to ignore the noise that surrounds herding and resist the temptation to jump onto the bandwagon when a broker calls with a hot tip, a coworker recommends an investment based on last year's great performance, or your mutual fund company introduces a hot new fund in a hot new sector. A better strategy is to construct a diversified portfolio that includes several types of investments and then rebalance that mix occasionally. More information on specific investment strategies can be found in Parts Two and Three of this book.

Mutual Fund Cash Flow Data

The 1990s brought that most prevalent herding behavior we have seen in 75 years. It was a time of fabulous growth in the markets and astounding growth in the mutual fund industry. Hundreds of mutual fund companies brought thousands of new funds to the market, all hoping to capture investor interest and investor assets.

Although the average U.S. equity mutual fund performed well in the 1990s, investors in equity mutual funds did not fare so well. The typical equity mutual investor averaged only 8.5% during the period from 1991 through 2000, according to a study by DALBAR, Inc.[1] (Figure 4-1). During the same period, the average return from U.S. equity mutual funds was 15.6% and the return from the Vanguard 500 Index Fund was 17.3%. (The Vanguard fund basically mirrors the performance of the S&P 500 Index.)

A second research study of cash flow, by the Financial Research Corporation, confirms the shortfall.[2] Here is a synopsis of those findings by Gavin Quill, senior vice president and director of research studies, from the *Journal of Financial Planning*, November 2001:

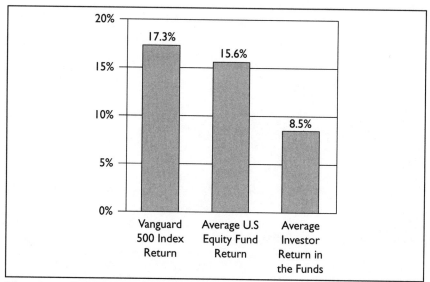

Figure 4-1. DALBAR performance analysis, 1991-2000
Data Source: DALBAR, Inc.

The data shows quite convincingly that there is a massive disconnect between what investors say they prefer to do and what they believe they are doing, versus what history has shown they have actually done with their mutual fund investments. They are simply churning their investments more than they think, and if the academics are right, far more than should be consistent with the achievement of their long-term financial goals. ... The average investor consistently underperforms as a result of excessive turnover.

The top journalists in the popular press understand the shortfalls of trying to pick the hottest mutual funds. In the June 2002 issue of *Money* magazine, Jason Zweig analyzed the flow of money into and out of U.S. stock funds from 1998 to 2001 ("What Fund Investors Really Need to Know"). His results showed the same gap between the average U.S. equity fund return and the average investor's return in those funds (Figure 4-2).

The basic mistake that causes the poor performance is that investors typically do not follow an investment strategy long enough

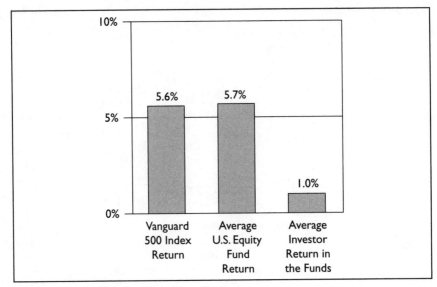

Figure 4-2. *Money* magazine study, 1998 -2001
Data Source: *Money,* June 2002

to allow it to work. Figure 4-3 illustrates that the average hold time for equity mutual funds ranges from two to three years, depending on current market conditions. There is greater turnover of funds during a bear market and less during bull markets. Investors typically sell funds that have underperformed the market and they move on to other funds that have beaten the market. Often, disappointed investors often blame their advisor or even the fund manager for the poor performance; however, the poor performance is more likely a result of the cyclical nature of investment styles. In other words, investment strategies tend to go in and out of favor during natural cycles that occur in the markets and the economy.

Researchers have found some interesting gender bias data about mutual fund turnover. In general, men have a 50% higher investment turnover rate than women, which means they change investment strategies more often. Financial economists Brad Barber and Terrance Odean quantified those results by examining the investing habits of nearly 35,000 households from 1991 to 1997 and dividing the accounts up by gender. They found that, on average, men earned

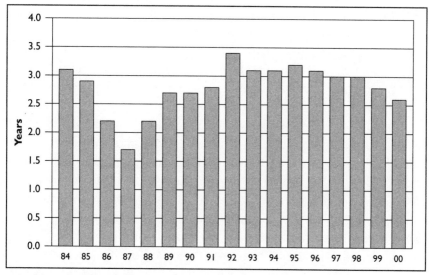

Figure 4-3. Retention rate of equity mutual funds
Data Source: DALBAR, Inc.

several percentage points lower on their investment portfolios than women did.[3] Their results are consistent with what psychologists say about men—we are overconfident, which is a detriment to our success as long-term investors.

Fund Styles Shift in and Out of Favor

Most equity mutual funds have an investment style that the manager is following. When a fund performs significantly better or much worse than the stock market, the style of the fund is usually the main factor. The investment style a manager is following is supposed to be clearly communicated in the mutual fund's prospectus and sales literature, although some fund companies do not do very good job of disclosing this important information.

In general, equity styles can be classified into six categories: U.S. and foreign stocks, large company and small company stocks, and growth and value stocks. U.S. companies have their headquarters on U.S. soil and foreign companies have headquarters outside of U.S. territory. Large companies have a value of roughly $10 billion and more and small companies are under $10 billion. Growth companies have higher earning expectations than average and include companies in technology and other rapidly growing industries. Value stocks have low growth expectations and include basic material companies like steel and industrial companies like automotive. A growth stock fund might include Microsoft while a value stock fund may include International Paper.

One equity style will always perform better than the others based on economic conditions. For example, 1998 and 1999 were great years for large-growth funds and terrible years for small-value funds. In 2000 and 2001 the trend reversed: small-value funds were top performers while large-growth funds were at the bottom of the barrel.

It seems plausible that beating the market merely entails predicting future economic conditions. Then one could position a portfolio to take advantage of a style that does well during that particular part of the economic cycle. However, it is difficult, if not impossible, to predict future economic conditions, so it is difficult, if not impossible, to predict the next hot style with the degree of accuracy needed to beat the market.

The typical investor does not understand the concept of investment styles. Investors see only that other mutual funds are doing well when their fund is not. As a result, they sell a fund whose style is out of favor and follow the crowd into a popular fund whose style is in favor. Investors consistently make the mistake of believing that somehow the hot fund manager is smarter than the cold fund manager. But that is rarely the case. 90% of the time, the difference in return can be explained by the style of the funds.

Chasing popular investment styles is a losing proposition, so investors need to find a better way. Typically, a majority of investors get into a style at or near the peak and participate in only a fraction of the gains. But they are fully invested when the reversal hits and suffer major loses. Instead of chasing styles, it is better to stay diversified across all styles and let the markets go where they may. Occasionally an investor should rebalance those styles to keep an appropriate amount in each one. By staying diversified and rebalancing occasionally, an investor is sure to earn the average return of all the styles, plus a little extra. (See Chapter 12, Asset Allocation Explained.)

Studies of Herding

The study of behavioral finance focuses on the investor decision-making process. Wall Street firms have always been interested in the drivers of investment decisions and conduct numerous behavioral studies in an effort to understand investors so they can promote the right products at the right time. In addition, Wall Street firms are always looking for new gimmicks to stay ahead of the crowd with their own trading activities.

During the last 25 years, behavioral finance research has spread from Wall Street to the clinics and classrooms of major universities. The merging of clinical psychology and investment decisions has yielded some interesting data, which may help people understand why following their natural instincts of fear and greed does not yield high investment returns. Most of the academic research centers on the trading of individual securities; however, the conclusions can be applied to mutual fund investing as well.

One finding is universal across all investment types: roaming with the herd from one popular investment to another may make investors feel secure about their decisions, but it invariably leads to below-average investment results. The data suggests that one reason people roam is to profit from what they perceive as a higher-returning fund. It seems equally important to disassociate from a losing fund. People want to think of themselves as smart and nice, winners not losers. An investor who feels hurt needs to heal. After selling a poorly performing fund, the investor starts rationalizing and minimizing the loss. Over time, the loss becomes tolerable because it is in the past and a new fund with better recent performance has replaced it. This allows investors to view themselves as winners, even though they did not actually own the new fund when it went up. Psychologists call this feeling "cognitive dissonance."

Here is one example of cognitive dissonance. Several years ago, I was working as a stockbroker with a large Wall Street firm. One investment I was using for my clients was a Standard & Poor's Depository Receipt (SPDR) S&P 500 Unit Trust—a "Spider." Spiders track the S&P 500 Index nearly dollar for dollar, so they perform the way the market performs. One October, a client called and informed me that he owned State Street Aurora mutual fund and that it was beating the pants off Spiders. He told me that *his* fund choice was up over 30% for the year, while *my* fund choice was up only about 8%.

After doing a little research, I found the client's claim to be quite impossible. According to a research report by Morningstar, the State Street Aurora fund had been open to the public for only a couple of months. Prior to that, it was only for State Street employees and this man was not a State Street employee. So, it was impossible for him to have earned a 30% return since the beginning of the year. A couple of weeks later, when the client called back and started boasting about his Aurora Fund again, we had this conversation:

"My Aurora Fund is doing so much better than your Spiders."

"When did you actually buy that fund?"

"Oh, I don't know. About a month ago."

"And, how much money have you made in the fund since you owned it?

"Well, nothing, yet. But I will. It's a great fund."

People want to maintain a good self-image. By purchasing stocks and mutual funds that have recently soared in value, they feel like they are doing the right thing and are therefore good investors. The new owners typically enjoy telling friends, relatives, and co-workers or anyone who will listen that they own one of the hottest stocks or hottest mutual funds on the market. They then receive praise and envy from their peers for their investment acumen, even though so far they have not made any money. None of these acquaintances are going to ask when the fund was purchased or how much profit the investors have actually made.

Herding Behavior in the Late 1990s

If history is any indication, the positive self-image gained by purchasing a hot investment does not last. Many times, investments that are top-ranked one year fall to the bottom ranking the next year. This leaves investors with a large loss and a sore ego and it puts them back into a herding mentality. This is exactly what happened to growth stock investors in the late 1990s. Many people felt compelled to buy aggressive growth stock funds during the period because not owning them made them feel left out. It would be like missing a good party. Not only would you miss the fun, but also you don't get to talk about it the next week. So, in 1998 and 1999, people bought anything that was remotely connected to technology, computers, and the Internet.

To illustrate what happened in the late 1990s, Figure 4-4 shows the growth of $1 invested in new-economy growth stocks and old-economy value stocks during of the period from December 1997 to March 2000. As you can see, growth stocks clearly outperformed value stocks by about 4 to 1. One dollar invested in growth grew to nearly $2.00, while during the same period $1 invested in value stocks grew to only $1.25.

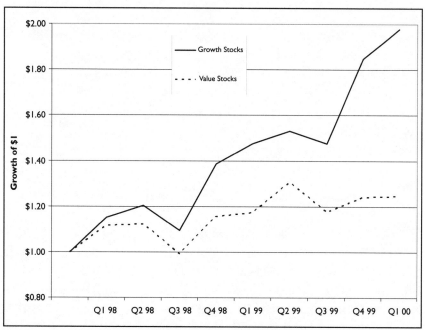

Figure 4-4. Growth stocks versus value stocks, December 1997 to March 2000
Data Source: Russell 1000 Growth and Russell 1000 Value Indexes

Compare the performance of growth stocks in Figure 4-4 with the flow of mutual fund money in Figure 4-5. Growth stocks outperformed value stock during the first three quarters of 1998; however, it was not until the fourth quarter of 1998 that investors took notice and started putting more into growth. In 1999 a huge shift took place. By the fourth quarter of 1999, not only was most new money going into growth funds, but investors were also shifting money out of value funds to buy growth.

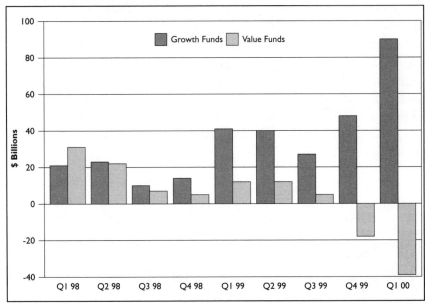

Figure 4-5. Quarterly money flow into growth funds and value funds
Data Source: The Investment Company Institute (ICI)

The mutual fund industry was more than happy to sell investors all the growth stock funds they wanted. As Figure 4-6 illustrates, over 80% of all new equity mutual funds created during the period were growth-oriented funds. For every new growth fund launched, the media extravaganza that went along with it was extensive. Investors were relentlessly pounded with the idea that growth funds were the only way to make money and the red-hot technology and communication sectors were the only games in town.

In the spring of 2000, when companies started announcing cut-

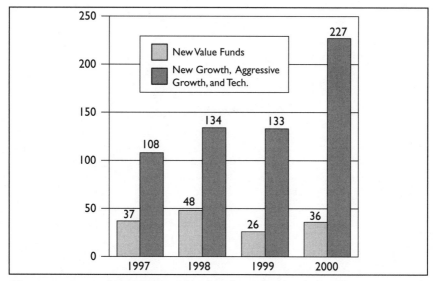

Figure 4-6.. Number of new value funds and growth funds
Data Source: Bogle Research Institute

backs on technology purchases, the prices of aggressive growth stocks began to tumble. At first, no one could believe it, especially the analysts on Wall Street making millions of dollars in bonus for hyping growth stocks. (At least they acted surprised.) In response, Wall Street encouraged individual investors to put more money in while prices were at bargain levels. Many people did, and the collapse that followed devastated a large number of individual investors. (See Figure 4-7.) It was especially harmful for people close to retirement or in retirement who tried to boost their wealth quickly by purchasing hot growth stocks and aggressive growth funds.

Most people say they are long-term investors, yet they routinely chase investment styles that go in and out of favor. Rarely do I find an investor who has held a mutual fund more than five years. The industry lingo for an investor exhibiting this type of behavior is "chasing a hot dot." Occasionally an investor can recognize a trend early and make excess profits. However, over a lifetime, moving from one investment style to another results in increased risk and lower returns.

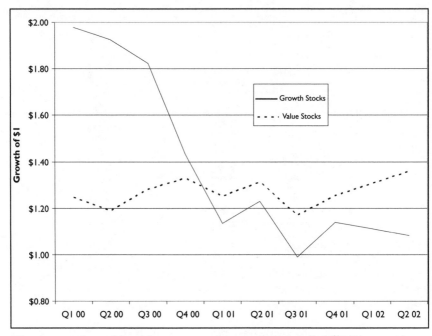

Figure 4-7. Growth stocks versus value stocks, March 2000-June 2002
Data Source: Russell 1000 Value and Russell 1000 Growth Indexes

A Classic Example of Chasing

My favorite example of chasing the hot dot is the Munder Net Net Fund. This high-flying mutual fund exemplifies the disaster that can happen to your savings if you get caught up in the euphoria of a hot fund, which eventually becomes a black hole that sucks up your money.

In August 1996, the investment firm of Munder Capital Management in Birmingham, Michigan, decided to create a unique and unusual sector fund. The fund was to invest in the companies that were in the Internet business. Investments included Internet service providers like AOL, Internet retailers such as Amazon.com, browser software companies such as Netscape, and companies that sold modems and equipment to hook up to the Internet.

The headquarters for Munder Capital Management was about five miles from the brokerage office where I worked at in the 1990s.

The brokers in my office had several client relationships with Munder at the time and we typically obtained information on new fund offerings before they became public knowledge. When we learned that Munder was going to offer a mutual fund that invested exclusively in Internet-related stocks, we had a good laugh. How much more ridiculous could the prices of Internet stocks get? I felt they were clearly overvalued. That was in late 1996.

Well, the joke was on me—at least for a while. After respectable first-year results, over the next two years the performance of the Munder Net Net Fund blew the doors off of every mutual fund in the country. The fund earned a 98% return in 1998 and 176% in 1999. This spectacular show grabbed the hearts, minds, and wallets of mutual fund investors far and wide. By late 1999, tens of millions of dollars per day were pouring into the Munder Net Net Fund. Assets exploded from just under $300 million at the beginning of 1999 to over $10 billion by March 2000.

Figure 4-8 charts the discrepancy between investors' investments in the Munder Net Net Fund and the subsequent performance of the fund. As luck would have it, billions of dollars of newly invested capital vanished between March 2000 and the end of that year as the fund tumbled 54% in value. The massacre continued though 2001 with a 48% drop and billions more were lost. In 2002, the loss was 45%. Over the three-year period, the Munder Net Net Fund lost nearly 90% of its starting value and billions of dollars in investors' money. Some people were lucky: they sold early and salvaged a portion of their invested capital. Others hoped for a rebound: they stayed in for the full onslaught, as no rebound ever materialized.

A casual observer might conclude that the Munder fund was a dismal failure from its beginnings in September 1996 to the end of 2002 because of the amount of money that was lost in the fund. But, that is not the way the mutual fund industry sees it. The method of performance measurement used by mutual fund companies is quite different from what first meets the eye.

According to the Morningstar *Principia* database, the annualized return of the Munder Net Net Fund class A share since inception was *positive* 2.15% annually, which was about the same as the typical

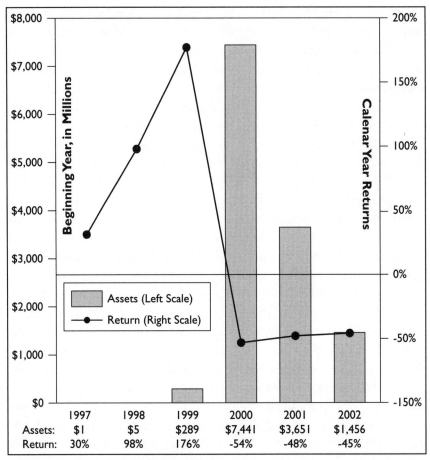

	1997	1998	1999	2000	2001	2002
Assets:	$1	$5	$289	$7,441	$3,651	$1,456
Return:	30%	98%	176%	-54%	-48%	-45%

Figure 4-8. Munder Net Net Fund
Data Sources: Morningstar, Munder Capital Management

technology fund, but lower than the 6.4% compounded return for the S&P 500 during the same period. As a result, Munder might say the fund "made money" since inception, which is not bad given the environment for technology companies. If you were an investor in the fund, would you feel the same way?

The Munder Net Net Fund reported return numbers are a classic example of performance reporting shenanigans. The standard method of performance measurement used by the investment industry is called *time-weighted returns* (TWR). Fund performance is calculated by placing a hypothetical $100 in that fund and then tracking the performance of that $100 over the years. Actual deposits and withdrawals in the mutual fund have no bearing on the reported performance number; only the original $100 matters. For example, if $10,000 were invested in the Munder Net Net Fund on October 1, 1996, it would have grown to $115,600 by February 2000. That is a total return of 1006% and an annualized return of 98.7%. But by the end of 2002, the original $10,000 investment was worth only $11,786, a total gain of only $1,786. However, a $10,000 investment in December 2000 would be worth only $1,314, a loss of $8,686.

When calculating total return since inception, Munder is not concerned with the investor who lost $8,686. What is important is only the hypothetical investor who made $1,786 since inception. The fact that billions of dollars were invested in the Munder Net Net Fund near the peak of the market and subsequently lost is irrelevant.

The problem with the TWR method is that it does not tell us how much money was made or lost in the fund over the period. It tells us only how much the return would have been if someone had held the fund for the entire period being measured—which is relatively useless in this particular case, because the amount of money in the fund at the start of 1997 was insignificant.

Munder does not have to disclose actual money gains and money losses in a fund. Nor does it have to disclose important items like risk measurements. Like all mutual fund firms, Munder can advertise fund performance over any period it wishes, as long as the time-weighted return is calculated correctly. Without the help of independent services like Morningstar to track fund performance and analytics, investors would be totally in the dark as to which funds made investors money and which ones did not.

The Three Axes of Style Chasing

There are three basic ways people chase returns. First, there are shifts between growth and value stocks; second, there are shifts between large and small stocks; and third, there are shifts between U.S. and foreign stocks.

The Growth and Value Axis

The growth stock boom of the late 1990s and bust of the early 2000s is still fresh on minds of investors because it occurred so recently. In addition, a lot of new investors got hurt in the cycle because there were tens of millions of new people in the market at the time. However, what happened with growth stocks during the period was not unique or even unusual. There have several growth stock booms and busts over the years.

Figure 4-9 illustrates the rolling three-year return differential between the Russell Growth Index and the Russell Value Index. When the chart is positive, growth stocks outperformed value stocks over the previous three years; when the chart is negative, value stocks beat growth stocks. Realize that this is only a 20-year period.

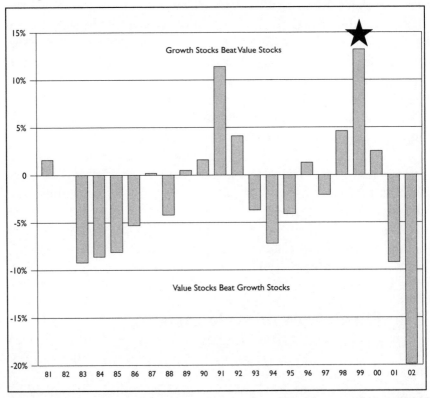

Figure 4-9. Growth stocks versus value stocks, rolling three-year annualized
Data Source: Frank Russell Company

The star in Figure 4-9 marks the period from 1997 to 1999 when growth beat value by an annualized rate of 13% per year. It is also the point in time when most investors were dumping value stock mutual funds for growth stock funds. Flip back to Chapter 3 and look at Figure 3-3. The mass migration to growth did not start until the first quarter of 1999 and the biggest movement of money occurred later in the year.

Working backwards in Figure 4-9, we see that value stocks handily beat growth stocks in 1992 and 1993. That caused investors to load up on value mutual funds a year later, in late 1993 and 1994. The money to purchase value funds came in part from growth stock funds that were purchased after the growth stock burst from 1989 to 1991.

Unknowing investors chase growth and value as the market flows back and forth between the two styles in an unpredictable pattern—and they do it late in the game. That sets a portfolio up for disappointing results when the tide turns. Long-time observers of the market know these style shifts are going to happen; they just do not know when. The best course of action is to not try to predict the shift. Simply buy and hold a diversified portfolio that contains both growth and value stocks.

The Large and Small Axis

A second form of chasing is based on the size factor in mutual funds. The stock market is made up of thousands of companies, some big but mostly small. The biggest companies dominate the major indexes, such as the Dow Jones Industrial Average and the Standard and Poor's 500 Index. Small companies represent less than 25% of the value of the overall market. Nonetheless, sometimes the stocks of smaller companies achieve significantly greater rates of return than larger stocks. When small stocks beat large stocks, mutual funds that hold small stocks beat funds that hold only large stocks.

Figure 4-10 represents the differences in returns over continuous three-year rolling periods between the S&P 500 and the Russell 2500 Indexes. The S&P 500 tracks mostly large company stocks and the Russell 2500 is composed of approximately 2500 small and medium-size companies not in the S&P 500. The star in Figure 4-10 marks

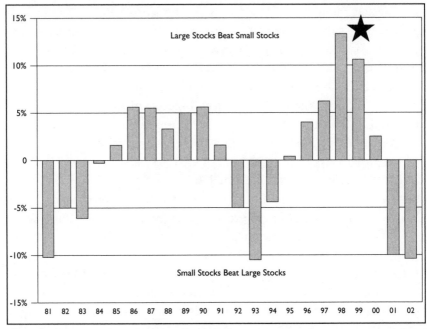

Figure 4-10. Large stocks versus small stocks, rolling three-year annualized
Data Sources: S&P, Frank Russell Company

the period in the late 1990s when large stocks were significantly out-performing small stocks. Most of the new mutual funds being created at the time were large growth funds, to meet the demands of investors.

Periods of superior performance shift back and forth between large stocks and small stocks in the same unpredictable manner as flows between value and growth stocks. Since average investors are particularly aware that size makes such a difference in mutual fund returns, they mistakenly chase mutual funds that hold smaller stocks after that sector of the market has had a couple of years of superior performance. This tendency sets investors up for poor performance in the future, when large stocks outperform and investors turn over their portfolios again.

The U.S. and Foreign Axis
The third factor that causes performance differences in stock mutu-

al funds is the choice of allocation between domestic stocks and foreign stocks. The value of U.S. stocks makes up about half of all stocks traded around the globe; the rest of the world's markets make up the other half. The returns of various markets around the globe are not in perfect synch with each other. This is due to currency fluctuations, economic factors, laws, customs, trading procedures, and other issues. As a result, there are times when U.S. stocks perform better than foreign stocks and there are times when foreign stocks perform better than U.S. stocks. Some investors try to follow the flow of money into various regions of the world. For example, there was huge demand for Japanese stocks in the late 1980s; then the demand shifted to emerging markets like Latin American stocks in the early 1990s, and then again to Europe in the late 1990s.

Figure 4-11 illustrates the annualized three-year rolling difference between stocks in the U.S., represented by the S&P 500, and foreign stocks, represented by the MSCI (Morgan Stanley Capital International) Europe, Australia, and Far East (EAFE) index. As you can guess by the location of the star on the chart, U.S. investors had a gigantic appetite for foreign investment in the late 1980s. This was particularly true of the markets in the Far East, where Asian countries were on track to dominate world trade and banking and Japan was heralded as an economic miracle.

As people try to make the best investment decisions they can with the minimum information they have, they tend to focus on past performance numbers. If investors notice their funds are not keeping pace with the more popular trends in the market, they will sell their funds and buy funds that are in style. Not only will investors buy a hot fund style near its peak, but they are also likely to sell an out-of-favor style near its low.

The major factors affecting the performance of a stock mutual fund are its size bias, growth or value bias, and its country bias. Table 4-1 lists how these factors have moved in relation to one other over the years. Studying this table is educational, but using it to predict the future is impossible.

Just when you think you see a pattern in the numbers and feel you can predict where the next gains will be made, you notice anoth-

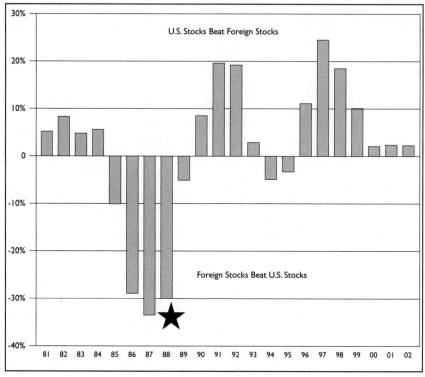

Figure 4-11. U.S. large stocks versus foreign stocks, rolling three-year annualized
Data Sources: S&P, Morgan Stanley

er time period where following that strategy would have resulted in a loss. For example, Japanese stocks had miserable performance during most of the 1990s, but they looked like they were staging a comeback in 1999. Based on this observation, you may have decided to invest heavily in Japan. Bad move. Japanese stocks were the worst-performing market in 2000 and 2001. Trying to time sectors and styles does not work.

Chapter Summary

This chapter illustrates the dangers of selling one type of mutual fund style and buying another simply because the investment strategy is out of synch with the short-term thinking of a herd mentality. Chasing the hot dot may feel right at the time, because that is what

	LG	LV	SG	SV	JPN	UK
1979	3	4	1	2	6	5
1980	3	6	1	5	4	2
1981	6	3	5	1	2	4
1982	3	4	2	1	6	5
1983	6	2	4	1	3	5
1984	5	2	6	4	1	3
1985	3	4	6	5	2	1
1986	4	3	6	5	1	2
1987	3	4	6	5	1	2
1988	5	3	4	2	1	6
1989	1	2	4	5	6	3
1990	2	3	4	5	6	1
1991	3	4	1	2	6	5
1992	4	2	3	1	6	5
1993	6	4	5	3	2	1
1994	2	5	6	4	1	3
1995	2	1	3	4	6	5
1996	2	3	5	4	6	1
1997	3	1	5	2	6	4
1998	1	2	5	6	4	3
1999	3	5	2	6	1	4
2000	4	2	5	1	6	3
2001	5	2	3	1	6	4
2002	5	4	6	2	1	3

Table 4-1. Comparing stock market returns (1 = best, 6 = worst)
LG = Large growth stocks (Russell 1000 Growth Index)
LV = Large value stocks (Russell 1000 Value Index)
SG = Small growth stocks (Russell 2000 Growth Index)
SV = Small value stocks (Russell 2000 Value Index)
JPN = Large Japanese stocks (Tokyo Stock Exchange)
UK = United Kingdom (Financial Times Actuaries All Shares Index)

everyone else is doing, but it is almost always the wrong decision. Trying to catch the wave on a hot style guarantees poor performance in a retirement account. The most reliable strategy is to own all types of mutual funds, all of the time, and keep the amounts you have in those funds balanced. Broad diversification is a key to success in any long-term investment plan.

Key Points

1. The overall performance of mutual funds is much higher than the average investor experiences. Every two to five years, the public herds from one fund type to another, chasing the best-performing funds. During this migration, investors tend to sell out-of-favor funds at low prices and buy in-favor funds at high prices, undermining the long-term performance of their retirement accounts.
2. The three elements of equity mutual fund holdings that explain nearly all the return of a given fund are size (large vs. small stocks), style (growth or value stocks), and geographic region (U.S. or foreign stocks).
3. It is impossible to predict which type of fund will outperform the others. Therefore, the best strategy is to hold a diversified portfolio that contains all types of stocks and stick with a constant mix.

Notes

1. DALBAR Inc., *Quantitative Analysis of Investor Behavior, 2001 Update*, DALBAR, Inc., Boston, MA.
2. Gavin Quill, "Investors Behaving Badly: An Analysis of Investor Trading Patterns in Mutual Funds," *Journal of Financial Planning*, November 2001.
3. Brad M. Barber and Terrance Odean, "Boys Will Be Boys: Gender, Overconfidence, and Common Stock Investment," *Quarterly Journal of Economics, February* 2001, pp. 261-292.

Chapter 5

The High Cost of Low Returns

He who will not economize will have to agonize.

—*Confucius*

A DOLLAR SAVED is a dollar earned. The old axiom, updated for inflation, applies particularly well to investing your savings. Every dollar unnecessarily spent on mutual fund fees, custodial charges, commissions, advisor fees, and other expenses is one dollar less you have for retirement, plus interest. Scrutinize your accounts. Get rid of the excessive costs.

Let's assume you were asked to give a 24-year-old some investment advice. A young woman you know just landed her first full-time job at a large company and her starting pay is $36,000. The company has a 401(k) plan. She intends to put 10% of her salary into the plan each year. The plan has two investment choices. Both are balanced stock and bond mutual funds. Your analysis of the investment options reveals that the only difference between the two funds is the management fee. One fund charges 1.5% and the other charges 0.5%. Which mutual fund would you recommend to the young woman? This is not a trick question.

Naturally, you would recommend the fund with a 0.5% fee. All else being equal, that option will likely yield a 1% higher rate of return each year because the fee is 1% less than the other option. You might think that this is a poor hypothetical example because it does not happen in the real world. But, in fact, this situation is very common among 401(k) and other employer-sponsored retirement plans.

Many plans I have looked at offer two nearly identical investment options whose only difference is the fee. For example, a corporate retirement plan may offer the Smith Barney Growth and Income Class A shares with a 1.17% fee and the Vanguard S&P 500 Index Fund with a 0.18% expense ratio. Both funds invest in the same group of large-cap, blue-chip companies and have basically the same weighting to industry sectors. The performance of each fund also moves up and down at the same time. In other words, the funds are highly correlated. In the investment industry, we would call the Smith Barney fund a "closet" index fund because it has the look, feel, and performance of the S&P 500, but with expenses. As you would expect, the Vanguard fund has performed much better than the Smith Barney fund because the Vanguard fee is almost 1% lower and there is no commission to buy shares.

Over several years, a 1% difference between fund returns can add up to large difference in the value of a retirement account. Consider the example of the young woman who starts saving 10% of her $36,000 salary. Assume she saves 10% throughout her career and gets a 3% pay raise each year until retiring at age 65. A 1% difference in investment fees adds up to several hundred thousand dollars at retirement. Table 5-1 provides those calculations.

If most people would recommend a low-fee investment to someone else, why do a majority of investors opt for the high-fee invest-

Retirement at 65	6% Return	7% Return	Difference	% Increase
Total savings at 10% salary	$1,471,394	$1,943,699	$472,305	32%
Annual withdrawal at 4%	$58,856	$77,748	$18,892	32%
Monthly withdrawal	$4,905	$6,479	$1,574	32%

Table 5-1. What a difference 1% makes in retirement!

ments in their own portfolios? That makes no sense, unless people are not paying attention to costs. In reality, typical investors are not aware of much they are paying in investment expenses. Many costs in investing are hidden or hard to quantify. I have seen many large 401(k) plans that give employees a periodic list of investment options and returns, but do not mention fees and expenses. As a result, people buy investments that are recommended by co-workers or financial advisors or that had the best short-term performance, regardless of the fee.

Most mutual funds and pooled investment products charge over 1% per year in expenses, before commissions. The December 2002 edition of the Morningstar *Principia* database listed 14,674 mutual funds of all types from all fund families. About 70% of those funds are in equity investment and about 30% are in bonds. The average annual expense of all the funds was 1.40%. There is no reason to pay that much to invest.

Compare the 1.40% fee with the expenses of one low-cost fund company, The Vanguard Group. Vanguard has 159 funds listed in Morningstar database, which hold about 63% in equity and 37% in bonds. The average expense of the combined Vanguard funds is only 0.27%. Vanguard's fund expenses are 1.13% less than the overall industry average. That means Vanguard funds are going to earn higher returns over time than the average mutual fund. Most other funds cannot make up the difference in fees because, on average, the managers picking stocks and bonds are not able to add enough return. I use Vanguard as an example, but there are other low-fee funds and fund companies.

My question is not why Vanguard fees are so low, but why the other fund companies' fees are so high. Unfortunately, the answer is money. Let's face it: most investment companies are in business to make money *from* you, not *for* you. Do investors really need over 1000 Growth and Income funds to choose from, all investing in essentially the same stocks and all earning basically the same performance, less their fee? There is no need for all those funds to exist—except as a source of fee income for the 400 or so mutual fund companies that provide them. I suggest finding the cheapest ones and putting your money there.

Figure 5-1 clearly illustrates how mutual fund expenses reduce performance. The figure is derived from a sort of the Morningstar *Principia* database. It is a list of the 97 mutual funds in the Growth and Income fund category that have been around since 1987. Two funds with the highest fees were left off the list because the performance was so bad it skewed the results. The 97 funds were then sorted into four buckets based on their current expense ratio. The low-fee funds are on the left and the high-fee funds are on the right. The return on the left is an average of the 15-year annualized return in each bucket. This analysis does not include commissions.

The Growth and Income category was chosen for this comparison because many of the big, well-known mutual funds are part of that group. This category includes Fidelity Magellan, Vanguard 500, Washington Mutual, the Windsor Fund, and the Investment Company of America.

The results shown in Figure 5-1 are clear. The more a fund charges in fees, the lower the expectations of returns. This cost-versus-return relationship is not restricted to only funds in the Growth and Income category. It stretches across all stock categories. Figure 5-2 illustrates the low-fee advantage of funds that invest in small company stocks and foreign stocks.

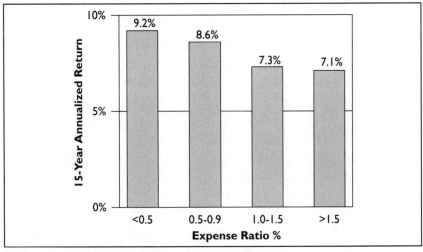

Figure 5-1. 97 growth and income mutual funds with a 15-year record
Source: Morningstar *Principia*, December 2002

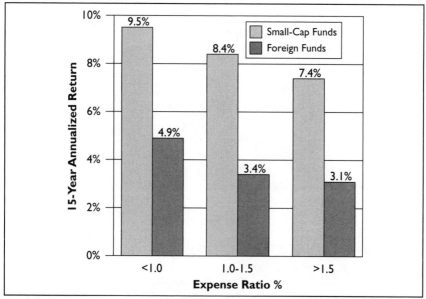

Figure 5-2. Small-cap funds and foreign funds with a 15-year track record
Source: Morningstar *Principia,* December 2002

The fee-versus-return relationship also extends to corporate bonds funds, government bonds funds, and tax-exempt municipal bond funds.

As previously explained, Figures 5-1 through 5-3 address only expense ratios within mutual funds, not the cost to buy the funds. About 70% of all mutual funds charge a commission of some sort to buy in. A commission can be charged in a variety of ways, but the most common is either upfront (front-loaded) or annually through a large 12b-1 fee. The average commission to buy a mutual fund is about 5.2%. However, commissions are rising. Over the last few years, commission rates have increased 0.35%, according to Financial Research Corporation, a Boston-based financial services research and consulting firm.

There is an early conclusion to this chapter, if you care to take it. To earn a higher rate of return on your retirement account, simply select mutual funds that have rock-bottom fees and do not charge a commission to buy or sell. These funds are called *pure no-load funds.* The lowest-cost pure no-load funds are index mutual funds from

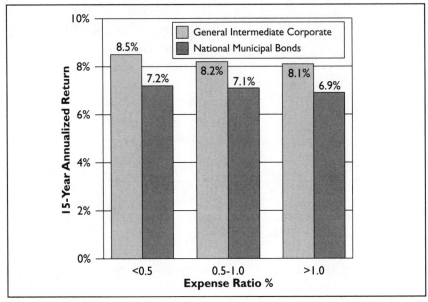

Figure 5-3. Corporate bond and municipal bond funds with a 15-year track record
Source: Morningstar *Principia,* December 2002

companies like the Vanguard Group. They have no tricks and no gimmicks, just pure dollar for dollar savings.

Getting Your Money's Worth

When a stockbroker or financial advisor recommends an investment, you should ask how much money he or she is going to make off the recommendation. The amount needs to include everything: front-end commissions, annual trailing commissions, including the broker's portion of the 12b-1 fee, and possibly a separate consulting fee on top of everything else. In addition, ask if there are any sales contests going on. There may be hidden benefits for the broker as well. Many times, if a broker or commission-based advisor sells enough of a particular investment, he or she may be entitled to free trips, sporting events, theater passes, a more prestigious title, and maybe even a better office. Insurance companies are notorious for giving away exotic vacations and an occasional sports car to salespeople who push fee-laden investment products.

Early in my career as a broker, I won a mountain bike for selling $5,000 worth of a limited partnership and a trip to Florida for selling $100,000 worth of annuities in one month. I admit that none of these extras were disclosed to the clients who bought those investments, but that is part of Wall Street culture. My former office manager was fond saying the clients do not need to know everything.

After the Enron and WorldCom scandals, there should be no doubt in investors' minds that most financial firms are not in the business of offering financial advice to small clients. They are in the business of distributing financial products to small clients—and getting paid a lot of money on those sales. This is especially true of brokerage firms that will distribute almost any new mutual fund, limited partnership, annuity, or new company stock if it appears legitimate and the commission is high enough. Management backs this charade because the profit potential for the firm is so great. Office managers encourage brokers to sell the products because they receive bonuses for reaching certain sales goals for new products. Sometimes a firm will run a special; in general, that means a broker can get a higher commission by selling one product over another. The way investments are sold is a major reason a lot of investors own mutual funds with 1.4% in fees rather than comparable funds with 0.3% in fees.

I recommend Vanguard mutual funds to many people. The fees are very low and The Vanguard Group is the only nonprofit investment company that is owned by investors in the funds. The Vanguard Group is owned by people who invest in its mutual funds, not a separate group of stockholders. If Vanguard has a profit at the end of the year, the management fees in the mutual funds are lowered. In this way, the more money that gets invested with Vanguard, the greater the economy of scale and the lower the fee. Over the years, Vanguard's mutual fund fees have fallen to the lowest in the industry. Another low-cost, no-load mutual fund company is the Teachers Insurance and Annuity Association-College Retirement Equities Fund (TIAA-CREF), New York, NY. Although it is a private company, the fees of most mutual funds and annuity products are very low.

While low-cost, no-load investing is the place to be, the number of funds that fall into this category is appalling low. As of December 2001, fewer than 300 no-load mutual funds had fees of 0.5% or less. Fortunately, a new concept is evolving that is helping to drive fees lower.

A number of mutual fund companies have introduced exchange-traded funds (ETFs) into the marketplace. These are low-cost mutual funds that trade during the day on a stock exchange, rather than at the close of business like a typical open-end mutual fund. There are disadvantage in ETFs. For example, you have to pay a brokerage fee to buy them and there may be a spread between the buy price and the sell price. However, the cost is nominal if you hold the fund as a long-term investment. Detailed information on ETFs can be found in another book that I authored, *All About Index Funds* (New York: McGraw-Hill, 2002).

Fees, Fees, and More Fees

The expense ratio of mutual fund management covers only the mutual fund itself. There could be many be other investment costs. If you use a broker, an insurance agent, or a commissioned financial planner, there will certainly be commissions and other fees attached to anything you buy or sell. If your plan is through an insurance company, the investment recommendation may be in the form of variable annuities, which are like mutual funds with an insurance wrapper that adds cost. An insurance-based retirement plan using variable annuities will have a mortality and administrative (M&A) expense on top of the standard mutual fund fees. The M&A fees range from 0.30% to 1.50%, depending on the insurance company.

In addition to the basic cost of investing, an investor may decide to hire an independent investment advisor to help make investment decisions. The typical independent advisor fee is 1.0% per year of assets, but fees vary depending on the advisor. Some firms (like ours) charge only a small amount. Others charge as much as 2% per year.

The custodian of your retirement account also charges an annual administrative fee for Individual Retirement Accounts that are below a minimum dollar level. That annual fee runs between $10 and $100 per account per year, depending on where your account is held.

In addition, most people now have employer-sponsored 401(k), 403(b), and 457 plans where they work. For simplicity, I will refer to all of these defined contribution plans as 401(k)-type plans. The day-to-day operation of these plans involves expenses for basic administrative services—such as plan record keeping, accounting, legal and trustee services—that are necessary for administering the plan as a whole. Today 401(k)-type plans may also offer a host of additional services, such as telephone voice response systems, access to a customer service representative, educational seminars, retirement planning software, investment advice, electronic access to plan information, daily valuation, and on-line transactions.

In some instances, the costs of administrative services will be covered by investment fees that are deducted directly from investment returns. Otherwise, if administrative costs are separately charged, they will be either borne by your employer or charged directly against the assets of the plan. When paid directly by the plan, administrative fees are either allocated among individual accounts in proportion to each account balance (i.e., participants with larger balances pay more of the allocated expenses) or passed through as a flat fee against each participant's account. Either way, generally the more services provided, the higher the fees.

In addition to overall administrative expenses, there may be individual service fees associated with optional features offered under a 401(k)-type plan. Individual service fees are charged separately to the accounts of individuals who choose to take advantage of a particular plan feature. For example, individual service fees may be charged to a participant for taking a loan from the plan or for executing participant investment directions.

Sometimes 401(k) plans use collective investment funds instead of mutual funds. A collective investment fund is one big account managed by a bank or trust company that pools investments of 401(k)-type plans and other similar investors. Each investor has a proportionate interest in the trust fund assets. For example, if a collective investment fund holds $10 million in assets and your investment in the fund is $10,000, you have a 0.1% interest in the fund. Like mutual funds, collective investment funds may have different investment objectives. There are no front- or back-end fees associated with a collective investment fund, but there are investment management and administrative fees.

All the Fees Add Up

Depending on where and how you invest your retirement money, expenses can run 3% or more annually. Consider an investor who pays a financial advisor 1.5% per year to select variable annuities that have expenses of 2.2% per year and administrative costs of 0.3% per year. That brings the total investment costs of this plan to 4% per year. During the 1980s and 1990s, it may have been easy to overlook 4% in fees because the markets were booming and people were generally making money. Over the next decade, 4% in fees will stick out like a pink-haired punk rocker at a monastery. There is no chance an investor who pays 4% in fees will achieve performance results anywhere close to the returns of the stock and bond markets. Bill Bernstein, author and investment manager, summed it up in a recent issue of *Barron's*, "Given low equity returns, high expenses, and poor planning, it is likely that most 401(k) investors will obtain near-zero real returns in the coming decades."[1]

Looking back at Figure 5-1, it is clear that high costs are negatively correlated with rates of return. The more you pay in commissions, fees, and expenses, the less money you will have for retirement. That is a law of economics that no wizard financial advisor can change.

Unfortunately, many people have no option at work except to invest in high-cost investment plans because their employer has chosen a high-cost provider for the company. However, workers at many firms have successfully petitioned management to add lower-cost investment options to their plans. Every dime saved on investment expenses is a dime straight into your pocket. It is worth a phone call.

I highly recommend you find out what the total fees are in all of your retirement accounts, including your employer's plan, and start working on reducing your cost. If that means frequent visits and e-mails to your plan administrator and trustees, then that is what you need to do. This is your retirement money—and you cannot afford to waste it.

Chapter Summary

High costs hurt. The more you pay in expenses, the less money you will have for retirement. It is a law of economics that no one can change. It is little wonder that most people get poor returns on their retirement accounts. The fees eat away much of their gains. It is imperative that you scrutinize every nickel of your retirement savings expenses and cut costs wherever possible. Your well-being in retirement depends on keeping costs low.

Key Points

1. Costs matter. The more you pay in fees, the less you make in return. There is no advantage to paying more for some investment products and advice when the same products and advice can be found for less expense elsewhere.
2. When starting to work with a financial advisor, be clear on how he or she gets paid and ensure that he or she discloses any conflict of interest.
3. Most 401(k)-type employer-sponsored savings plans are overburdened with administrative and management costs. Know the total cost of your plan and work with your employer to reduce expenses when possible.

Note

1. William Bernstein, "Riding for a Fall; The 401(k) Is Likely to Turn out to Be a Defined-Chaos Retirement Plan," *Barron's*, November 26, 2001.

Chapter 6

Advice About Investment Advice

The cheapest commodity in the world is investment advice from people not qualified to give it.

—Louis Engel

IT APPEARS ON THE SURFACE that two major causes of inferior investment performance among individuals are poorly timed decisions and high costs. While there is ample evidence that people lower their returns by market timing, style shifting, and paying high expenses, these mistakes are also symptoms of a much deeper problem. The main problem plaguing poor returns is that people are not getting good investment advice.

Issues concerning the quality of advice have many facets, but the main issue stems from the fact that many of those giving advice have ulterior motives. They are trying to better themselves in one way or another.

Consider this recent memo from the management at American Express Financial Advisors to its sales representatives about increasing the fees they are charged for selling certain outside mutual funds: "our goal is to balance the needs of the clients, advisors/employees, and stockholders." Basically, the memo was trying to push brokers into selling more in-house mutual funds with higher fees, thereby producing higher profits for the firm. The fact that the outside mutual funds performed better was irrelevant. Brokerage firms are not in business to make money *for* you, but to make money *from* you any way they can.

Selling Lies

To be successful, an advisor service must tell people what they want to hear, not necessarily what is the truth.
—Nicolas Darvas

Here is the hard truth. Wall Street firms are paid a lot of money to create and distribute many questionable investments that ultimately end up in the hands of individual investors. Most of the time they get away with acts that border on fraud, but sometimes the losses are so large that politicians demand investigations. In 2002 alone, two major Wall Street firms paid fines of $100 million each to the federal and state governments to settle misrepresentation and fraud charges out of court. Citigroup will soon up the stakes by paying hundreds of millions in fines for misrepresenting the prospects of several investments and has also promised to change the way it sells products to the public. While a $100 million fine sounds like a lot of money, it is a slap on the hand to big firms like Merrill Lynch, Credit Suisse First Boston, and Citigroup. Those firms made far more money when they sold the investments in question than they will ever pay in fines. (As a matter of record, none of the settlement money is being paid back to investors as restitution. The cash goes into government coffers.)

Over a period of years, the U.S. economic system has experienced a gradual breakdown of the institutions that investors relied on for accurate financial information. Research analysts on Wall Street have promoted rather than analyzed companies. This has occurred because underwriting new investment banking business generates bigger profits than giving accurate information to consumers. When the fellow on the Morgan Stanley Dean Witter commercial says, "We measure success one investor at a time," he is not talking about you or me. He is talking about profitable investment banking clients.

Enter the Poorly Trained Advisor

You may not believe this, but anyone can get paid to give investment advice. You do not need a license and do not need to take any exams. You do not need a background in the subject, or a college degree, or special training. Heck, you could have flunked out of the third grade, gone bankrupt seven times, lost everything you ever owned to a Ponzi scheme, and still make a great living managing other people's money.

An investment advisor is a person who claims to be one: it is that simple. Once you have a certain number of clients who pay you to manage their money, then you need to register. That means sending in a form to the state or federal government with a modest filing fee and possibly taking a state test. If you are selling investment advice through a newsletter or a Web site rather than managing accounts directly, there are no registration forms, fees, or tests, regardless of how many subscribers you have.

In this surreal world of investment advice, anyone can claim to be an expert and get paid for it. The problem is, most investment advisors are borderline incompetent. Thousands of them lack the basic investment skills and knowledge of a first-year business student.

With so many investment advisors running around claiming to have unique insight into the financial markets, how do you tell a good advisor from a bad one? Most people start by checking an advisor's education, experience, and references. This is possible only if you understand all the titles and acronyms in the business and can separate fact from fiction.

There are literally hundreds of investment titles used in the investment business, but only a few have real meaning and denote years of study and professional commitment. The best designations include Certified Financial Planner (CFP) and Chartered Financial Analyst (CFA). Unfortunately, most designations and titles represent very little academic work and can be purchased by paying a fee to a marketing organization or by selling a lot of high-commission products. For example, the title of vice president (VP) is the most overused and meaningless title in the financial services industry. The title is earned based on the amount of commission dollars a salesperson generates, not by exhibiting skill or expertise. It seems that every salesperson at every brokerage firm and insurance company sports a VP title.

Improper training in the investment industry is widespread. This leads to poor advice, misrepresentation of products, and a genuine lack of business ethics. As a result, thousands of individuals file complaints and claims against their financial advisors each year. These claims involve everything from peddling inappropriate products to excessive trading (churning). According to the National Association of Securities Dealers (NASD), broker-customer claims alone rose over 40% in 2001 and climbed steadily higher in 2002. Most of these cases tend to fall into three main areas: unsuitability (brokers placing clients in investments clients later deemed too risky), misrepresentation (brokers misleading clients on the nature and risk of the investments sold), and breach of fiduciary duty (brokers misusing customer funds). Each week, *The Wall Street Journal* lists the settlements and penalties of these cases; recently the section has taken up nearly a full page using microprint. It is not a pretty sight.

I believe the large numbers of cases against financial advisors occur for three reasons:

- Investment advisors are poorly trained by the firms they work for.
- Advisors become overly greedy and opt to sell high-commission products that are inappropriate for most clients.
- Management pressures the advisors to sell certain products without the advisors knowing or understanding the inherent risks.

As a general rule, most financial advisors know about enough to be dangerous to their clients. To become a salesperson for a Wall Street firm, you simply need to be a U.S. citizen, be able to read and write English, have no criminal record, and pass one basic investment exam. Depending on what products the firm wants you to sell, the licensing exam is either a few hours long or all day. These NASD-administered exams are designed so that anyone with a high school equivalency can pass, although you do not need a high school diploma to take the exams. If you fail an exam, you can retake it every 30 days forever until you pass.

Once you pass an NASD exam, the next step is to attend a short, in-house sales training course. Training is provided over the course of a few weeks and it is all about selling investment products. That means learning about the products the firm wants to you sell and learning how to overcoming a client's objections to buying. After this training period is over, the brokers are let loose on the public to sell investments that they barely know anything about.

Since it is easy to make a lot of money selling investment products, the greed has spread from brokerage firms and insurance companies to banks, accounting firms, and law firms. The partners at some accounting firms and law firms can become intoxicated with the idea of adding quick and easy revenue to their bottom line by selling investment products and insurance directly or referring to someone who does and collecting a cut of the fees. Industry professionals will tell you that most accounting and law firms should not be in the investment advice business. It is a huge conflict of interest.

H&R Block used to be an income tax preparation firm. It is now H&R Block Financial Advisors. The advisors now sell tax preparation services along with a range of investment and insurance products. That is a great combination for H&R Block, because the advisors have full access to a client's financial information. However, it is lousy deal for unsuspecting tax clients who visit the firm to get their taxes done. Many end up buying high-commission whole life insurance, variable annuities, loaded mutual funds, and other products that have high fees and commissions. This is all done under the banner of "independent financial advice."

Meet the Press

Nobody has more to answer for in today's complicated investment climate than financial journalists, who were clearly on record during the bubble spreading the message that 'this time it's different.'
—Warren Buffett, *Fortune*, December 2001

The problem of poor advice extends well beyond brokers and investment houses and into the media. Magazines, newspapers, and financial entertainment TV shows are all supported and heavily subsidized by advertising dollars from the investment industry. In return for the money, the media quotes and promotes various financial firms in news stories and on the television. It is a quid pro quo relationship. What magazine editor or television director is going to probe deeply into the problems of poor advice that plague the country when the culprits are providing the advertising revenue that pays their salaries? Granted, there are token stories about the latest scandal on Wall Street, but those stories stop after the guilty firms take out full-page ads in the most widely read magazines and newspapers and pay for a few extra commercials on financial entertainment TV shows.

The subtle message from the media is that you can easily make money in the markets by following their wonderful guidance. In reality, most of the investment recommendations you hear or read about are mediocre at best and some are just plain bad. Nearly all the recommendations are trend-following. Financial journalists sometimes criticize financial advisors for selling the "flavor of the month," but that is exactly how newspapers and magazines sustain their readership.

Case in point: the March 18, 2002 cover of *Forbes* proclaims, "The World's Billionaires: You Can Still Get Rich (even in tech)." That's a catchy headline, but your chances of becoming a billionaire in tech stocks are about the same as picking all six numbers in the PowerBall lottery. So, what's the point? The point is to get people to buy the magazine so that *Forbes* can continue to sell advertising space to mutual fund companies and brokerage firms.

An anonymous journalist wrote a classic article in the April 26, 1999 issue of *Fortune*, "Confessions of a Former Mutual Funds Reporter." A couple of excerpts from the story say it all:

> Mutual funds reporters lead a secret investing life. By day we write "Six Funds to Buy NOW!"... By night, however, we invest in sensible index funds.

> I know, because I was once one of those reporters—condemned to write a new fund story every day—when I covered funds for an online publication. I was ignorant. My only personal experience had been bumbling into a load fund until a colleague steered me to an S&P 500 index fund. I worried I'd misdirect readers, but I was assured that in per-

sonal-finance journalism it doesn't matter if the advice turns out to be right, as long as it is logical. ...

Unfortunately, rational, pro-index-fund stories don't sell magazines, cause hits on Websites, or boost Nielsen ratings. So rest assured: You'll keep on seeing those enticing but worthless SIX FUNDS TO BUY NOW! headlines as long as there are personal-finance media.

Another interesting source of investment information is newsletters that you can buy for a few hundred dollars per year. The investment results of some of these newsletters look impressive—and they should. In 1985, The U.S. Supreme Court ruled that newsletters were exempt from the Investment Advisors Act of 1940 and therefore not subject to SEC regulation. That means courts view newsletters as journalistic works and not investment advice. As a result, newsletters can claim they have achieved any performance number they wish, even if it is not true, and their claim is protected under the First Amendment.

A perfect example of this is the *California Technology Stock Letter*, published by Michael Murphy. In advertisements for this newsletter, Murphy claims incredible stock-picking ability, routinely touting stocks that had climbed 700% to 900% after his recommendation. Unfortunately, Murphy must not be taking his own advice. The Monterey Murphy Technology Fund, personally managed by Murphy, was one of the worst-performing technology funds in the country from its inception in 1993 though August 2002, when it was finally liquidated. The performance of this disaster was negative 14.1% annualized since inception, meaning a $10,000 investment in the Monterey Murphy Technology Fund in 1993 would have been worth only $2,615 at the closing. The average technology fund gained 7.2% annually over the same period and $10,000 would have grown to $18,475 over the same period, according to Morningstar.

Book writers have not fared any better. We have more than our fair share of con artists and swindlers in the book publishing business.

Take Wade Cook, for example. Cook writes and sells a series of investment books, tapes, and classes. The books and tapes are sold in national bookstore chains as well as seminars that Cook puts on around the country. According to a Federal Trade Commission complaint in 2000, Cook's advertising and promotional materials contain expressed or implied false claims that he had earned high returns using his strategies and that his customers would earn an extremely high rate of return of 20% or more per month on their portfolios using Cook's trading secrets. SEC reports show that Cook's stock portfolio lost 89% in 2000 and 60% in 2001, before commissions.

I am not about to get involved in a libel lawsuit with Cook, so here is the text of a report that came directly from the Federal Trade Commission Web site. You can draw your own conclusions:

> February 21, 2002: Despite collecting millions from consumers over the past five years pitching his "Wall Street Workshop" to investment-minded consumers, financial "guru" Wade Cook and his company, Wade Cook Financial Corporation (WCFC), allegedly have failed to comply with an October 2000 U.S. District Court order. Among other things, they have failed to disclose the current rate of return for their stock trading investments, substantiate all promotional claims, and make redress payments to compensate eligible customers who did not make more money trading stocks than they had paid to attend the workshop. Accordingly, the FTC today announced it is seeking civil contempt against Cook, WCFC, and Stock Market Institute of Learning, Inc. (SMIL), the successor to Wade Cook Seminars, Inc.

Trying to find updated information on the company is difficult. Even WADC board members cannot get data. According to Bloomberg, on Sept. 12, 2002, board member Everett Sparks quit, complaining he couldn't obtain information about the stock seminar company's finances. Sparks was the last member of the company's audit committee to quit, after three others left in June 2002. The price of the WADC stock fell from approximately $55 in 1997 to approximately 12 cents by the end of 2002.

Here's an example of how media hype can spin out of control. On April 25, 2002, Wade Cook appeared on Pat Summerall's television show, "Summerall's Success Stories,"® The show claims to profile corporate leaders and innovators, which is why they said they spotlighted Wade Cook Financial Corporation. I am sure the pending FTC hearing was not discussed, nor the dismal performance of WADC stock, nor the poor financial state of the company, nor Mr. Cook's earnings in light of the meltdown. By the way, Cook has a new book out, *Wade Cook's Stock Picking Handbook*. I'll pass on that one.

Here is one more interesting book story. Henry Blodget is a former Merrill Lynch stock analyst who wrote bullish research reports about failing Internet stocks so his firm could reap millions of dollars in investment banking fees. At the same time, he was sending private e-mail to friends telling them to avoid these same stocks. In one e-mail, he said the CEO of InfoSeek was a "sleazebag" and the company was "a piece of junk." Other stocks got equally brutal private assessments while investors were told that the stocks were Merrill's top picks. Excite@Home was "such a piece of crap." Internet Capital Group provided "nothing positive to say." Two others were each assessed as "a piece of s—t." You would think that Blodget would go to jail for spreading lies that caused countless number of investors to lose billions of dollars. That is not what happened. Blodget left Merrill Lynch in late 2001 and decided write a book that tells why he was a victim of Wall Street and the Internet bubble.

In early 2003, the National Association of Securities Dealers informed the analyst that he could face regulatory charges over his research picks while at Merrill Lynch. The NASD was also investigating his supervisors as part of its probe into conflicts of interest on Wall Street.

How good are most investments touted in newspapers, magazines, books, and investment newsletters? They may be entertaining and informative, but they offer investors little hope for beating the markets.

While interviewing Nobel Prize Laureate Merton Miller for a *Barron's* article, journalist Gene Epstein asked the economist what advice he would give the average investor. Miller gave Epstein a surprising answer:

"What advice would you give the average investor?"

"Don't quote me on this, but I'd say don't read Barron's.*"*

"Why!?"

"Because it will only tease you about investment opportunities you'd best avoid."

Hats off to *Barron's* for printing Miller's honest and accurate answer.

Mutual Funds Follies

Mutual fund marketing is a high-stakes game. Fund companies do whatever it takes to make their funds look good. One big fund can make or break a fund company. There were 14,747 mutual funds listed in the December 2002 release of the Morningstar *Principia* database, including funds with multiple class shares. If you limit the count to distinct portfolios, meaning counting only once those funds with multiple class shares, then the database listed 5,842 stock, bond, and balanced mutual funds. With so many funds, it is impossible for people to keep track of the horserace. As a result, companies that monitor and evaluate mutual funds have become increasingly important.

The largest and most familiar fund evaluation service is Morningstar in Chicago. Morningstar develops a fact sheet on each fund, which keeps track of portfolio characteristics, risk and return numbers, and manager changes, among other things. Once a mutual fund has been in existence for three years, it gets a star rating. The star system is similar to the star system used by the travel agencies: a five-star hotel earns honors as a top-of-the-line establishment while a one-star hotel is a hangout for cockroaches.

Morningstar has done an excellent job of compiling information for investors. In addition to the *Principia* database, I go to the Morningstar.com Web site almost every day. Much of the information on the Web site is free, and the "conversation rooms" are partially interesting. If you have specific question about an investment or retirement topic, you can post your question under one of the conversations and you are sure to get a lots of free advice. The conversation topic I frequent is the Vanguard Diehards.

Is There Information in Mutual Fund Ads?

Mutual fund advertisements are plastered all over magazines and newspapers and even aired on television. The ads typically boast a top rating in one thing or another or they try to signal superior performance in other ways. Are mutual fund companies trying to tell us something important with these ads? Do they advertise funds with superior results because the fund company believes the fund managers will continue to provide investors with superior returns in the future? Or do fund companies advertise the returns of their hottest products simply to attract new capital with a full understanding that past performance is not an indication of future results?

A study published in *The Journal of Finance* (April 2000), "Truth in Mutual Fund Advertising: Evidence on Future Performance and Fund Flows," helps shed light on the disadvantage of investing in heavily advertised funds. Prem C. Jain of Tulane University and Joanna Shuang Wu of the University of Rochester examined 294 mutual fund advertisements to find out if buying the funds would have led to superior returns. In their controlled study, Jain and Wu measured the performance of the funds one year prior to the first advertisement date and one year after. The study found the advertised funds performed about 4% higher than the average fund in its category prior to the advertisement date—and about 0.8% below average in the period after the advertisement.

The study clearly demonstrates that past performance is not an indicator of future returns. Following the advice of the fund companies led to returns below those of the average mutual fund. If these fund companies do know something about the future of the funds they manage, they are not telling investors.

Mutual Fund Accounting Tricks

Business is tough for most mutual fund companies. There is a lot of competition, advertising is expensive, and the recent bear market dragged revenues down. Who can blame management for trying to spice up the performance of their companies by using an assortment of shady reporting techniques? Other industries do it all the time and, until the Enron debacle, creative accounting was considered acceptable on Wall Street.

Don't get me wrong. Fund companies are not doing anything illegal like Enron, but what they are doing borders on being unethical and misleading. The next three sections of this chapter cover three tricks used by active fund companies to dress up firm-wide performance: incubator funds, me-too funds, and priming the pump. These techniques describe only a few blatant examples. There are many others.

Incubator Funds. Incubator funds are small, actively managed individual accounts or private investment pools run by a mutual fund company. These funds are not available to the public, but may be available to employees of the firm or a large private investor. The company manages these private assets using new or improved investment methods. If a new strategy works, the fund opens to the public. If it does not work, the fund is shut down, in most cases.

The idea of testing a new strategy before selling it to the public makes sound business sense. However, the problem is that the SEC allows the performance of the incubator fund to be used as part of the performance history of the new public mutual fund. That means a brand new mutual fund can claim a fabulous multi-year track record and, if the track record covers more than three years, the new fund will likely get a coveted five-star rating from Morningstar. Figure 6-1 shows that a five-star Morningstar rating will bring in cash faster than anything else.

In addition to Morningstar, Lipper Analytical Services and Value Line Mutual Fund Survey also rate mutual funds using independent methods. That gives mutual fund companies plenty of opportunity to get investors herding in their direction.

Do fund companies have many eggs in the incubator at one time? *The Wall Street Journal's* October 9, 2000 "Mutual Funds Quarterly Review" section noted that one fund company had 19 funds in incubation at that time. All the funds were less than three years old. This same fund company launched no less than 18 incubator funds three years prior. Exactly half of the 18 were liquidated and the other half

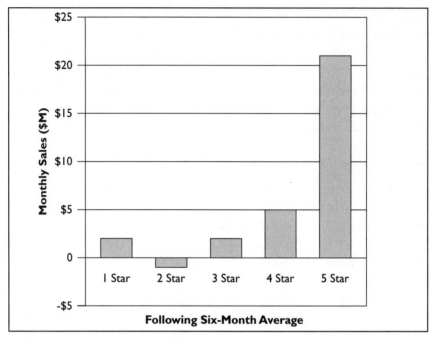

Figure 6-1. Impact of initial Morningstar ratings on sales, 1998-1999
Source: Financial Research Corporation

introduced to the public. No one knows the performance of the funds that were closed. We only know how the public funds performed in the past. Is this fair disclosure? No. Is it legal? Yes.

Vanguard founder Jack Bogle isn't a big fan of the SEC's decision to allow fund companies to attach a fund's previous record as an incubator fund to its new record as a public mutual fund. Bogle says that a regular open-end fund record provides "little enough" useful information that allowing even shakier records is a bad idea.

Me-Too Funds. Mutual fund companies don't want to miss out on collecting investor assets for lack of a fund that covers a trendy investment style. If one fund company introduces a successful new fund, the entire major fund industry creates dozens of "me-too" funds. The largest companies will introduce two to three funds with similar styles, but different names. Most funds are introduced with multiple share classes. Soon, the market is flooded with hundreds of me-too funds. The issuance usually peaks right about the time the bubble bursts on the style.

As you might expect, most "me-too" funds do not survive very long. More than half are closed or merged by the third year. That way a fund company can claim success with its best-performing new fund, while sweeping the performance of losing funds under the rug. Typically, about 5% of all mutual funds disappear during any 12-month period; 2002 was a big year, however, with a record number of funds disappearing. Hundreds of funds vanished and many more are on their last leg.

In 2002, Merrill Lynch pruned four technology and growth funds that it introduced during the technology boom in the late 1990s. Merrill said it closed the funds because investors don't need three aggressive-growth options from one family. Although the company would never admit it, poor performance and dwindling assets were the biggest factors in its decision about which funds to close.

Putnam closed two funds during the same time and merged nine others. The funds shut down were the Technology Fund and the New Century Growth Fund. Both of these funds were less than three years old. Lawrence Lasser, Putnam's President and CEO, commented on the disappearance act by saying, "We would never say 'make this [poor performance] go away' by retiring the fund."

Priming the Pump. Many technology and aggressive growth funds launched during the tech boom in the 1990s had huge one-year gains from hot initial public offerings (IPOs) of new stock. An IPO is hot when the stock is issued to investors at $15 per share and the first trade on the stock market opens at $60 per share. Investors who are lucky enough to get $15 shares on the offering from the underwriter can "flip" the new stock at $60 and make a huge one-time gain. This gain can really pump up the performance of an incubator fund or a fledgling me-too fund.

Receiving shares of a hot IPO is like free money to a mutual fund company, if it can get shares from an underwriter. Unfortunately, the way Wall Street distributes hot IPO shares is a disgrace—and the SEC has taken a keen interest in the way shares are distributed. Basically, the shares go to fund companies that do a significant amount of routine stock trading with the brokerage firm that is the lead manager of the IPO underwriting. The commissions on these routine trades are much higher than if the mutual fund used a deep discount brokerage firm. However, fund companies gladly pay the price of entry into the IPO market. The more commission dollars a fund company pays to a brokerage house, the greater the likelihood of getting an IPO allocation. In other words, the mutual fund companies pay off brokerage firms using the assets of mutual fund investors.

Flipping IPO shares would be fine if gain from the trades went to the mutual funds whose shareholders paid for the privilege of getting the shares, through the high cost of commission dollars those shareholders paid. But that is typically not the case. Despite the fact that the shareholders of the big funds paid the entry fee, most of the allocation of a hot IPO will go into one or two small incubator funds or a fledgling me-too fund. A hot IPO can easily pump up the performance of a small fund, but it barely puts a dent in the performance of a big fund. So, why waste it?

When a new fund is stuffed with hot IPOs and other good deals, there is an excellent chance it will be a Morningstar five-star fund and bring in lots of money. This is how the Munder Net Net Fund went from practically nothing in 1997 to over $8 billion in early 2000. Unfortunately, nothing fails like success. The small fund gets large and stealth performance pumping gives way to routine money management. It would take an impossible number of hot IPOs to keep the performance going in a big fund. Like the Munder Net Net Fund, whose rise and fall from fame is reported in Chapter 4, the air can quickly escape when the fund gets too big and the pumping stops.

There are always new funds being created. So, when a pumped-up fund becomes popular and gets big, fund company management shifts the good deals to a new small fund and the process begins again. This practice ensures that there will be at least one fund in a family that is a five-star performer.

Caveat Investor! This section barely scratches the surface on the shenanigans in the mutual fund business. As fund companies struggle to survive by scrambling for new investors and new assets, we are likely to see many more creative ways to hide poor-performing funds and pump up the numbers of other funds. Let the buyer beware.

Lots of Noise, No Information

Something that everyone knows isn't worth knowing
—Bernard Baruch

So far in this chapter I have said that your financial advisor does not have superior information or skill, the media does not have superior information or skill, and mutual fund companies do not have superior information or skill. I have not discussed friends, relatives, or co-workers because it should be obvious by now that they have no superior information or skill either.

Since superior information is needed to earn a superior return, where do you get it? I have bad news. It does not exist in your world or in mine. It is not possible to consistently pick winning investments based on skill, because you can never have the right information fast enough or act upon it well enough to make an excessive gain. You need timely, accurate information on the economy, industries, and corporations before anyone else and know what to do with that information before anyone else. If that data and insight do exist, they are not available in any public venue and buying them privately would cost a sizable fortune.

A few years ago, it was amazing to listen to people living in Michigan who thought they had superior information about a dot-com company starting up in Silicon Valley, California. In talking with those people, I found that most of the "superior" sources of information turned out to be Internet chat rooms, stock charts, and real-time prices provided by their on-line brokers. There is nothing superior about gossip that passes in a chat room or a chart that tell syou what the stock did 10 minutes ago. Everyone on the entire planet has access to that information.

Maybe Alan Greenspan and Warren Buffett get some superior information about the economy and companies, but not you and me, and certainly not your co-worker or your brother-in-law. Clearly, an overwhelming majority of investors would be better off with no information at all. They should simply buy the entire market using low-cost, market-matching index funds, which happens to be one topic in the next part of this book.

Chapter Summary

Experienced investors recognize Wall Street for what it is—a gigantic marketing machine that pumps out investment products by the truckloads. It is no coincidence that Madison Avenue, the hub of the advertising industry in the U.S., is only a few blocks away from the New York financial district. Madison Avenue and Wall Street are cut from the same fabric.

In all fairness, Wall Street plays a major role in our capitalist system. Without analysts inflating growth prospects of fledgling new companies and mutual fund managers clamoring to buy IPOs for their hot little funds and under-trained brokers peddling investment products to trusting clients, how would promising young companies ever raise capital? Granted, most of these companies will not survive, but business failure sometimes does some good ultimately for the economy. For example, we have a plenty of bankrupt technology and communications companies, but we have also put in place millions of miles of fiber-optic cable that is now operating as the backbone of a nationwide communications infrastructure.

The purpose of this book is to help you protect your wealth from all the dogs of the investment world and from errors in human judgment. This entails creating a sensible plan involving constant saving and investing. Part of that plan includes a well-defined long-term investment strategy of low-cost mutual funds. It is the only rational method of growing and protecting your financial future.

Key Points

1. Take caution where you get your financial advice. An overwhelming majority of investment advice is not advice at all. It is salesmanship by a person or company trying to profit from the public's ignorance.
2. The education and training of our nation's financial advisors is dismal. There are no educational requirements needed to

become a fee-only financial advisor, while commissioned stock-brokers and insurance salespeople only need to pass elementary exams.

3. Personal investing is a very important matter. Do an appropriate amount of research before committing your money. If the expected return on an investment sounds too good to be true, it is.

Part Two

Building Blocks to Success

Chapter 7

Types of Retirement Accounts

You can be young without money but you can't be old without it.
—Tennessee Williams

WhﬆEN IT IS TIME to start saving for retirement, you will want to put the money into a special type of account that gives you tax advantages and retirement income in the future. There are many different types of tax-advantaged retirement accounts created by Congress and administered by the Treasury Department. All of these account options allow your money to grow without being taxed while it stays in the account. The tax treatments of the money going in and the money coming out differ among various types of accounts. This chapter provides a brief outline of the major types of retirement savings plans, including similarities and differences among them.

After reading this chapter, you can get an idea of which accounts may be appropriate for your situation. Before making a final decision, you will need to gather more information from your employer, tax advisor, and the Internal Revenue Service (IRS) to make sure that you know all the facts before you make a final decision. Typically, a combination of different accounts will lead to the best tax-saving strategy, which in turn leads to a larger nest egg in retirement.

Terminology

The words, phrases, and definitions used to describe various retirement accounts and features can sound very similar, but differ greatly in meaning. For example, there is a big difference among the terms "account," "custodian," and "investment." There are also big differences between "tax-free" and "tax-deferred" and between "pre-tax" and "after-tax." This guide should help you put the terms into perspective.

Accounts, Custodians, and Investments. What is an account? An account is an empty box that has a name slapped on the side. That name may be an Individual Retirement Account (IRA), 401(k) account, joint account, or any number of titles. Standing alone, an account has no value. It is simply an empty box.

A custodian is the place where your account resides. Typical custodians are brokerage firms, banks, insurance companies, and mutual fund companies. All accounts need a custodian, who provides statements and tax information and performs other administrative duties.

An account takes on value once money is deposited in it. After an account is funded, you can buy investments with the cash. Basically, investments go into the account (the box) and the cash deposited in the account pays for them. These investments may include stocks, bonds, mutual funds, or other things of value. For example, your IRA account may be invested in stock mutual funds. When you put this all together, you may own 100 shares of IBM (investment) in your IRA (account) at Charles Schwab (custodian).

Sometimes, people get the terminology mixed up. I have been asked more than once, "Should I put my money into an IRA account or a mutual fund?" I answer that mutual funds are investments that may be purchased in an IRA account. First, you contact a custodian and open an IRA account. Then, you fund the account by putting money into it. Finally, you buy mutual funds as an investment in the account.

Pre-Tax and After-Tax Savings. Contributions to retirement accounts can be made with either pre-tax dollars or after-tax dollars.

Investing pre-tax dollars is a good option, because you can subtract the amount of the contribution from your gross income this year, which lowers the amount of federal income tax you pay. If you reduce your taxes when you put money into a retirement account, then the money is taxable when it comes out. Although investing pre-tax savings gives you an immediate benefit by lowering your income taxes, the government restricts the amount you can deduct each year, based on the amount you earn. In addition, if you take the money out before age 59½, you pay taxes and a penalty for early withdrawal (with some exceptions). You cannot keep the money in the account indefinitely either. At age 70½ you have to start taking minimum distributions and paying income taxes.

If you invest after-tax dollars, it means you have already paid income tax on the money being invested. There is no deduction on your tax form. Unless the money is going into a special account called a Roth IRA, you can put away as much after-tax money as you want. There are no restrictions.

Tax-Deferred, Taxable, and Tax-Free. The tax treatment of the money once it is *within* an account can differ greatly. It can be tax-deferred, taxable, or tax-free.

Tax-deferred means the dividends, interest, and capital gains accumulate in the account without being subject to income tax as long as the money stays in a tax-sheltered account. However, all of these earnings are taxed as ordinary income when you withdraw them from the account. Normally, you must be at least 59½ years old to withdraw any money from the account or you incur a penalty.

Taxable accounts are regular savings accounts, which are subject to ordinary income and capital gains tax every year. The advantage is that you can access your money at any time: there is no minimum age and no penalty. You can put tax-free investments into taxable accounts, which creates tax-free income, but the interest rate on those investments is quite low compared with the interest on investments that are taxable.

Finally, there are tax-free accounts. There are a few special accounts set up by Congress that allow your money to grow tax-deferred in the account and then withdraw the money tax-free later on. Two types of tax-free accounts are the Roth IRA and the Educational IRA (see Appendix). The money that goes into these accounts does not currently qualify for a tax deduction.

Numbered Plans and Acronyms. Congress decides the names of retirement accounts and, as you may know, the government loves to use numbers and acronyms. The numbers come from the section of the tax code where details of the legislation can be found. For example, information on 401(k) plans can be found under Income Tax Regulations Section 401 of the Internal Revenue Code of 1986.

Sometime it is easier to assign an acronym to a type of retirement account, although this can be confusing because several types of accounts have part of the same acronym. For example, an Individual Retirement Account (which the IRS calls an Individual Retirement *Arrangement*) is an IRA for short, but there are contributory IRAs, rollover IRAs, Roth IRAs, SEP IRAs, and even education IRAs, which are discussed in Appendix A. You can rest assured that if the account has IRA in the title, the growth in the account will be tax-deferred. However, there are large variations in the tax treatment of the contributions and withdrawals in each type of account.

Types of Retirement Accounts

The following section is designed to answer most introductory questions about the common retirement accounts. It is by no means complete. The tax code detailing each of these accounts can run several hundred pages. In addition, Congress can change any part of the tax code at any time and the IRS can interpret the regulations differently depending on the circumstances.

Before choosing one retirement savings plan over another, my recommendation is to consult with a tax accountant or a qualified financial planner. There are several advantages to opening one or more tax-advantaged retirement accounts, but you do not want to make a mistake. The penalties and back taxes for over-funding retirement accounts can be harsh.

Employee-Funded Retirement Plans

Over 50 million U.S. workers are eligible to participate in an employer-sponsored, employee-funded savings plan. The titles and benefits of these plans differ depending on the employer. If the employer is a for-profit company, the plan is a 401(k). If the employer is a non-profit organization, such as a hospital or school, the plan is a 403(b). If the employer is the government, the plan is a 457.

401(k) Plans. A 401(k) plan is sponsored by a corporate employer for the benefit of the employees. By the time you enroll in your company's 401(k) plan, your employer is already working with a plan administrator and has selected a number of investment options to choose from within the plan. Typically those options will include a guaranteed fixed income account, a few stock mutual funds, a bond mutual fund, and possibly the employer's own stock, if the company is publicly traded.

All of the money that you put into the plan is deducted from your normal compensation. This reduces your income tax, because it decreases your income. (However, all your wages are still subject to Social Security, Medicare, and federal unemployment taxes.) By delaying taxes on your contribution, it's like giving yourself a pay raise. For example, if you earned $50,000 last year and contributed $5,000, or 10% of your income, you reduce the amount subject to federal and state tax to $45,000. That reduction could save you about $1300 in federal tax.

There are limits on contributions. The amount that an employee is allowed to contribute into his or her account in the plan is limited. In 2003, the maximum is $12,000; it is scheduled to go up to $15,000 by 2006.

When you delay taxes by contributing to your 401(k), there is a hidden benefit. Since taxes aren't deducted before you invest, you are putting your full $5,000 contribution to work earning money. That makes a big difference. For instance, if you had paid 27% in taxes, you would have had only 73 cents on the dollar to invest—only $3,650. And that 73 cents would need to earn nearly a 40% return before it would equal $5,000.

The money is in the 401(k) plan grows tax-deferred until you withdraw it from your account. Withdrawals from a 401(k) plan become part of your ordinary income the year they are withdrawn. If you take money out of a tax-sheltered account before age 59½, you'll face a 10% penalty, except for certain loan options. If you leave the company before age 59½, the money can be rolled into an IRA account. (See the section on rollover IRAs.) Many plans allow employees to make a hardship withdrawal because of immediate and heavy financial needs. But you cannot access all of your account balance. Hardship distributions from a 401(k) plan are limited to the amount of the employee's elective deferrals (the technical term for "contributions") and do not include any income earned on the deferred amounts.

Some companies offer to match a portion of your contribution. For every $1 you contribute, they'll add 25 or even 50 cents. What that means is that you will get an immediate 25% to 50% return on your money before the investment does anything. That is certainly a deal you want to make sure you take advantage of.

403(b) Plans. 403(b) plans, also known as a tax-sheltered annuity (TSA) plan, is a retirement account for certain employees of public schools, tax-exempt organization 501(c) employers such as some hospitals, and tax-exempt ministries. 403(b) plans work very much like 401(k) plans, in that both individuals and employers can contribute to the account on a pre-tax basis.

The following types of contributions can be made to 403(b) accounts.

1. **Elective deferrals.** These are contributions made under a salary reduction agreement that allows your employer to withhold money from your paycheck to contribute directly into your 403(b) account. You do not pay tax on these contributions until you withdraw them from the account.

2. **Non-elective contributions.** These are employer contributions that are not made under a salary reduction agreement. Non-elective contributions include matching contributions, discretionary contributions, and mandatory contributions from your employ-

er. You do not pay tax on these contributions until you withdraw them from the account.

3. **After-tax contributions.** These are contributions you make with funds that you must include as income on your tax return and from which income tax has been withheld. You cannot deduct after-tax contributions on your tax return.

4. **A combination** of any of the three contribution types listed above.

A 403(b) account may make self-directed investments through allowed mutual fund investments or it may be invested directly in an annuity contract purchased through an insurance company. The annuity contract can be used to generate a guaranteed income stream at retirement. See IRS Publication 571 for complete information.

457 Plans. A 457 plan is a nonqualified deferred compensation plan that can be established by state and local governments and other tax-exempt employers. A nonqualified deferred compensation plan provides for the deferral of compensation, but does not meet the requirements for an IRS tax-qualified deferred compensation plan, which means the employer does not get a tax deduction for putting a match in the plan. But, since only government and tax-exempt employers use 457 plans, the tax deductibility does not matter. For Social Security and Medicare purposes, a 457 plan is treated the same as a 401(k) or 403(b) plan: wages are included for determining Social Security and Medicare taxes.

In many cases, employers that allow employees to participate in 403(b) plans also offer their employees a 457 plan. If you participate in both a 403(b) plan and a 457 plan, the 457 plan limits are applied to the total combined contributions under both plans. This means that the total contributed to both your 403(b) and your 457 for the year cannot be more than the limit for the 457 plan.

SIMPLE Plans. Savings Incentive Match Plan for Employees (SIMPLE) retirement accounts are the small business owner's answer to a 401(k) plan. SIMPLE programs combine features that make them attractive to both employers and employees. With a SIMPLE plan:

■ The employer avoids many of the administrative costs of a traditional 401(k) plan.

- Eligible employees can defer up to $8,000 (for 2003) of compensation annually, indexed annually for inflation.
- The plan assets grow tax deferred until withdrawal.
- All participants are 100% vested immediately.
- Participants have complete discretion over their own retirement assets held in individual employee accounts.

There are some limits on a SIMPLE plan:

- Only SIMPLE contributions can go into the plan. No rollover contributions (see below) are permitted unless the rollover is from another SIMPLE.
- Employers must contribute either matching contributions of up to 3% or a 2% non-elective contribution to all eligible employees.

SEPs and Other Plans for Small Business Owners. Simplified Employee Pension (SEP) plans save taxes and build retirement wealth for small business owners, their employees, and self-employed individuals. SEPs are the workhorse of small business retirement plans, for the following reasons:

- They are easy to establish and have no administrative costs.
- They can be established after the close of the business year and after April 15 with extensions.
- New employees can be vested out of the plan for up to three years.
- They do not require the employer to file with the IRS or report on Form 5500 (Annual Return of Fiduciary of Employee Benefit Trust).
- Contributions are tax-deductible and elective: contributions are not required from year to year.

SEPs are effective for either an individual with a part-time business with no employees or any type of business or professional practice with many employees. A SEP plan is a business-sponsored Individual Retirement Account (see below) with higher contribution limits than an individual IRA.

Surprisingly, a SEP plan can be established and funded up to April 15 for the previous tax year. A business can start a SEP plan and make the contributions with two extensions (four and two months) up to October 15 and receive a tax deduction for the previous year. If the business is a corporation, the maximum extension is September 15.

The typical SEP is placed with a brokerage firm, bank, or mutual fund family with a diversified group of funds. The business owner selects a custodian and then uses that company's SEP documents at no cost. The employees have their own SEP/IRA account at the custodian used by the business. The investment decisions, control of the account, and IRA fees, if any, are the responsibility of the employee. All the business does is send one monthly check to the custodian with a listing of each employee's SEP/IRA account information and the amount of contributions into each account. The custodian takes care of everything else. In addition to employer contributions, participants may make up to a $3,000 personal contribution into their SEP/IRA account.

As an alternative to a SEP plan, self-employed individuals can open a Keogh plan. Keogh plans are the self-employed equivalent of corporate retirement programs. They come in two basic flavors: profit-sharing plans and defined-benefit pension plans. To get a deduction for the current tax year, the plan must be established before year's end. Once that's done, contributions can be deferred until the extended due date for that year's return. These plans allow a self-employed person to save more than the SEP limit. Profit-sharing plans allow a maximum contribution of 25% of wages up to $40,000 per year in 2003. Defined-benefit pension plan contributions are based on the age of the business owner. The older a person is when starting the plan, the more he or she can contribute pre-tax.

Limits on 401(k), 403(b), 457, SEP, and SIMPLE Plans. The individual, annual limit for pre-tax, payroll deduction contributions to 401(k), 403(b), and 457 plans is 100% of wages, up to $12,000 for 2003. This limit will increase by $1,000 per year until it reaches $15,000 in 2006. The limit on both employer and employee contributions is the lesser of $40,000 or 100% of compensation.

A SEP contribution for self-employed individuals is limited to the lesser of $30,000 or 15% of wages, including the SEP contribution (about 13% of net). The individual limit for contributions to employee SIMPLE plans in 2003 is $8,000 and will also increase by $1,000 per year to a maximum of $10,000 in 2005. The limits will then be adjusted for inflation in $500 increments. In 2001, "catch-up" provisions were put into place that allow people over the age of 50 to contribute more until 2006. The catch-up amount in 2003 is $1,000. See a tax advisor or qualified financial planner for more details on annual limits.

Individual Retirement Accounts

This section briefly summarizes different types of Individual Retirement Accounts (IRA) created by Congress to help people save for the future. This book is designed only to familiarize you with some of the highlights of IRAs. Everything you want to know about IRAs can be found in Publication 590, Individual Retirement Arrangements.

Traditional IRA. The first IRA was proposed by President Nixon in 1971 and created by Congress in 1974. It allowed workers not covered by an employer pension plan to save up to 15% of their earnings per year pre-tax, to a maximum of $1,500. In 1981, Congress raised the limit to $2,000; in 2001, Congress authorized an increase to $3,000, which started in 2002, and a gradual increase of that amount to $5,000 in 2008, and subsequent adjustments for inflation in $500 increments.

This is a brief summary of the highlights of traditional IRAs, also called ordinary IRAs or regular IRAs. The three advantages of a traditional IRA are as follows:

- You may be able to deduct some or all of your contributions from ordinary earnings on a pre-tax basis, depending on your circumstances.
- Generally, amounts in your IRA, including earnings and gains, are not taxed until they are distributed.
- Under the Tax Relief Act of 2000, money can be withdrawn prior to age 59½ without penalty either to pay for higher education costs or, up to $10,000, to buy a first home.

You can set up a traditional IRA and contribute to it if:

- You or your spouse (if you file a joint return) received taxable compensation during the year, and
- You were not age 70½ by the end of the year.

You can have a traditional IRA whether or not you are covered by any other retirement plan. However, you may not be able to deduct all of your contribution if you or your spouse are covered by an employer retirement plan. If both you and your spouse have compensation and are under age 70½, each of you can set up an IRA. You cannot both participate in the same IRA.

There are limits and other rules that affect the amount that can be contributed to a traditional IRA. The most that can be contributed to one or more traditional IRAs in a year is $3,000 for 2003 and 2004, $4,000 for 2005, 2006, and 2007, and then $5,000. In addition, individuals age 50 and older are allowed a "catch-up" contribution, up to $500 for 2002-2005 and $1,000 for 2006 and later.

If neither you nor your spouse was covered for any part of the year by an employer retirement plan, you can take a deduction for total contributions. The limit is reduced by any contribution you make to a section 501(c)(18) plan (generally, a pension plan created before June 25, 1959, that is funded entirely by employee contributions).

There are many other options in IRA accounts. For example, contributions can be made to an IRA for a non-working spouse. In addition, if you are ineligible to deduct the IRA contributions on your taxes, you may be entitled to make a nondeductible contribution to the account. This does not reduce your taxes today, but the amount contributed grows tax-deferred. Please talk to your tax advisor or read IRS Publication 590 for more information on traditional IRA eligibility and funding.

Rollover IRA. A rollover occurs when you withdraw cash or other assets from a qualified employer retirement plan and contribute all or part of it to a traditional IRA within 60 days. This transaction is not taxable, but it is reportable on your federal tax return. You can roll over most distributions, with the following exceptions:

- Normally, the nontaxable part of a distribution, such as your after–tax contributions to a retirement plan.

- A distribution that is one of a series of payments based on life expectancy or paid over a period of 10 years or more.
- A required minimum distribution or a hardship distribution from a 401(k) plan.

Any taxable amount that is not rolled over must be included as income in the year you receive it. If the distribution is paid to you, you have 60 days from the date you receive it to roll it over. Any taxable distribution paid to you is subject to a mandatory withholding of 20%, even if you intend to roll it over later. If you roll it over and want to defer tax on the entire taxable portion, you will have to add funds from other sources equal to the amount withheld. You can choose to have your employer transfer a distribution directly to another eligible plan or to an IRA. Under this option, taxes are not withheld.

If you are under age 59½ at the time of the distribution, any taxable portion not rolled over may be subject to a 10% additional tax penalty on early distributions. Certain distributions from a SIMPLE IRA will be subject to a 25% additional tax.

Previously, a maze of rules governed the transfer of retirement plan distributions from one plan to another. In 2001, these rules have essentially been repealed, allowing a transfer of distributions from any type of retirement plan—401(a)/(k), 403(a), 403(b), 408 (IRA, SEP, SIMPLE)—to any other plan.

The direct rollover and withholding rules also extend to 457 plans. Government employees can roll over 457(b) plan distributions to a traditional IRA or a qualified retirement plan such as a 403(b) or 401(k) when they retire or change jobs. The only exception to this rule is a 457 plan of a nonprofit employer. Employees of tax-exempt non-profit organizations can roll over their plan distributions only to another non-governmental 457(b) plan.

Roth IRA. Once there was only the traditional IRA. Then there was the SEP IRA. With the Taxpayer Relief Act of 1997, there are now two additional IRA options: the Roth IRA and the Education IRA (see Appendix A). Both of these options are made with after-tax contributions, but the growth is tax-deferred and the withdrawals may be tax-free.

Some of the benefits now available by saving or investing using a Roth IRA include:

- Tax-deferred growth within the Roth IRA account.
- Tax-free earnings upon withdrawal after age 50½.
- Higher income phase-out ranges for contributions.

After you've put money into a 401(k) or similar plan (especially if there is an employer match) and funded your IRA with tax-deductible dollars, turn to a Roth IRA if you qualify. Your adjusted gross income must be less than $110,000 or less than $160,000 if you're married. These income levels change periodically. Check with your tax advisor for an update.

In some cases, it may be better to forgo the employer-sponsored plan if there is no employer match or you hit the match limit; if so, go straight to the Roth IRA. This is especially true for a younger worker in a low tax bracket without the match. You won't get a tax deduction on your contributions, but the tax-free status of your Roth returns later on, when you're likely to be in a higher tax bracket, out-weighs any gain you'd get from a tax deduction now.

Personal Annuities. Annuities are personal investments that resemble mutual funds. All the money you put into a personal annuity is after-tax, so there is no deduction on your income taxes. However, once the money is in an annuity, it is sheltered from taxation. This means the growth in an annuity is tax-deferred. When you take money out of an annuity, the growth comes out first and it is taxed as ordinary income. You can withdraw from the principal only after all the gain comes out and is taxed.

There is a tax advantage to having personal annuities, but the big disadvantage is cost. Most annuities are sold through stockbrokers and insurance agents, who tend to push high-commission products. That cost comes right out of your pocket in the form of annual expenses that are very high compared with those for other invest-ments, such as no-load mutual funds. However, there are a few low-cost annuity providers, including the Vanguard Group and TIAA-CREF. As a result, there may be a time when it almost makes sense to invest in one.

William J. Bernstein, author and president of Efficient Frontier, a Portland, Oregon investment management company, wrote a very informative article on the viability of variable annuities, "A Limited Case for Variable Annuities." Bernstein concludes his article with the remarks below. I have made some word changes with the permission of the author. (You can read Bernstein's report in its entirely at the www.efficientfrontier.com Web site.)

It's clear that an annuity makes sense *only* if all four of the following conditions are met:

- The investment class is highly tax-*in*efficient.
- The investment's expected return is significantly higher than that of a comparable tax-efficient stock or bond expected return *after reducing it* by the higher expenses incurred in the annuity.
- The investment is held for a long period of time.
- You have run out of other tax-advantaged retirement accounts in which to put the investment.

Personal Savings in a Taxable Account. Personal savings accounts are simply titled in your name, the name of your spouse, joint name, or the name of a trust. They are funded with after-tax dollars. All interest and dividends are taxed as ordinary income each year. Capital gains are taxed at the lower capital gains rate if the investment is over one year old, if a gain has been realized, meaning the investment has been sold at a profit.

Table 7-1 summarizes the savings plans we've been reviewing.

Investments that are placed in taxable accounts should be tax-efficient. These may include tax-free municipal bonds, index mutual funds, and other investments to be covered in later chapters.

Levels of Contributions

We have covered all of the basic types of retirement savings accounts. To put it all into perspective, here is the order in which the typical person should fund those accounts:

1. Max out the employer match. Each year, put as much into your deferred savings plan at work as your employer will match. What

Type of Account	Contributions	Growth	Withdrawal
401(k), 403(b), 457	Pre-tax	Tax-deferred	All taxable
SEP, SIMPLE	Pre-tax	Tax-deferred	All taxable
Keogh Plans	Pre-tax	Tax-deferred	All taxable
Traditional IRA[1]	Pre-tax	Tax-deferred	All taxable
Traditional IRA[2]	After-tax	Tax-deferred	Growth taxable
Rollover IRA	Pre-tax	Tax-deferred	All taxable
Roth IRA	After-tax	Tax-deferred	All tax-free
Personal Annuity	After-tax	Tax-deferred	Growth taxable
Personal Accounts	After-tax	Taxable	Gains taxable

Table 7-1. Summary of savings plans
1. Pre-tax contributions contingent on income and other factors.
2. All taxpayers can contribute to an IRA on an after-tax basis.

other investment gives you the equivalent of a 25% or 50% return on the very first day?

2. Continue to fund the employer plan to the maximum of your salary limit. (See note below.)

3. After your employer plans are fully funded, if you are still eligible to contribute pre-tax to a traditional IRA or a spousal IRA, those are the next accounts to fund.

4. The next level is a Roth IRA. The contribution levels for a Roth IRA are more liberal than for a traditional IRA, but contributions are on an after-tax basis.

5. If you can't open a Roth IRA because of your income level, then consider a nondeductible IRA. Everyone can contribute to a nondeductible IRA. There are no income limits. Like a traditional IRA, the maximum annual contribution amount is $3,000 in 2003, with a extra $500 "catch-up" provision for people over the age of 50. The contributions limit rises to $4000 in 2005, and to $5000 in 2008. In addition, the catch-up amount rises to $1000 in 2006. Taking advantage of a nondeductible IRA can be significant: after 20 years, the tax-deferred compounding will give you

5% to 15% more to spend during retirement than the same investment in a taxable account.

6. When you've exhausted all these options, the next best thing is a taxable investment. The key to choosing taxable investments for retirement is to keep your expenses down and get the most benefit from the 20% capital gains break. That means holding your stocks for more than 12 months—longer, if possible—and choosing mutual funds with a low annual turnover (the rate at which the fund manager buys and sells holdings).

7. Variable annuities are last on the list, because their exceptionally high expenses often counteract their tax benefits. Variable annuities make sense only for investments that pay a lot of taxable income, such as high-yield bond funds or real estate investment trusts (REITs), and only if you are saving for many years. In that case, the gains from compounding your interest free of income tax eventually outweigh the drag created by higher fees.

Note: There are times when contributing to a 401(k) is not a good idea. The most common circumstance is when *all* of the following are true:

- The contribution is not matched.
- All of the investment choices include funds with high expenses.
- You have reason to believe you will be in at least the same tax bracket during retirement as you are now.
- You will be disciplined enough to save outside the 401(k), rather than just waste the money.
- You will invest that money in a tax-savvy manner.

If all of the above are true, it may make sense to fund a Roth IRA to the $3,000 maximum before making unmatched 401(k) contributions. Consult your tax advisor first, though, before making this decision.

Chapter Summary

The benefits and limitations of the various retirement savings accounts can be very confusing. Make sure you understand the tax benefits and limitations of each plan and don't over-fund your account or the taxes and penalties can be high. Your employer and the IRS have lots of free literature available to help you make the right decision for your needs. CPAs and financial planners can also guide you in the right direction and the Internet is full of information.

Key Points

1. Save as much as possible pre-tax, so you lower your tax bill each year.
2. Take advantage of any employer matching contributions, because that is the easiest money you will ever earn.
3. Once you have used all the pre-tax options, select for your personal account tax-efficient investments that are taxable each year. Use annuity products sparingly, if at all.
4. One size does not fit all. Consult your tax advisor to discuss your best option.

Chapter 8

Investment Choices: Stocks

To achieve satisfactory investment results is easier than most people realize; to achieve superior investment results is harder than it looks.
—Benjamin Graham

T HE ROAD to a secure retirement starts by establishing a savings account and developing a plan to fund the account on a regular basis. Once an account is funded, the money should be placed in investments that will grow more than the rate of inflation over the years. To achieve long-term inflation-adjusted growth, most people look to the stock and bond market as their primary investments of choice. This chapter focuses on stock investing and explains why index mutual funds are one of the best choices for achieving satisfactory returns in the stock market.

Stocks: A Partner in Business

There are only two ways to invest your money. First, you let someone else borrow your money, for which they will pay you a user fee known as interest. Second, you can purchase an asset at one price and sell it at a higher price.

Sometimes the assets you purchase also earn income that can be paid out to you periodically in cash. For example, if you buy antiques, coins, or a stamp collection, the only way to make money is if you sell those assets for more than you paid. But if you invest in rental real estate or another business, the business may generate a profit for which you are entitled to your fair share and, depending on profitability and outlook of the enterprise, you may be able to sell your share of the business for more than you paid.

Buying the stock in a company is a way of investing in that business. As part owner, when the company earns money, some of that profit belongs to you. However, you cannot demand that the earnings be paid out in the form of a cash dividend. Some companies retain all earnings and reinvest it in projects or buy new business. Others use part of the earnings to buy back stock in the open market, which increases the percentage of the company you own. Either way, if the management of the company continues to do a good job and earnings continue to rise, your stock becomes more valuable.

If the company is expected to be successful in the future, the price of the stock will likely go up in value. How much more you are expected to earn is a matter of debate. However, the entire stock market has historically performed better than the bond market and money market funds, although with more risk. See Chapter 11, Realistic Market Expectations, for more information on historic returns and future expectations of stocks and bonds.

One advantage of owning stocks over owning a business outright is that you have no management responsibility and limited liability. This means the amount you can lose is limited to the cash you invested in the stock; you have no personal liability above that amount if a lawsuit is filed against the company. For example, the unaffiliated shareholders of WorldCom stock are not liable for the accounting fraud that took place in that company and have no fear of being forced to pitch in more money to clean up the mess. The bad news is that long-time shareholders lost all of their investment. The disadvantage of owning stock is a lack of control. Since you are only a very small owner, you have practically no say in management decisions, one of which is whether or not the company will pay a dividend.

Stocks are bought and sold on stock exchanges and in stock markets. An exchange is a location where shares trade hands; a market is a conceptual term and does not have to be a physical location. The New York Stock Exchange (NYSE) is the largest open stock exchange in the U.S. It is located on Wall Street in Manhattan's financial district. The building is a large, white, bank-like structure that has big columns in the front and resembles a Roman forum. Every day hundreds of billions of dollars worth of stock change hands at the NYSE. Shares also trade around the corner from the NYSE at the American Stock Exchange (AMEX). Stocks that are not listed on one of the physical exchanges trade in cyberspace via the over-the-counter dealer market (OTC). Literally tens of thousands of securities trade OTC.

Companies must apply to have their stock traded on a market or exchange. The OTC requirements are least stringent. As a result, the OTC markets trade many of the newer technology and biotech companies, because these firms did not qualify to be on the NYSE "big board" when the shares were first issued to the public. One segment of the OTC market is the National Association of Securities Dealers Automated Quote system, known more commonly as the NASDAQ. The NASDAQ covers more active companies whose stocks are priced higher than $1, have some tangible net worth, and trade several thousand shares per week.

Stock Mutual Funds

There are several ways to participate in the stock market. You can buy individual stocks of companies that you deem to have potential for gain. You can hire someone else to pick individual stocks for you and pay commissions or an ongoing management fee. Or you can buy a stock mutual fund, where everything is done in one package.

Mutual funds are a wonderful investment idea and a great convenience. They offer diversification across a wide range of companies with one easy purchase. Mutual funds are easy to buy and sell, the fees are generally less than trying to buy a portfolio of individual stocks, and the tax reporting is simplified to one Form 1099. The general operations behind a mutual fund are as follows:

1. A large group of investors pool their money in an account that is held by a bank trust department. A professional investment manager is hired to pick stocks that go into the account. (There are also bond mutual funds.)
2. The bank trust account is divided into shares. Each investor is allocated a certain number of shares based on the amount of money he or she puts into the trust.
3. The manager of the mutual fund is given the right to buy and sell stocks or bonds as he or she sees fit, following the strict guidelines that are laid out in the fund *prospectus*. This legal document explains in nauseating detail how the money in the trust account will be allocated among various securities.
4. An investor who wants to sell shares sells them back to the trust at the end of each trading day at the valuation price, also known as the *net asset value* (NAV). At that time the fund manager will sell stocks or bonds to raise the cash needed to pay off the investor.
5. Investors who want to buy shares in the fund pay money to the trust and new shares are created. The portfolio manager then uses the money to buy more securities.

A mutual fund prospectus is free to all interested parties, even to a person who is not considering buying shares in the mutual fund. People considering investing in a mutual fund should read and understand the prospectus before purchasing the fund, because it details how their money will be put to work. Government regulations require that the fund mail an annual update of the prospectus to all shareholders.

Many mutual funds hold several hundred securities, but investors in the fund will not get detailed information on each individual stock from the fund. An annual report is sent to shareholders listing the holdings in the fund as of a certain date, but the information is limited to names and the amount of shares held. If you want more information about a particular company held in the fund, you would have to do more research on your own.

Securities held in a mutual fund may pay dividends or interest during the year, which is a taxable event to people who hold the fund in a taxable account. In addition, the fund manager will buy new securities and sell old ones, which may create capital gains or capital losses. This may also have tax consequences. To simplify tax accounting, mutual fund companies send investors a Form 1099 at the end of each year. This form details for each investor the cash distribution from the fund that has been assigned to the individual shares that he or she holds in a taxable account. Form 1099 is a standardized document that lists all of these items, and makes year-end tax preparation very simple. The only item missing is your personal cost for each share of the fund you buy, so you will have to keep records or your custodian may offer that service.

Mutual funds are a great way to diversify your stock investments in one easy package. However, contrary to what some people believe, mutual funds do not offer protection from a downturn in the stock market. Since most funds own many stocks, a rising stock market will generally lift most funds and a falling market will sink them. Some mutual fund prospectuses give the fund manager the authority to reduce the amount of stock exposure in the fund if the manager thinks a bear market is coming. Unfortunately, most fund managers have never been successful in doing so. It is impossible to predict successfully the tops and bottoms of the market, even for professionally trained mutual fund managers. If a manager is wrong on a prediction, it can cost shareholders a lot of money and result in that manager losing his or her job. As a general rule, most managers keep 90% to 95% of the money invested at all times, which means most stock funds will go up and down with the market.

Since you probably do not have the time or expertise to sift through thousands of stocks or read thousands of financial publications and annual reports, mutual funds are the most convenient stock investment a person can make. They offer a clean and simple solution to a complex problem of portfolio management. The only problem is that there are so many mutual funds that it is difficult to pick the best ones. I have a simple and cost-effective solution—stock index funds.

Active Funds and Passive Funds

Mutual funds can be divided into two broad types: actively managed and passively managed. In an actively managed stock fund, the manager attempts to select stocks that he or she believes will deliver superior investment performance, beating the return of the overall stock market. One example of a large and popular active fund is Fidelity Magellan. The goal of the Fidelity Magellan fund is to beat the performance of the S&P 500 Index. The S&P 500 is an index that measures the total return of 500 mostly large U.S. stocks, weighted by market value, representing about 70% of the value of all stocks that trade on U.S. markets.

The second type of mutual fund is managed passively. In a passively managed stock fund, the manager replicates a particular stock index, thus matching the performance of that index. Index funds are constructed by purchasing nearly all stocks in an index, using the same weights as the index. One example of a passively managed index fund is the Vanguard 500 Index. The fund was established in 1976 and is the oldest index fund on the market. Its objective is to match the performance of the S&P 500, less a small management fee.

There are thousands of active funds, but only a few hundred passive funds. Most passive funds have come to the market in the last 10 years. Several index funds have been developed to mirror the performance of the S&P 500 index; others have been designed to match the performance of other indexes, such as those that track small company stocks, foreign stocks, and the bond market.

Index Funds Versus Active Funds

Most investors, both institutional and individual, will find that the best way to own common stocks is through an index fund that charges minimal fees. Those following this path are sure to beat the net results (after fees and expenses) delivered by the great majority of investment professionals.
—Warren Buffett

Index funds make a lot of sense for most investors because they cost very little compared with active funds. For this reason, index funds tend to beat the performance of active funds over time. Granted, there are a few actively managed mutual funds that have done very well over the years, but in general active fund managers have a very difficult time beating the performance of index funds because of the extra costs.

Finding a superior active fund is more difficult than trying to select superior stocks. One reason is because there are more mutual funds on the market than there are readily available liquid stocks to invest in. A second problem is the limited talent pool.

John Spence, Associate Editor of Indexfunds.com, recently interviewed Roy Weitz, founder of FundAlarm.com, an investment newsletter. The entire interview is available on the Indexfunds.com Web site, but one exchange caught my eye:

> *Q: What's the most important challenge facing the mutual fund industry today?*
>
> **A:** Competence. Simply, the talent pool in the mutual fund industry is so diluted, and the number of offerings is so vast. The results are generally so poor that I think people are losing faith in the competence of the mutual fund industry. In order to prosper, the fund industry needs to show it can pick stocks—that it knows when to buy stocks, and when to sell stocks. Ultimately, fund managers need to show that they can produce performance that beats the unmanaged indexes. Until they do that, they really have no reason to exist.

There are thousands of stock mutual funds, but only a few great mutual fund managers. Unfortunately, it is nearly impossible to know which managers are going to be great in the future and which are going to be mediocre at best. Granted, there will always be a few new managers who beat the market each year, but they seem to be different managers each year and there is no way to pick the stars in advance. Buying last year's winning fund is risky business, because a great majority of hot funds turn out to be style-specific—and styles do not stay in favor very long. (See Chapter 4, Getting Trampled by the Herd.)

Top universities and academic researchers have spent years searching for a reliable method for picking future top-performing mutual fund managers. The best and the brightest financial researchers from colleges across the country have sliced and diced a seemingly endless number of facts and figures looking for clues to future performance. They have even studied which schools the managers attended and tried to categorize managers based on SAT scores during high school. All of this research has led basically nowhere, except for two conclusive facts. The first fact is that mutual funds with low fees have a greater likelihood of beating the mutual funds with high fees. The second fact is that, factoring out fees, it is unreliable at best to assume that managers who have beaten the market or their peers in the past will do so over the long term.

As a group, active mutual fund managers do not beat the market. But they are not bad investors, just handicapped. The reason most do not do well is because of high fees and expenses charged to the funds they manage. This is where index funds have a huge advantage. On average, index mutual funds have the lowest fund expenses in the industry—and low fees for fund companies mean higher returns for investors.

The Performance Numbers

The best way to illustrate the advantage of investing in index funds is with actual performance results. But first, it is important to understand that, while index funds are consistently good performers, they are rarely the best-performing mutual funds in their categories. There have always been and will always be several actively managed mutual funds that beat the returns of index funds in the short term. However, by delivering consistently good returns over time, index funds have become the clear winners long-term. As the saying goes, over time the cream floats to the top.

In August 1976, the Vanguard 500 Index Fund became the first index fund available to the general public. The fund is benchmarked to the S&P 500. Vanguard set the fund management fee very low and, as a result, the performance was consistently good. A search of the Morningstar *Principia* database generates a list of U.S. stock mutual funds that invest in the same group of stocks as the Vanguard 500, have been around for 20 years or more, and are available to the public. The *Principia* search turned up 57 competing funds that invested mainly in large U.S. companies over the period. Table 8-1 compares the performance of the competing funds with the Vanguard 500 fund over the 20-year period.

20 Years Ending 2002	Vanguard 500 Fund	57 Competing Funds
Annualized Return (load adjusted)	12.5%	10.9%
Growth of $10,000	$104,704	$78,760
Vanguard 500 percentile rank	Top 20%	

Table 8-1. Performance of Vanguard 500 versus peer group
Data Source: Morningstar *Principia*

The annualized return of the 57 funds in Table 8-1 is load adjusted. Investors in some funds had to pay a commission to buy them 20 years ago. Load-adjusting the returns factors in this sales expense to show a true net investment return. The Vanguard 500 Index Fund is a pure no-load mutual fund, which means there is no commission charged to buy or sell shares.

The Vanguard 500 Index beat the average actively managed fund by 1.6% per year, after adjusting for all commissions and fees. As a result, a $10,000 investment in the Vanguard 500 Index in 1983 would be worth almost $26,000 more than the average competing fund by 2002.

But this is not the whole story. When the Vanguard 500 began in 1976, there were 211 competing U.S. equity funds on the market. Most of those funds no longer exist, due to poor performance and company mergers. If we included the performance of the non-surviving funds in the table for the period that they existed, the average competing fund would have performed about 2.6% less than the Vanguard 500 Index.[1]

Figure 8-1 is a histogram that gives a clear picture of the dispersion of the returns around the Vanguard 500 Index. Overall, the fund was tied for seventh in the group. Nine competing funds performed better than the Vanguard 500 Index by an average of 0.9%, one fund tied, and 48 fell short by an average of -2.1%. Fund num-

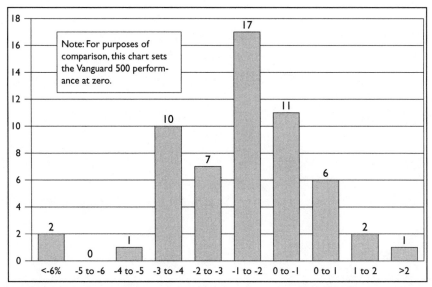

Figure 8-1. Vanguard 500 returns versus 57 competing funds, 20 years ending December 2002

Data Source: Morningstar *Principia*

ber 28, which is the median (middle of the group), performed 1.6% less than the Vanguard 500. You can clearly see that there were several big losing funds, with two falling over 6% short of the Vanguard 500 Index Fund. It is very difficult for mutual fund managers to beat a passively managed index fund over the long term.

Why did the Vanguard 500 Index Fund fare so well and why can you expect it to continue to be in the top of its category in the future? The biggest reason the fund performed well against its peers was its cost advantage. Currently the expense ratio of the fund is only 0.18%, while the average expense of active funds is about six times higher. Figure 8-2 compiles the average fee and 10-year return from all load and no-load growth and income funds and compares them against the average large-cap index fund in the Morningstar database. As we learned in Chapter 5, The High Cost of Low Returns, there is a definite advantage to having a low-fee mutual fund.

In addition to low fees, index funds have a second advantage over active funds. Their turnover of stocks tends to be low. Typically, in an attempt to keep ahead of the markets, managers of active funds

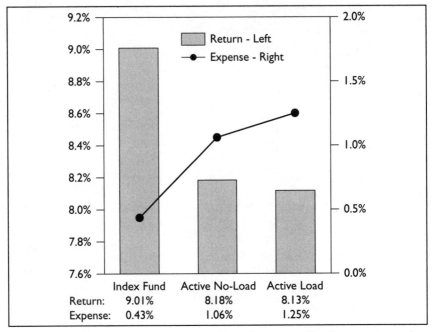

	Index Fund	Active No-Load	Active Load
Return:	9.01%	8.18%	8.13%
Expense:	0.43%	1.06%	1.25%

Figure 8-2. Index funds versus growth and income funds, 10 years ending December 2002
Data Source: Morningstar *Principia*

buy and sell securities often. These frequent transactions can create higher trading costs than incurred by index funds. As we have learned, costs matter—and the lower cost of low turnover adds to the index fund performance advantage.

More Stock Index Funds

Index funds are not limited to just large U.S. stocks. About 30% of the 10,000 stocks in the U.S. market are mid-cap and small-cap companies, and there are many index funds that cover that segment of the market as well. Companies with values between about $2 billion and $10 billion are considered mid-cap stocks and account for roughly 20% of the market. The remaining stocks, with market values below $2 billion, are called small-cap stocks and make up the final 10% of the market. In all categories there is a cost advantage to using index funds over active funds. Figure 8-3 compares the average

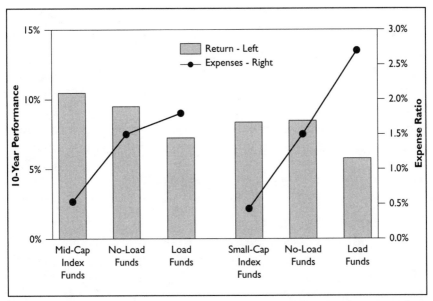

Figure 8-3. Index funds versus no-load versus load funds, 10 years ending December 2002

Data Source: Morningstar *Principia*

fee and return of an index fund with the fees and returns of the average no-load and load mutual fund in the mid-cap and small-cap stock category.

Instead of buying an S&P 500 index fund and a small stock index fund, you can cover all your U.S. stock investments with one mutual fund. A total U.S. stock market index fund mirrors the performance of the Wilshire 5000 index, which is a complete composite of all actively traded U.S. stocks. Depending on market conditions, between 70% and 85% of the Wilshire 5000 is large stocks; the remainder is small to mid-size stocks. There are several advantages to purchasing a total stock market fund. First, it is simple: you own the entire market in one fund. Second, the management fee is minimal and turnover of stocks in the fund is exceptionally low. Third, owning the whole market reduces your desire to chase fund styles, since you already own all the styles. Fourth, the low turnover of stocks in the fund is also good for taxable accounts because it delays capital gains.

There are several total stock market funds on the market. The oldest is the Vanguard Total Stock Market Index Fund, which has been on the market since 1992. Competitors to Vanguard include the TIAA-CREF Equity Index Fund, T. Rowe Price Total Stock Market Fund, and the Schwab Total Stock Market Index Fund. If I were to choose one U.S. stock fund for a lifetime, it would be a U.S. total stock market fund. The funds mentioned above are slightly different in construction and fees, but they all hold 3000 stocks or more.

Indexing Foreign Equity Markets

The U.S. market is one part of the global stock market. According to the latest data, the U.S. stock market accounts for roughly 50% of the value of all stocks traded around the world. (See Figure 8-4.) There is a good chance the U.S. share of the global market will shrink as major countries like China, Russia, and India privatize large government-controlled companies.

Generally, the foreign stock market is divided into two categories: *developed* markets, in countries with established economies

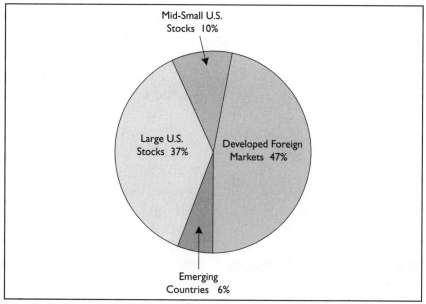

Figure 8-4. The global equity markets
Data Source: Morgan Stanley Capital International

such as Japan and Germany, and *emerging* markets, in countries such as Mexico and Korea. A wide variety of index funds are now available that cover all geographical locations. You can invest in an index fund for a particular country, for a geographical region, with all non-U.S. stocks, or to cover the globe. There are several good foreign stock index funds available, including the Vanguard Total International Stock Index Fund. Vanguard also offers index funds that invest in the Pacific Rim, Europe, emerging markets, and developed markets.

Investing in foreign stocks has several benefits. Over the long term, maintaining about a 30% position in foreign equities helps round out a well-diversified U.S. index fund portfolio. Owning foreign stock index funds also gives you a partial hedge against a decline in the U.S. dollar. Global diversification also proves to be effective for diversification, which reduces portfolio risk and leads to slightly higher returns. For more information on using foreign stock index funds in a portfolio, see Chapter 12, Asset Allocation Explained.

Equity Index Fund Guide

Table 8-2 is a partial list of equity index funds to consider for your portfolio. For more complete information about index mutual funds, including exchange-traded funds, read *All About Index Funds*, by Richard A. Ferri (McGraw-Hill, 2002). You can also contact the Vanguard Group at 800 662-7447 or visit the company's Web site at www.vanguard.com.

Chapter Summary

Von Baron once wrote, "The way to win is by not losing." Stock index funds are such a concept. By reducing the cost of stock investing, you can ensure that your index mutual funds will eventually float to the top of the mutual fund performance list. This strategy will add greater stability to retirement savings and give you the time and money for more important things in life. Investors who embrace the idea of using index funds will save time, money, and the frustration of trying to pick the next winning stock or the next hot mutual fund manager.

	Symbol	Fee
Total U.S. Stock Market Funds		
Vanguard Total Stock Market	VTSMX	0.20%
Vanguard Total Stock Market VIPERs**	VTI*	0.15%
Fidelity Spartan Total Market	FSTMX	0.24%
TIAA-CREF Equity Index Fund	TCEIX	0.26%
iShares Russell 3000	IWV*	0.20%
iShares DJ U.S. Total Market	IYY*	0.20%
Large Company U.S. Stock Funds		
Vanguard 500 Index Fund	VFINX	0.18%
iShares S&P 500	IVV*	0.09%
iShares Russell 1000	IWB*	0.15%
Small Company U.S. Stock Funds		
Vanguard Extended Market	VEXMX	0.25%
Vanguard Extended Market VIPERs**	VXF*	0.15%
Fidelity Spartan Extended Market	FSEMX	0.24%
Vanguard Small Company Index	NAESX	0.25%
Value Style U.S. Stock Funds		
iShares Russell 3000 Value	IWW*	0.20%
iShares Russell 1000 Value	IWD*	0.20%
Vanguard Value Index (S&P / Barra)	VIVAX	0.22%
Real Estate Investment Trust (REIT) Funds		
Vanguard REIT	VGSIX	0.33%
streetTRACKS Wilshire REIT	RWR*	0.25%
iShares DJ U.S. Real Estate	IYR*	0.60%
Foreign Stocks		
Vanguard Total International	VGTSX	0.40%
Vanguard Developed Markets	VDMIX	0.31%
Fidelity Spartan International Index	FSIIX	0.25%

* Exchange-Traded Funds **Vanguard Index Participation Equity Receipts

Table 8-2. Equity index funds

10 years ago, only a handful of index funds existed and it was not possible for individual investors to build a globally diversified index fund portfolio. Fortunately, the number of index funds has grown by popular demand. As of this writing, there are nearly 700 index funds covering a wide variety of markets, including small-cap stocks, foreign markets, and the entire globe. The number includes over 200 exchange-traded index funds, which you can buy and sell during the day through a stockbroker.

Key Points

1. Historically, the stock market has earned greater returns and exhibited more volatility than the bond market or the money market and it is expected to earn higher returns in the future.
2. The easiest way to own a diversified portfolio of stocks is through a mutual fund.
3. The least expensive mutual funds generally deliver the highest returns. Index mutual funds are the least expensive of all.
4. For complete information on index mutual funds, including exchange-traded funds, read *All About Index Funds*, by Richard A. Ferri (McGraw-Hill, 2002).

Note

1. Several independent researchers have concluded that the average survivorship bias in large-cap mutual fund composites inflates the return by more than 1%.

Chapter 9

Investment Choices: Bonds

Credit is the pavement along which production travels.
                                        —*John Maynard Keynes*

Bonds are nothing more than loans issued by corporations, government entities, banks, and people like you. When you take out a home mortgage, you are issuing a bond. You owe interest for each day you use someone's money. Eventually a bond needs to be paid off. This is done periodically over the life of the bond (serial payments) or all at once at maturity (bullet payment). Mortgages are serial bonds because you pay a little principal back with each mortgage payment.

If you lend someone money in the form of a bond, you are entitled to collect interest on that money while it is being used. Eventually, you get your principal back, if the borrower is creditworthy.

When a bond issuer puts up backing or collateral to borrow money, it is called a *secure* bond. Your mortgage is backed by the equity in your house, so it is secure credit. When the only thing that backs a bond is a promise to pay, it is called a *debenture*. Debentures are subordinate to secure bonds, meaning that if the issuer went into bankruptcy, the secure bondholder would be paid first.

In general, investing in bonds is less risky than investing in stocks, because if a company goes bankrupt, the stockholder is the last to get any money. Since the risk of owning bonds is lower than the risk of owning stocks, the expected returns are also lower.

The expected total return of a bond is called its *yield to maturity* (YTM). The YTM of a bond is based on variety of factors, including the cash interest payments, the length of time the money is borrowed, and the creditworthiness of the borrower.

Interest Rates and Market Conditions

Yields move around every day based on market conditions. In addition, the banking industry plays a major role in setting current yields. Banks use money in checking accounts and time deposits (certificates of deposit) to make long-term mortgages and commercial loans. The banks earn revenue on the spread between the interest they pay on deposits and the interest they collect on longer-term loans. Obviously, the spread between short-term interest paid and long-term interest collected is very important to bank profits. That is why the Federal Reserve Bank, a quasi government/private partnership, directly controls short-term interest rates. Representatives from government and the banking industry form the Federal Reserve Board (Fed) and work together to set the inter-bank "Fed funds" rate.

When the Fed has an easy money policy, short-term rates are low compared with long-term rates and banks step up lending, which increases economic activity. When the Fed is tightening credit, short-term rates are high and banks stop lending money, which slows economic growth. This policy is called *central banking*, which was designed in the early 1900s to smooth out the ups and down in the economy. (Some would argue with the success of the program.)

Interest Rates and Time

The longer the *maturity* of the loan, the higher the interest rate.

Money market mutual funds are a type of short-term lending. Generally, money market funds are invested in a large portfolio of bonds that have maturities between one day and one year. These short-term bonds, typically called "cash" or "cash equivalents," include securities such as Treasury bills and commercial paper. Money market funds are convenient: all of your money is available within one day. But the interest on your investment is generally lower than you would receive from investing in longer-term lending. However, money funds can provide good yields when short-term interest rates are rising, because money funds invest in short-term instruments and their managers can capture higher-interest investments as interest rates rise.

At the other extreme, bond maturities can be as long as 30 years. Bonds of greater maturities generally offer higher expected yields. Take, for example, a two-year Treasury note and a five-year Treasury note. Normally, the five-year note should yield higher than a two-year note, because you have to tie your money up for three more years. That means that you are taking a greater risk that fluctuations in interest rates could make other investments more profitable—and that inflation could outpace the interest rate you are earning.

Interest Rates and Risk

The greater the *default risk* of the borrower, the higher the interest rate.

Bonds that have credit risk are also expected to pay a higher return. For example, compare the yields of a five-year Treasury note and a five-year Ford Motor Company bond. The Ford bond will yield more than the Treasury note because its credit risk is greater. Generally, corporate bonds are a greater risk than government bonds, but usually offer higher yields. Also, state and city municipal bonds are a slightly greater risk than U.S. government bonds.

Variety Is the Spice of Portfolios

There are many different bonds, notes, mortgages, and other types of loans that you can invest in. This chapter will discuss several types of securities and ways to include them in your portfolio. Investing in bonds may not be as glamorous or exciting as investing in the stock market, but their steady return serves as a stabilizer in a portfolio.

The Nature of Bond Pricing

Interest rates change daily based on changing economic conditions. If you own a bond or bond mutual fund, daily fluctuations will affect the market value of your portfolio. As a general rule, bonds and bond funds go up in value as interest rates go down and vice versa.

If you sell a bond before it matures, you may gain or lose on its value, depending on interest rates at the time. On the other hand, if you hold a bond to maturity, it will be redeemed at its original *face value*, also called *par value*, whatever the current interest rates. Sometimes a bond is *called* prior to the maturity date; this means that the issuer is redeeming or retiring the bond by buying it back from investors. If a bond you own is called, you will get the par value back sooner than expected and you may be paid a slight premium over par value as a reward for the inconvenience of losing your investment.

A company's bonds are generally less risky than its stock. If a company experiences financial difficulties, stockholders may suffer losses as the price of its stock drops, but the interest on its bonds will be paid. Consequently, the price of the bonds should stay fairly stable unless a serious financial problem develops. The federal government also suffers financial difficulties in an economic downturn, but it simply goes further into debt by issuing more bills, notes, and bonds.

(The terminology used for government borrowing is primarily a matter of maturity. Treasury *bills*—T-bills—have maturities of one year or less. Treasury *notes*—T-notes— have maturities of more than a year but not more than 10 years. Treasury *bonds*—T-bonds—have maturities greater than 10 years. I should add that the Treasury Department hasn't issued a bond since its decision in October 2001 to suspend issuance of the 30-year bond. Finally, bills, notes, and bonds are generally together called *bonds*.)

The government has unlimited taxing power that ensures that it never defaults on any of its obligations. That is why Treasury bonds are considered credit-risk-free.

When a company falls on hard times and its viability comes into question, there is a risk that it will not uphold its obligation to bondholders. In other words, the company may default on its obligations. At that point the creditworthiness of the company will likely fall to *junk* status. That does not mean the company is junk; the term is slang used by Wall Street to mean the rating of the bond is less than quality investment grade, usually indicating a credit rating of BB or lower.

(A credit rating is an indication of a corporation's credit history and ability to pay its obligations. Standard & Poor's and Moody's are two services that rate bonds. Their ratings are basically the same, but use different letter codes: Standard & Poor's rates the highest as AAA and the lowest as C, while Moody's rates the highest as Aaa and the lowest as D.)

As the crisis unfolds, the market price of a company's bonds may go up and down dramatically. If the company misses an interest payment, it is technically in default and must take one of three actions: file for bankruptcy, restructure the covenants of the loan, or immediately pay off the entire issue.

Junk bonds are a very tricky market and I do not recommend buying individual bonds for your portfolio. However, a well-diversified mutual fund holding better-quality junk bonds may have a small place in your portfolio. I like the Vanguard High-Yield Corporate Bond Fund (VWEHX) and the TIAA-CREF High-Yield Bond Fund (TCHYX).

Bond Market Structure

The U.S. bond market is the largest in the world. Every day billions of dollars in U.S. bonds trade at hundreds of bond-trading desks across the globe, while corporations and government agencies issue new bonds to finance projects or refund maturing bond issues. The Treasury is constantly issuing new bills and bonds through regularly scheduled auctions to meet the government's needs for working capital and refinance maturing debt. States and cities constantly issue tax-free municipal bonds to help build roads, schools, and parks. As stated earlier, if you take a mortgage out on your home, your loan will likely become part of a large mortgage pool that will trade in the bond market. In total, the U.S. bond market is worth over $25 trillion, of which $5 trillion is U.S. Treasury issues.

The fixed income market (securities that pay a specific interest rate) is divided into two general types of bonds—taxable bonds and tax-free municipal bonds. In this book we cover mainly taxable bonds, because they are the only type that should go into your tax-sheltered retirement savings accounts. However, for your taxable money, municipal bonds may be an ideal way to generate the best after-tax return. You have to take into consideration your tax bracket and the state tax where you live. To learn more about municipal bonds, there are several good books that can be found at your local library and bookstores, including the following:

- *Keys to Investing in Municipal Bonds*, by Gary M. Strumeyer (Barron's, 1996)
- *Municipal Bonds: The Basics and Beyond*, by David Logan Scott (Probus, 1992)
- *The Fundamentals of Municipal Bonds*, by the Bond Market Association (John Wiley & Sons: 2001, 5th edition).

Taxable bond funds can be categorized along two axes (Figure 9-1). On the horizontal axis is the average maturity of the bonds and on the vertical axis is the average creditworthiness of the bonds.

Short-Term	Intermediate	Long-Term	
SH	IH	LH	High-Yield Corporate
SI	II	LI	Investment-Grade U.S.
SG	IG	LG	U.S. Government

Figure 9-1. A bond matrix

The average maturity of a bond can be divided into three ranges. Short-term bonds have an average maturity of three years or less, intermediate bonds have an average maturity of four to nine years, and long-term bonds have an average maturity of 10 years or more.

Under normal economic conditions, you should expect to get a higher return in a long-term bond because the interest rate risk is greater. This means the value of a long-term bond will fluctuate more with changes in general interest rates.

The credit risk on the vertical axis in Figure 9-1 is more complex. On the bottom of the chart are the least risky government bonds. The bonds that fall into this category are direct obligations of the U.S. government or indirect obligations of quasi-government agencies such as the Federal National Mortgage Association (FNMA). The middle credit level includes investment-grade U.S. corporate bonds and foreign "Yankee" bonds. U.S. corporations with sound fundamental characteristics receive an investment-grade rating from credit rating agencies Standard & Poor's and Moody's. Yankee bonds are foreign bonds issued in U.S. dollars on a U.S. exchange. At the top risk level are high-yield bonds—low-quality bonds, also known as non-investment-grade or junk bonds. As discussed earlier, these companies have a questionable ability to repay their obligations. Historically, over 90% of junk bonds are paid off without the company going into bankruptcy. However, the risk of default certainly justifies a higher return in this asset class.

By putting the two factors together in Figure 9-2, you can see the expected return of a bond is a function of its average maturity and average credit rating. Figure 9-2 illustrates the spread in the rate of return among the various types of bonds based on these two factors. Short-term government bonds have the lowest interest rate risk and the lowest credit risk; therefore, they are expected to produce the lowest long-term return. On the other hand, long-term and high-yield bonds have the highest interest rate risk and highest credit risk; therefore, they are expected to generate the highest long-term return.

Fixed Income Indexes

In the bond market, Lehman Bothers (LB) is the most recognized name. LB indexes are on par with S&P 500 and the Dow Jones Industrial Average in the stock market. LB constructs hundreds of fixed income indexes covering all the global bond markets. The most common U.S. indexes cover the following categories:

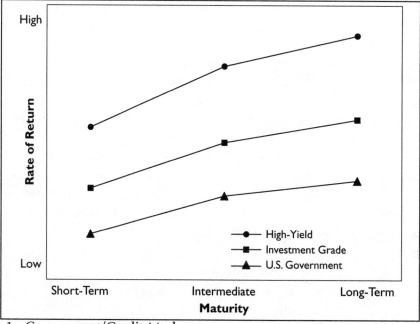

1. Government/Credit Markets

Figure 9-2. Fixed income risk and return comparison

    a. Government
       i. Treasury
       ii. Agency
    b. Corporate (investment grade, BBB or better)
       i. Industrial
       ii. Finance
       iii. Utility
       iv. Yankee Bonds (foreign bonds trading in U.S. dollars)
2. Mortgage Market
    a. Government National Mortgage Association (GNMA)
    b. Federal Home Loan Mortgage Corporation (FHLMC)
    c. Federal National Mortgage Association (FNMA)
3. Asset-Backed Securities
    a. Credit card receivable
    b. Auto loans
    c. Home equity loans

The broadest and most popular index in the LB fixed income series is the Lehman Aggregate Bond Index. This index tracks the prices of over 6,600 bonds—U.S. Treasury, government agency, corporate, and foreign. The bonds in the index have an average maturity of less than nine years, which places the index average in the intermediate-term category. It is also a highly rated index, with over 60% of its holdings in U.S. Treasuries, agency, and government-backed securities. The rest of the bonds are investment-grade corporate and Yankee bonds. There may be a handful of non-investment-grade bonds in the index, due to credit downgrades by the rating agencies during the middle of a reporting period. Those bonds will eventually be deleted from the index. In 2002, the average asset weightings held in the LB Aggregate Bond Index were as shown in Table 9-1.

Short-Term	Intermediate	Long-Term	
SH	**IH**	**LH**	High-Yield Corporate
SI	**II**	**LI**	Investment-Grade U.S.
SG	**IG**	**LG**	U.S. Government

Table 9-1. Lehman Brothers Aggregate Bond Index

A Very Special Treasury Bond

A new type of Treasury bond was introduced in 1997. They are called Treasury Inflation-Protected Securities (TIPS) and are designed to protect against the damaging effects of inflation. As with other Treasury notes and bonds, TIPS pay interest semi-annually and pay principal back at maturity. Unlike the traditional Treasuries, however, the semi-annual interest payments and the par value at redemption of TIPS are linked to the rate of inflation. If inflation goes up, your interest payment goes up with the rate of inflation and the par value at maturity goes up with the rate of inflation as well.

This makes TIPS free from inflation risk, which is unique among all fixed-income securities.

The inflation adjustment in TIPS is based on the Consumer Price Index (CPI), the leading measurement of inflation. Each month the bond price is adjusted based on the previous month's CPI. In all likelihood, inflation will occur over the life of the security and you will be paid more at redemption than you paid at purchase. I recommend buying new issue TIPS rather than bonds that have been out for a few years. If you buy new issue TIPS, in the unlikely event of deflation (a drop in prices), you don't have to worry about losing principal. The Treasury has built a safeguard into the system: the final payment cannot be less than the price when the bond was first issued. Therefore, if you buy a new issue TIP, at worst you'll break even on the principal amount and still collect your interest payments.

Before investing in TIPS, there are a few items you need to know about the interest adjustment. Like other notes and bonds, TIPS pay a fixed coupon (interest rate). However, this fixed rate of interest is applied to the inflation-adjusted price, not the original issue price. So, if inflation occurs throughout the life of your security, every interest payment will be greater than the previous one. On the other hand, in the rather unusual event of deflation, your interest payments will decrease over time.

Bond Accounts and Bond Mutual Funds

Now that you know what is available in bond land, you have two investment strategies to choose from. Either you can buy individual bonds and build your portfolio or you can purchase a bond mutual fund. In some cases, buying bonds directly can lead to higher returns than investing in mutual funds. On the other hand, some classes of bonds are too complex or illiquid to buy directly and should be purchased only through a fund.

Buying Individual Bonds

Building and managing an individual bond portfolio can be a simple undertaking, although I recommend using individual bonds only for liquid securities such as Treasuries and government agency debt. With Treasury and government agency bonds, you don't have to worry about default risk and the resale market for these bonds is very high. In addition, when you buy a bond from a friendly broker, make sure he or she *fully* discloses the commission. Brokerage firms tend to stick individual investors with fees on bond transactions. You should not pay more than a couple of dollars commission per $1000 bond.

Although you can buy individual bonds through any brokerage firm, you can also purchase new issues from the Treasury Department through TreasuryDirect. This will eliminate the commission charge by a brokerage firm. If you buy $5,000 worth of a new bond direct from the Treasury, you get the same yield and pay the same price per bond as a billion dollar mutual fund. To find out more, contact TreasuryDirect at 800 722-2678. The Web site is www.treasurydirect.gov.

Building a Bond Ladder

The simplest type of portfolio to manage is called a *bond ladder*. A laddered portfolio is put together by purchasing an equal number of bonds with maturities from one to anywhere between five and 10 years. You then hold the bonds until maturity and collect interest each year. When a bond matures, you roll out to the end of the ladder and buy another bond. Thus, the ladder continues.

To establish a ladder, take the size of your account and divide it by the number of years in the ladder. For example, using a five-year Treasury bond ladder and a $100,000 investment, you will buy $20,000 worth of bonds maturing each year for the next five years. Table 9-2 illustrates a sample portfolio.

In a bond ladder, you are interested in the yield to maturity (YTM) or total return. For all practical purposes, the coupon on the bond is not that important. It does not matter if the bond pays 4% or 6% interest; the price of the bond will adjust according to current interest rates. What matters to you is the yield on a bond, which is a function of the coupon rate, the price you pay, and the time to maturity.

Once you have established the ladder, you simply hold the bonds and collect interest. When a bond matures, you reinvest the

Quantity	Bond	Maturity	Coupon	Price Paid	Yield to Maturity
20	T-Note	Dec. 2004	6.25%	102.14	5.00%
20	T-Note	Nov. 2005	6.63%	104.02	5.12%
20	T-Note	Sep. 2006	4.25%	96.10	5.14%
20	T-Note	Nov. 2007	5.38%	97.17	5.24%
20	T-Note	Dec. 2008	5.25%	99.75	5.30%

Table 9-2. Five-year treasury bond ladder; average yield: 5.20%
Note: Rates are not accurate.

$20,000 principal and $5,000 accumulated interest into another five-year bond. The results are in Table 9-3.

Quantity	Bond	Maturity	Coupon	Price Paid	Yield to Maturity
20	T-Note	Nov. 2005	6.63%	104.02	5.12%
20	T-Note	Sep. 2006	4.25%	96.10	5.14%
20	T-Note	Nov. 2007	5.38%	97.17	5.24%
20	T-Note	Dec. 2008	5.25%	99.75	5.30%
25	T-Note	May 2009	5.31%	100.02	5.30%

Table 9-3. Continuing a bond ladder; average yield: 5.16%
Note: Rates are for illustration only and do not reflect market prices.

Notice in the example how the yield to maturity of the portfolio increases from 5.16% to 5.22% after the first year. This jump in yield occurs because the original one-year bond had a low yield of only 5.00%, and the new 2006 bond has a 5.30% return. If interest rates remain constant over the next several years, all the new bonds will be purchased at the higher yield. This will cause the portfolio yield to increase to 5.30%.

A bond ladder can be five years, seven years, 10 years, or longer. I do not recommend building a ladder greater than 10 years for a couple of reasons. First, the longer the ladder, the more the portfolio is subject to interest rate risk. That means if interest rates move higher, the value of a long-term bond portfolio will fall much more than the value of a short-term bond portfolio. Second, many bonds are callable after 10 years. If the issuer redeems your bonds early, then the total return usually falls.

If you buy bonds from a brokerage firm, ensure that you are getting a fair yield on a bond by checking a few sources for current interest rates. *The Wall Street Journal* is a good place to begin. It includes comprehensive bond listings where you can gauge the market. There are several Web sites that give up-to-the-minute bond yields. Check www.bloomberg.com for current yields.

The Mutual Fund Alternatives

In general, individually managed bond portfolios perform better then most bond mutual funds, because the fee for mutual fund management is generally high. The average fee for a bond fund is 1% before commissions, according to Morningstar. However, there are several low-cost alternatives. For example, the Vanguard Group of mutual funds offers a variety of low-cost bond funds.

One of the widely diversified bond mutual funds you can own is a bond index fund. There are dozens of mutual fund companies offering hundreds of stock index funds, but only a handful offer bond index funds. The Vanguard Group currently manages four open-end bond index funds. In July 2002, Barclays Global Investors introduced several exchange-traded funds benchmarked to the Lehman Brothers Treasury bond indexes. In November 2002, ETF Advisers introduced Fixed Income Trust Receipts (FITRs, aka "fighters"). FITRs track Treasury securities with one-, two-, five-, and 10-year maturities. Each Treasury FITR portfolio matches the performance of a consistent-maturity Ryan Treasury Index less a 0.15% annual fee.

One bond index fund that may be appropriate to use for a portion of your retirement account is the Vanguard Total Bond Market Index Fund. The fund is made up of a well-diversified portfolio of corporate debt, government agency bonds, and Treasury bonds. The objective of the fund is to match the performance and risk of the LB Aggregate Bond Index. The portfolio has an average weighted maturity of about seven years.

Depending on your situation, you may prefer bonds with a shorter maturity. The Vanguard Short-Term Bond Index Fund has an average maturity of about 2½ years, which is similar to a five-year bond ladder, described earlier.

Unfortunately, there are not many bond index funds available. Despite the efforts of Vanguard and Barclays, a lack of funds leaves many holes in the fixed income market where no index funds exist. To fill the gaps, low-cost actively managed bond funds are the next best thing to indexing. Some types of bonds—such as junk bonds, mortgages, and international bonds—are complex and should be purchased only through low-cost mutual funds. Although there are no index funds in these categories, Vanguard and other mutual fund companies have diversified low-cost funds that cover these market sectors.

Table 9-4 is a partial list of bond index funds and low-cost bond funds from *All About Index Funds,* by Richard A. Ferri (McGraw-Hill, 2002). You can also contact the Vanguard Group at 800 662-7447 or visit the Web site at www.vanguard.com.

As you can see from the list, there are lots of bond funds to choose from. Selecting the funds that are right for your portfolio will depend on the time frame you have for investing and the risk you are willing to take. Those subjects are covered in Part Three of this book.

	Symbol	Fee
Total Bond Market Index Funds		
Vanguard Total Bond Market Index	VBMFX	0.20%
Summit Apex Lehman Aggregate Bond Index	SALAX	0.30%
Schwab Total Bond Market Index	SWLBX	0.35%
Short-Term Bond Index Funds		
Vanguard Short-Term Bond Index	VBISX	0.20%
Schwab Short-Term Bond Market	SWBDX	0.35%

Table 9-4. Recommend bond mutual funds (continued on next page)

	Symbol	Fee
Treasury Bond Funds		
Vanguard Short-Term Treasury	VFISX	0.27%
Vanguard Intermediate Treasury	VFITX	0.27%
iShares 1- to 3-Year Treasury Index*	SHY	0.15%
iShares 7- to 10-Year Treasury Index*	IEF	0.15%
iShares 10- to 30-Year Treasury Index*	TLT	0.15%
ETF Advisers Treasury 1 FITR*	TFT	0.15%
ETF Advisers Treasury 2 FITR*	TOU	0.15%
ETF Advisers Treasury 5 FITR*	TFI	0.15%
ETF Advisers Treasury 10 FITR*	TTE	0.15%
Vanguard Inflation-Protected (TIPS)	VIPSX	0.22%
Government Bond and GNMA Funds		
Vanguard Short-Term Federal	VSGBX	0.27%
Vanguard GNMA Fund	VFIIX	0.27%
USAA GNMA Fund	USGNX	0.32%
Corporate Bond Funds		
Vanguard Short-Term Corporate	VFSTX	0.25%
Vanguard Intermediate Corporate	VFICX	0.25%
iShares GS $ InvesTop Corporate Bond*	LQD	0.15%
High-Yield Corporate Bond Funds		
Vanguard High-Yield Corporate	VWEHX	0.28%
TIAA-CREF High-Yield Corporate	TCHYX	0.34%
Emerging Market Bond Funds		
Payden Emerging Markets Bond	PYEMX	0.90%
Fidelity New Markets Income	FNMIX	1.00%

*Exchange-traded funds

Table 9-4. Recommend bond mutual funds (continued)

Chapter Summary

Interest rates play a critical role in our lives, from the rate you pay on a mortgage to the rate you receive on a bank savings account. Over your lifetime, the bonds or bond funds you select as investments are an important part of the total return of your retirement portfolio. By spending a little time understanding bonds and the bond market, you can create an appropriate portfolio of bonds and bond mutual funds to help meet your retirement needs.

Managing an individual bond portfolio can be rewarding. However, the bond market can be full of pitfalls, such as hidden brokerage commissions and little-known call features on bonds. My recommendation is to stick with managing the most liquid and accessible bonds, which are U.S. government bonds, particularly U.S. Treasuries. These bonds can be purchased directly from the government. If you buy from a broker, ensure that you are not paying too much in trading costs: check the price with a reputable source such as *The Wall Street Journal*.

An easier solution to buying bonds is to select a low-cost bond mutual fund. This is practically true of mortgages and high-yield bonds. There are several bond funds on the market, but the Vanguard Group has the best variety at the lowest cost.

Key Points

1. Bonds are interest-bearing investments that offer safety of principal and a competitive return.
2. One method of investing in bonds is through a bond ladder. You purchase an equal number of bonds each year and roll the principal when the bonds mature.
3. The preferred method of investing in bonds is through low-cost mutual funds. This method offers convenience and wide diversification.

Chapter 10

Other Sources of Retirement Income

The meek shall inherit the earth, but not the mineral rights.
—J. Paul Getty

TRADITIONAL SELF-MANAGED retirement accounts, such as IRAs and 401(k)s, typically invest in stocks, bonds, cash equivalents, and mutual funds. These accounts will be used to generate income during retirement. However, most people also have wealth stored in property and other assets that can be used to help fund their retirement needs. This wealth includes such assets as the equity in their homes, private businesses, collectibles, and the present value of their future Social Security benefits.

Additional stores of wealth beyond individual self-managed accounts can be divided into three broad categories. The first category includes employment-related assets such as defined benefit pension plans, incentive stock options, restricted stock compensation, and Social Security benefits. The second category covers direct business ownership, including partnerships and income-producing real estate. The third category covers personal assets such as home equity, vacation property, precious metals, and collectibles such as fine art and rare coins.

All of the assets discussed in this chapter either will generate income in retirement or can be converted to income-generating assets if needed. Some of the assets discussed in this chapter are relevant to everyone and some are relevant to only a small segment of the population. Nevertheless, it is important, when putting together a retirement plan, to consider all the assets you own. This information will fall into place as you read Part Three of this book.

Employment-Related Assets

Employment-related assets are those benefits that you accumulate from an employer over a period of time. They do not include pay or cash bonuses or the savings that *you* contribute to an employee savings plan. These assets include defined benefit pension plans, Social Security benefits, and employer medical plans that extend to retirees. Although you never see the actual lump sum value of these benefits, in most cases they are worth several hundred thousand dollars.

Employment-related assets would also include the employer match portion of a deferred savings account such as a 401(k). In a corporation, assets may accumulate as part of a performance incentive and be paid in the form of restrictive company stock or stock options. Whatever the case, these assets become part of your overall retirement income plan and you should not overlook them.

Social Security

In 1935, after bank failures and a stock market crash that wiped out the savings of millions of Americans, the country turned to Washington to guarantee the nation's elderly a decent income. The solution was Social Security.

Since its inception, almost all working Americans have been corralled into the Social Security system. Half of the money going into the trust fund is a tax paid by employers and the other half is a tax paid by employees. Currently, the tax is about 15%, which includes a Medicare portion (see Chapter 15). A few employers are not required to pay into the Social Security system, since their employees are covered under a separate plan, such as that provided by the Railroad Retirement Act, some members of the clergy, and longtime federal employees who opted out of the system years ago.

Each year, hundreds of billion of dollars from millions of U.S. workers are paid into the Social Security Trust Fund and, as of this moment, slightly less goes out to retirees in monthly payments. That means the fund is running at a surplus, but it is not going to last. By about 2012, more money will be paid out in Social Security benefits than will be coming in from payroll taxes. So, the fund will start to run a deficit. There is enough money in the fund to run a deficit until the 2030s—and then the fund will be broke.

In some ways, the surplus in the Social Security Trust Fund is already gone. The extra money taken in each month is loaned right back to the government in the form of special government bonds. These special government bonds do not count as part of the federal deficit. Therefore, the Social Security Trust Fund becomes a neat way in which Washington hides the true size of the federal debt. (As an aside, if the CEO of any corporation tried to hide debt in this manner, he or she would be put in jail.)

Social Security faces a funding crisis. When the trust fund starts turning in its bonds for cash to pay for benefits, the government will no longer be able to borrow from Social Security, but will also have to start making good on the loans outstanding. The government can raise the cash to pay the loans in one of three ways: by increasing taxes, by cutting spending, or by running a deficit. Around 2032, the fund is predicted to be out of cash and out of bonds. Coincidentally, the money runs out about the time the average baby boomer turns age 75, which is about the age when part-time work becomes difficult. That means big cuts in Social Security benefits, little part-time work, and a lot less money for everyone. We are clearly heading for a huge retirement crisis in America—and yet our political leaders do little or nothing to stop it.

The history and general outlook for Social Security was provided to give you an idea of the risk in the system. Current retirees and those about to retire should get full benefits from the government, at least for a while. But it is painfully obvious that most baby boomers and younger will face large cuts in benefits and probably delays in benefits.

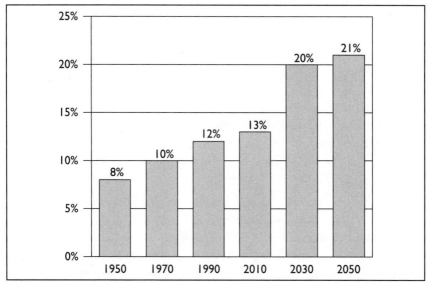

Figure 10-1. U.S. population over age 65
Source: Social Security Administration

How large will these cuts be? Each year the Social Security Administration sends all participants a statement that outlines their projected benefits under the current plan. If you are in your 50s, it may be wise to reduce those projections by 25%. If you are in your 40s, it seems plausible to reduce them by 50% and add three to four years to the full retirement age. For workers in their 30s and younger, a 60% to 70% reduction in benefits is likely and possibly a five- to seven-year increase in the full retirement age. The younger you are, the more you should discount any projections sent to you by the Social Security Administration.

Defined Benefit Plans

Some employers offer a defined benefit plan to employees who have met certain longevity and age requirements. This provides a worker with a steady paycheck after retirement. Employees typically become eligible for benefits after they finish a five-year vesting period and reach the age of 55 to 65. The size of the benefit grows with time on the job and level of base pay. The employer is the sole contributor to a defined benefit plan and must fund the plan on a regular basis, even if the company has no profits.

A defined benefit plan holds all employee assets in a pool, rather than in individual accounts for each employee. Record keepers keep track of each person's share of the pool. Since the pool is a liability of the employer, the employees have no voice in the investment decisions concerning defined benefit plans. The pension committee appointed typically hires consultants and investment managers to manage the portfolio. Since the employer makes a specific promise to pay a certain sum in the future, it is the employer who assumes the risk of fluctuations in the value of the investment pool and must make up any permanent impairments.

Annual contributions to a defined benefit plan can be very complex. They are based on actuarial assumptions regarding life expectancy during retirement, expected account growth, and future salary projections. If the account does well, then the company may not need to make a contribution, but if the accounts perform poorly, the company is required to fund the shortfall in the account.

Payouts from defined benefit plans can be divided into three categories:

1. Flat benefit plan—All participants receive a flat dollar amount as long as they have met a requirement of a predetermined minimum of years.
2. Unit benefit plan—Participants receive benefits that are either a percentage of compensation or a fixed dollar amount multiplied by the number of qualifying years of service.
3. Variable benefit plan—Benefits are based on allocating units, rather than dollars, to the contributions to the plan; at retirement, the value of the units allocated to the retiring employee would be the proportionate value of all units in the fund.

With a defined benefit plan, the employer is legally required to make sure there is enough money in the plan to pay the guaranteed benefits. If the company fails to meet its obligation, the federal government steps in. Defined benefit plans are insured under the Pension Benefit Guaranty Corporation (PBGC). The insurance works like the Federal Deposit Insurance Corporation insurance that backs up your bank accounts. If your plan is covered and the sponsoring company goes bust, the PBGC will take over benefit payments up to a maximum amount. The insurance protection helps make your pension more secure, but it is not a full guarantee that you will get what you expect. It is a good idea to check that your company is insured under the PBGC.

A Few Final Words on Social Security and Pensions

Some retirement plans adjust benefits for inflation (called the *cost-of-living adjustment,* or COLA). This means the amount of the retirement checks goes up each year with inflation. Most government plans provide for inflation protection, but most private defined benefit plans do not. Social Security is a type of government defined benefit plan that adjusts for inflation, at least for now. Very few corporate defined benefit plans provide for an adjustment each year for inflation. Therefore, over the years, the purchasing power of the retiree relying on a corporate pension shrinks considerably.

A second important item to understand is survivorship benefits. If the retired employee dies, his or her spouse gets either a reduced benefit or nothing at all. Sometimes, the retired employee can buy insurance to cover the spouse, but that means a lower retirement check for the retired employee. Ask your employer what the rules are for spouses. Social Security has one of the most generous survivorship benefit programs: a surviving spouse gets 100% of the highest amount of either spouse and any children under 18 also collect. While this is a noble practice, the generosity of Social Security is killing it.

The final word: there is a debate in the financial planning world as to whether these payments should be thought of as income from a bond or as a separate asset class. In my opinion, Social Security and defined benefit payments should be treated as a separate and distinct asset class and not as a bond. If you treat Social Security and a defined benefit pension as a bond, then you may feel like being more aggressive when buying stocks in an individual account. The problem with getting aggressive in a individual account is that most people cannot handle the volatility in a down market and tend to trade their account much too often and make other mistakes as described in Chapter 3, Bear Markets and Bad Investor Behavior, and Chapter 4, Getting Trampled by the Herd. In addition, it is nearly impossible to put a present value on future benefits that may or may not be paid as expected. Benefits will likely be reduced in the future and the eligibility age will likely be extended. Since future benefits are largely unknown, the present value of those future benefits is also unknown, so you cannot treat Social Security as bond that pays a fixed rate. To be safe, keep Social Security and defined benefit pension plans separate from your investment portfolio. They are not bonds and should not be treated as bonds.

Corporate Stock Plans

Over the years, there has been a dramatic increase in the number of companies granting restricted stock and stock options far down their organizational ladders. Faced with rapidly changing business conditions, new technologies, global competition, tight labor markets, and a changing tax code, companies ranging from Internet startups to giants like PepsiCo, Bank of America, and Procter & Gamble decided that most or all of their employees belong in their equity incentive programs. The idea behind stock-based incentive programs is to strengthen and grow a company by encouraging employees to become partners in that growth.

While stock incentive programs work out well for some, the trend has been a double-edged sword. There have also been big winners, like Microsoft, General Electric, and Citigroup, but there are also big losers. Thousands of workers at Enron, WorldCom, Qwest, and hundreds of other firms suffered devastating losses in wealth by relying on the stock program of the companies they worked for. The moral of the story is simple: incentive programs that rely on corporate stock have significantly more risk than cash bonus programs. Workers in stock incentive programs may do irreparable harm to their wealth by not diversifying into other investments when they have an opportunity.

Types of Programs. There are three basic types of employer-funded stock programs:

- 401(k) matches
- stock option plans
- restricted stock awards.

401(k) Matches. The most common stock award program is the 401(k) match. In many cases, corporations will make a matching contribution to their employees' 401(k) plan in company stock instead of cash. This contribution is usually determined by matching a percent of the employee contribution, up to a predefined maximum amount. For example, an employer may elect to put in 50 cents for every dollar up to a $2,000 contribution. If an employee places $2,000 in the plan, the company will place $1,000 of company stock. That's an immediate 50% return on investment, regardless of how well the 401(k) money performs.

Many companies make their 401(k) match in corporate stock only if the employee chooses. In that case, it is better to act prudently and maybe restrict your allotment to half stock and half cash. Most of the time, the shares you receive in a 401(k) are restricted, meaning you cannot sell them for a certain number of years. This restriction on sales caused many Enron employees to lose years of accumulated company match value as the stock collapsed. Since the government became concerned about restrictions on sales after Enron, many companies have reduced the average number of years from five or more to about two.

According to a study by the Employee Benefit Research Institute, 401(k) participants whose employers match in company stock have over 50% of their total account balances invested in that single stock. In plans that offer company stock as an investment option on the employee contribution side, but where the employer doesn't match with company stock, on average just under 20% of the total account balances are in company stock. Both amounts are far too risky for most individuals. A good rule of thumb is to have no more than 10% of the account invested in company stock.

Stock Option Plans. Stock options are a way in which companies allow employees to acquire company stock and get a potential income tax break. When a company grants stock options to employees, it is essentially giving them a contractual right to purchase stock at a fixed price for a certain period of time. This is called the *grant price*. Most employees eventually decide to exercise the options and purchase shares when the market price of the stock is above the grant price. They can make an instant profit by buying the stock from the company at the grant price and reselling it on the market at the current price. An employee also has the right to hold the shares indefinitely after exercising the options.

When new options are granted, the price is typically set at or near the market value on the grant date. Companies typically impose vesting restrictions on grants. This means that an employee must continue to work for the company for, say, three to five years before he or she can exercise part or all of the options. If the company stock price never rises above the grant price, then the employee can simply let the unexercised options expire and owe nothing to the company. Thus, the employee does not risk any money by receiving an option grant or by exercising the options and immediately selling the stock. The only risk is if the employee exercises an option and then holds the stock instead of selling. In that case, the stock price may fall below the grant price. This is a double whammy for some employees, because they may owe taxes on the original gain, but now the stock is worth less than the purchase price.

There are two types of stock options, nonqualified and incentive.

The intrinsic value of nonqualified stock options is taxed as ordinary income on the day they are exercised. *Intrinsic value* is the difference between the strike price of the option (the stated price at which an employee may purchase stock when exercising the option) and the market price of the stock.

Incentive stock options meet the Internal Revenue Code rules for preferential tax treatment, but the rules are tricky and always changing. As of this writing, if an employee exercises an option and holds the stock for at least two years after the date of grant or one year after exercising the option, the gain made by the exercise is potentially taxed at lower capital gains rates; however, the company does not receive a tax deduction. If the employee sells the stock during the holding period, then it is treated as a nonqualified option, i.e., the spread is treated as ordinary income and the company receives a tax deduction. As we used to say in the Marine Corps, these rules are as clear as mud. Check with your tax advisor before proceeding.

During the technology boom in the late 1990s, many high-tech employees made millions by exercising their options. However, the only ones who kept the money were the people who sold stock before the tech bust from 2000 to 2002. Many employees never exercised or they held onto stock after exercising and ended up with nothing. Ironically, many who held the worthless stock were still liable for tax based on the gains they made on the exercise date. Stock options made millions for many employees and wiped out the savings of many others. It is a very risky venture to hold a large block of your net worth in stock after exercising options. If you exercise stock options, sell some of the stock and diversify.

Restricted Stock Awards. A restricted stock award is part of the compensation package generally given to a top-level employee or executive of a company. The granting of restricted stock means that the recipient's rights in the stock are limited over a period of time. He or she cannot sell the stock during the restricted vesting period. Vesting periods can be simply a matter of time (a stated period from the award date) or there can be conditions based on either company or individual performance (tied to achievement of specified goals).

The Securities and Exchange Commission (SEC) controls restricted stock under SEC Rule 144. When the vesting period is over and an employee wishes to sell restricted stock, he or she must obtain the written permission of the company and file a special form with the SEC. The SEC form becomes part of the public record. Once all the requirements are met, the stock becomes unrestricted and the employee is free to execute the trade.

Under federal income tax rules, an employee receiving restricted stock awards is not taxed at the time of the award. Instead, he or she is taxed at the time the restriction lapses. The amount of income subject to ordinary income tax is the difference between the fair market value of the shares at the time of vesting and the price paid for the shares, if any.

An employee can accumulate a significant amount of wealth in a restricted stock award program, depending on the performance of the stock and the amount of restricted stock granted to the employee. The risks in a restricted stock program are the same as in any other stock incentive plan. It pays to diversify if company stock becomes a large portion of your retirement savings, especially as your age and years of service increase.

Businesses and Partnerships

Over 85% of North American businesses are family-owned, including 35% of the *Fortune* 500. Business owners work hard to achieve success. They meet and overcome many challenges over the years. Yet, despite the experiences and success, most owners are not prepared for what is usually a once-in-a-lifetime experience, executing an exit strategy. This involves converting equity in the business into an income stream during retirement.

One option is to leave the business in the hands of family members. This allows the owner to retain some control over the business and to draw a salary or consulting fee for overseeing the business. But family succession does not guarantee success. Only 30% of businesses make it to the second generation, and just 15% to the third generation. Often it is because family issues get in the way, the successor is not qualified, or the succession is poorly planned. Nevertheless, a business placed in the hands of a competent sibling or relative is often a solution that offers a way to draw steady income from the assets.

Many small business owners opt to sell rather than finding someone in the family to take over. The sale can be to a larger company, to an unrelated third party, to a current partner, or to employees in the form of an employee stock ownership plan (ESOP). An ESOP is a type of defined contribution benefit plan that buys and holds company stock for the benefit of employees. The ESOP takes out a loan to pay for the shares and employee contributions eventually pay back the loan. ESOPs are often used in closely held companies to buy part or all of the shares of existing owners, but they also are used in public companies.

Most sales of businesses are structured as a lump sum payout, a multi-year payout, or some combination of the two. The profit from the sale is taxable to the former owner, but many times the bulk of the profit is taxed at a 20% long-term capital gains rate.

Selling a business creates problems. For instance, there are questions of loyalty. Will the customers stay with the new owners or will they leave? Will employees stay and work for the new owner or will the new owner bring in a new team of workers? Sometimes key employees have to be given a financial incentive to stay on, which may take away from a seller's profit.

The decision to sell is one of the most complex and difficult decisions a longtime business owner will make. The desire to pursue personal goals and the ability to achieve financial independence from the sale must be balanced against the challenges and stimulation of owning and operating a business. Family considerations, health, age, and concern for employees are all factors to be considered.

Despite the complexities, most owners should think about the succession of their business a few years prior to the sale. Property planning and positioning the business for sale will increase the value and enable the owners to get the best price and terms.

Rental Property

One interesting way to produce income up to and during retirement is to own rental property. Typically, this is in the form of a rental home or a small commercial building. Often a business owner will sell the business, but retain ownership in the building that houses the business. This allows the owner to reduce the tax consequence of selling the business and to produce rental income. In addition, the owner can take blocks of tax-free cash out of the property by periodically refinancing when interest rates are advantageous. Later in retirement, if real estate prices are favorable or if managing the property becomes too much of a chore, the owner can sell the property and invest the remaining equity in passive income-producing securities.

There are several advantages to owning rental real estate. First, well-managed and maintained rental real estate properties can be expected to generate an annualized pre-tax return of about 10%, according to *Property* magazine. This includes rental income and capital appreciation, net of maintenance costs. Second, there are tax benefits derived from the depreciation of rental property and other expenses. Third, owning rental property diversifies an investment portfolio, which is an important element in lowering overall investment risk.

The 10% average return does not come without risk. There can be many disadvantages to owning rental real estate. First, the property could remain empty while taxes and other costs mount. Second, the company renting the property could fall on hard times and file Chapter 11 bankruptcy, which would allow it to stay in the building and not pay rent. Third, real estate is an illiquid investment. Selling it takes time. The local economy could be in a slump or interest rates could go higher, thereby reducing the value of the property and making it more difficult to sell. Finally, many former owners help the new owner by personally financing the large down payment required by banks for a loan. If the new owner defaults on the bank loan, it leaves the seller with the obligation to pick up the bank loan on a building that is no longer generating enough income to cover the payments. These problems can create huge headaches for someone in retirement and reduce cash flow significantly.

Partnerships (Including Limited Partnerships)

Partnerships come in two forms, active and passive. An *active* partnership is a business that you participate in, but do not entirely own. It has all the advantages and disadvantages of owing the business outright, except that the exit strategy can be difficult if your partners do not want to cooperate. Active partnerships also include unlimited liability, meaning you can be personally held liable for any accident or act. A *passive* limited partnership, on the other hand, requires no participation except writing a check to the general partner. In addition, your personal liability is typically limited to the amount of the check you write, so there is no fear of being sued. Make sure you read the fine print on any limited partnership—and have your lawyer read it too.

Some active partnerships are in the form of a *family limited partnership*. This is a corporate structure that facilitates the succession of a business between parents and children. In a family LLC, the parents generally own a large percentage of the shares and the children own a small percent. Over time, the parents gift or sell more shares to the children. When the parents pass away, the remaining portions of the partnership are shifted to the children. The valuation of the limited partnership at death is at reduced for estate tax purposes. This is because the family limited partnership shares are illiquid. The rules are complex, so see an estate-planning attorney.

In a passive limited partnership, the partners have no management responsibilities. They place money into a pool along with other limited partners. A general partner manages the investments in the pool. Limited partnerships are the way hedge funds, venture capital funds, some real estate funds, and many other packaged investment products are structured. Not everyone can buy these funds because they may require a certain level of income or net worth to participate. This restriction of investors avoids providing detailed disclosures to the SEC.

The major problem with a limited partnership is not buying shares; it is selling them. It is very difficult to liquidate partnership shares, especially if you need to cash out early. Typically there are no buyers except for the other partners, and they are willing to buy only at a greatly discounted rate.

Tangible Personal Assets

During life we accumulate lots of things. The largest asset most people have is their house. In addition, you may own a vacation home, land, precious metals, artwork, antiques, coins, collectible cars, etc. Eventually, most people want to reduce the amount of stuff they own, which can result in money to be invested for income.

Homes and Vacation Property

We all live someplace, but you may not need as large a home in retirement as you did when the children were all home. After the children leave the nest, many retirees downsize and take equity out of their home. They then reinvest this equity in income-producing investments.

Retirees may take equity out of their home without selling. You could leverage the house through refinancing or doing a reverse mortgage. Leveraging means taking out equity in a house by borrowing against it. A reverse mortgage is a loan against your home equity that you do not have to pay back as long as you live in the house. A reverse mortgage can be paid to you all at once, as a regular monthly advance, or at the time and in the amount that you choose. The loan is paid off when you or your heirs sell the house in future years.

Millions of Americans have two homes, a primary residence and vacation property. During retirement, many people decide to sell one or the other or to sell both and buy one home that suits both purposes. All of these options provide capital that can be reinvested to supplement retirement income.

Occasionally, a family owns a tract of land that is no longer being used. This land is also a candidate for sale. Selling land converts cash outflows for property taxes into cash inflows from alternative fixed income investments.

When reviewing a retirement plan, it is important to consider the equity in personal real estate. It is there if you need it.

Collectibles

When I was growing up, my next-door neighbors collected antique art glass and ceramic figures. Later in life, those collections provided an important source of income for the couple. Without the added income, it would have been very difficult for this couple to live the lifestyle they wanted in retirement. Although they had been collecting for years, it was not too hard to sell the antiques because as the couple aged, they started having more accidents and breaking more objects. Clearly, selling was a smart option.

Collectibles may be almost any items. Some are more valuable than others. A lot of older people want to pass their collections on to their children and grandchildren. But in many cases, the collections are not really wanted. What is a valuable gift in the eyes of a grandparent can be worthless junk in the eyes of a grandchild. When that is the case, it is in the best interest of all to sell the collection and use the money for other things.

Gold and precious metals are thought of as a hedge against rising inflation. However, at some point late in life, no amount of inflation is going to matter to your standard of living, except possible health care inflation. At that point, is may be a good time to sell the silver and gold coins and use the proceeds for more important needs.

Chapter Summary

Retirement income can come from many sources. When you piece together your retirement plan while reading Part Three of this book, make sure you include employment-related assets, business assets, and personal assets. They all play an important role in funding the income-producing investments needed to live the lifestyle you want in retirement.

Defined benefit pension plans and Social Security benefits are important pieces of your retirement puzzle. Make sure you understand how these systems work, especially the COLA and survivorship benefits. Do not consider these payouts as a bond investment and then increase the risk on your personal savings. Look at them as a separate asset class.

Corporate stock in a 401(k) plan can lead to terrific gains and terrible losses. There are thousands of "Microsoft Millionaires" as a result of the stock incentive plans at that company. On the other hand, some 11,000 Enron employees lost about $1 billion within six weeks in October and November 2001 as shares sank from the $30s to pennies.

Stock incentive plans are one aspect of wealth accumulation. They have worked particularly well for some younger workers who could afford to take the risk. However, I recommend that older employees diversify away from company stock as much as possible. There is too much risk in placing your career and a large portion of your retirement savings in the hands of one company. In my opinion, 10% in company stock seems to be a prudent amount.

Equity built up in private businesses and partnerships can be used to generate income. The trick is an exit strategy: how to get cash out of the business. Once that issue is resolved, the equity taken out of the business can be used to buy more liquid and passive investments, such as stock, bonds, and mutual funds.

Home ownership has been one of the best investments a person could make in life. The equity in a home can be an ideal source of capital if needed in retirement. The home can be sold or the equity in the house can be borrowed using any of several techniques.

When we count our blessings, sometimes there are more there than we think. It helps to know the value of your valuables, from the value of a pension plan to the equity in your house. These stores of wealth will eventually provide extra income in retirement if needed.

Key Points

1. There are many potential sources of retirement income that need to be considered when developing a plan.
2. Social Security, defined benefit plans, and other work-related programs will help fund a retirement income need, but likely at a reduced rate for younger people.
3. Family businesses and partnerships can provide much-needed capital for retirement as long as there is an exit strategy.
4. Personal equity in homes and collectibles can help generate retirement income if needed.

Chapter 11

Realistic Market Expectations

In the short run, the market is a voting machine. In the long run,
it's a weighing machine.

—*Benjamin Graham*

EFFECTIVELY MANAGING your retirement account requires you to
have realistic expectations of future stock and bond market
returns. Having reasonable expectations requires knowledge of
the past market performance and, more importantly, an understanding of why those returns materialized. This chapter will help
you develop an appropriate portfolio that meets your needs.

The past 25 years have been unusually generous to investors,
despite the recent bear market in stocks. As a matter of record, it
was one of the most profitable periods in the economic history of
the United States. There is little chance the high returns of the '80s
and '90s will repeat over the next 25 years. In fact, based on current interest rates and low inflation, it is all but impossible for the
markets to repeat the performance.

Before we begin a detailed look at risks and returns of various
markets, there are a couple of issues you need to know about.

First, it is nearly impossible to accurately forecast stock and bond returns over the short term. There are too many unpredictable events and uncontrollable factors that can affect the near-term outcome. However, over the long term, the performance of the stock and bond market is fairly predictable, because it follows the growth of the U.S. economy. Therefore, to the extent that we can predict long-term economic growth, which is somewhat controlled by the Federal Reserve Board, we can predict long-term returns in financial markets.

The second issue surrounds the market-forecasting methodology used in this book. There are several methods used to make a market forecast, all requiring a certain amount of trust in the viability of American capitalism. Nevertheless, some people trust more than others and economists will agree to disagree on everything—inflation expectations, tax rates, trade issues, interest rates, and so on. However, in the end, the differences in most market forecasts still seem to fall in a 1% to 2% range and I believe the conservative market forecasts at the end of this chapter are at the lower end of that range.

There are two simple methodologies explained in this chapter that are used to determine long-term stock and bond forecasts: a risk-adjusted return model and an economic growth model. If you want to skip the details of the methodology and get to the forecasts, go to the end of this chapter. There you will find my market forecast based on 2002 data. Of course this forecast is subject to revision as the economy shifts and changes. If you are interested in how these forecasts were formed, read the rest of the chapter through to the end.

Using Historic Risk and Return Data to Forecast Returns

It seems only natural to study past returns of the markets in an attempt to forecast future returns. However, simply extrapolating past results into the future is not going to yield a reliable forecast, especially if you limit your observations to the last half century. Market returns can differ significantly from period to period, and no one can tell you what the next period will return based solely on the last period observed.

Over any 25-year period, the returns of the stock and bond markets will fluctuate with economic conditions, especially the rate of inflation. However, it is interesting to note that the period-over-period risk inherent in the financial markets tends to be more stable than the returns. If you observe the price volatility of stocks in the U.S. and abroad, the up and down movement of stock prices month over month and year by year seems to be fairly consistent over any 25-year period. Logically, and according to capital pricing theory, in the long run the risk of a market should be a good indication of the future return. Higher-risk investments should be expected to yield higher returns and lower-risk investments should be expected to yield lower returns. This is true in the stock market, the bond market, the real estate market, and every other business venture.

100 Years of Market History

It always helps to look at charts to view long-term trends. Figure 11-1 represents over 100 years of U.S. stock prices adjusted for inflation and Figure 11-2 represents over 100 years of dividend yields. Notice that from 1900 to 1950 stock prices basically ended in the same place as they started, on an inflation-adjusted basis. At the same time, dividends were very high, averaging 6% per year. The only real return of the stock market during this period was the high dividends and the reinvestment of those dividends.

After the Korean War, the market changed. Figure 11-1 illustrates that stock prices began to outpace the inflation rate by a wide margin. By 1967, the stock market was trading at seven times the inflation-adjusted level of 1950. For a clue as to why this happened, take a look at Figure 11-2. The dividend yield on stocks fell from 7% in 1950 to 3% over the same period. Corporations started retaining earnings rather than paying them out in dividends. One reason for this was changes in the tax code, which dictated higher taxes on dividend income than on realized and unrealized gains. The same phenomenon occurred in the 1980s and new highs were hit in the 1990s. By 1999, stocks prices were trading at over 10 times their 1950 level on an inflation-adjusted basis. At the same time, Congress was tinkering with the tax code and limiting tax-deductible

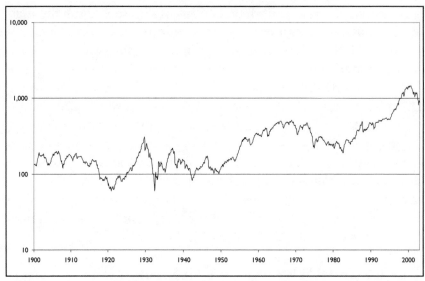

Figure 11-1. U.S. stock prices adjusted for inflation, logarithmic scale

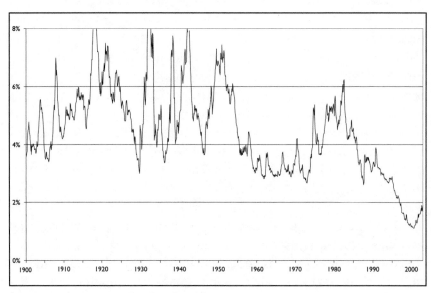

Figure 11-2. S&P 500 dividend yield

compensation to corporate executives. As a result, dividend yields fell almost as low as 1%, as companies retained more earnings, looking to boost stock prices and save the stockholders, the company, and the executives tax dollars.

Does this evidence above suggests that Congress is partially responsible for the booms and busts in the stock market through changes in legislation and the tax code? Yes. Did these issues come up in 2002 during congressional hearings surrounding the investigation of Wall Street stock manipulation claims and the bankruptcies of Enron and WorldCom? A few references were made, but they were not the focus of the investigations. My point is that Congress and the media jump all over corporate America every time the market dumps, but economic growth walks a fine line between government policy and corporate profitability. Each one dramatically affects the other.

Early in the first half of the 1900s, about 70% of all companies paid out to shareholders about 70% of the earnings they made in the form of cash dividends. As a result, dividend yields were in the 6% range. Today, due to changes in the tax code and the increased use of stock compensation, about 20% of companies pay only about 30% of corporate earnings in cash dividends, equaling about a 2% dividend yield. The rest is retained internally for corporate growth or used to buy back stock.

One can only guess how Congress will change the laws in the future concerning the taxation of dividends and the use of stock compensation, so we do not know how the market will react to those changes. In the long run, dividends and capital gains are all part of the stock market's "total return."

Modern finance predicts that, although dividend policy may shift, it should not affect the total return of the market in the long term. If capital gains rates fall again, then the market will react by cutting dividends and buying back stocks. This will cause the price of stocks to go up and dividend payout to continue to drop. If dividend payments become a tax deduction to a company (today they are not), then corporations will shift to higher dividend payouts and prices of stocks will decline. In the end, it all comes out in the wash.

Historic Nominal and Real Returns

Over long periods of time, stocks have made more money than bonds and bonds have made more money than money market funds. The interesting part of that observation is that everything made money—or so it seems. One problem with historic rates of return is that they are all biased by inflation. To get a clear picture of exactly how a market performed over time, we must strip out the inflation rate and look at the inflation-adjusted return.

Inflation is a hidden income tax that a government places on its people through faulty budgeting and poor monetary policy. Believe it or not, our government likes a 2% or so inflation rate, but anything over 3% makes people nervous and is not created intentionally. The problem with market returns and inflation is that the results are distorted. A 3% nominal return from a Treasury note is a 0% real return after taking out 3% for inflation. Nominal returns may look great on paper, but real returns are what count. One more point: since the IRS does not take inflation into account, taxes are due on the full 3% nominal gain, which makes the real after-tax return negative.

To gain an understanding of the future potential of the stock and bond markets, we need to begin with a historic look. Table 11-1 lists the nominal rates of return and historic price volatility of various financial markets. Subtracting the inflation rate from the nominal index return yields the real return. Since indexes have different starting dates, there are three groups. The year 1950 was chosen for the return of major U.S. indexes. By focusing on the second half of the 20th century, we concentrate on the returns of "regulated" markets. In the early 1900s, the stock market was only minimally regulated, and that had a large effect on the risk and return characteristics in the first half of the century. A start date of 1950 also takes us through two major bull markets and two major bear markets. While two complete market cycles hardly provide an adequate statistical sample, it is all we have to work with.

Forecasting Returns Using Risk

Table 11-1 has a lot of raw data, but we cannot take the numbers at

	Start Date	Nominal Return	Real Return	Annual Risk*
Select U.S. Indexes, 1950-2002				
S&P 500 (Large Stocks)	1950	11.8	7.9	14.5
Small U.S. Stocks	1950	12.9	9.0	19.7
Long-Term Govt. Bonds	1950	6.0	2.1	8.9
Long-Term Corp. Bonds	1950	6.2	2.3	8.0
U.S. T-Bills	1950	5.1	1.2	0.8
Consumer Price Index	1950	3.9	NA	1.1
Select U.S. Sectors, 1979-2002				
Russell 3000 Value	1979	14.0	9.8	14.8
Russell 3000 Growth	1979	11.6	7.4	18.8
Wilshire REIT Index	1979	13.1	8.9	14.3
Select International Indexes, various dates				
MSCI EAFE Index	1970	10.0	5.1	17.0
MSCI Emerging Markets	1988	10.0	6.9	24.2
JP Morgan Global Bond	1987	6.2	3.0	6.1

*Risk is measured by the annualized standard deviation of monthly returns.

Table 11-1. Historic market returns
Source: Russell, S&P, Federal Reserve Board, Bloomberg, Wilshire, MSCI

face value and project them into the future. That would yield erroneous results. As we learned earlier in the chapter, there were a lot of changes going on in the stock market during the last half of the 20th century. Those changes caused stock prices to jump dramatically over a normal rate of growth. Despite changing growth patterns and dynamics in the markets, the *risk* of each market was relatively stable. Therefore, risk can be used to calculate expected future returns.

The most common measure for risk in the financial markets is *standard deviation*, written as the Greek letter σ (sigma). Standard deviation is a mathematical formula that expresses the average amount of price volatility in a market. Standard deviation does not express the limit of market risk; it simply tells us the "average miss," how far the market return in any given year was from its historical average annual return.

Figure 11-3 uses the 1950 data from Table 11-1. As you can see, the markets with the highest risk have generated the greatest long-term returns. Using historic risk numbers for each market and plugging them into a pricing model that also includes the current interest rate on Treasury bills, we can estimate expected future rewards for all markets.

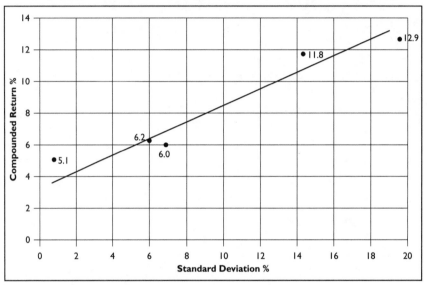

Figure 11-3. Risk as a driver of expected rewards: U.S. financial markets, risk and return, 1950-2002

The returns of stocks and bonds vary from period to period. However, the risk of a market tends to be much more consistent and more predictable than its return. Since the risk of a market is fairly constant, we can use that data to forecast an expected reward for taking this extra risk. Stocks have more risk than Treasury bills; therefore, stocks should have a "risk premium" over the return of T-bills. The financial equation used to forecast expected market returns using risk as a factor is called the Capital Asset Pricing Model (CAPM).

I will spare you the details of the CAPM equation and just provide an overview. Table 11-2 lists the predicted returns of various markets based on the CAPM equation. We know that the safest security you can own is a T-bill. The federal government has the power to print money and will pay off all T-bills. That makes the T-bill a "risk-free" investment. The return of T-bills can be forecasted to be 1.0% higher than the inflation rate over the long term. Since there is no investment as safe as a T-bill, you can estimate the return of other investments by adding a risk premium to the T-bill rate. The extra layer of return is directly related to the extra asset risk in the investment and is calculated in the CAPM equation.

Now, I am going to make a change to the CAPM, which might be considered heresy in academia, but you have to take a stand sometime. I do not believe T-bills are a good indicator for the risk-free rate. T-bill rates are artificial. They are very close to being directed by the dealings of the Federal Reserve Board. A better risk-free rate is to just use inflation itself. That takes all the biases out. Table 11-2 shows my projections of market returns using this method.

Asset Class	Long-Term Historic Risk Premium Over Inflation	Expected Return of Asset Class
T-Bills	1.2	Inflation + 0.5%
Long-Term Treasury Bonds	2.1	Inflation + 2.0%
Long-Term Corporate Bonds	2.3	Inflation + 2.5%
Large U.S. Stocks	7.9	Inflation + 5.0%
Small U.S. Stocks	9.0	Inflation + 6.0%

Table 11-2. Projected risk premiums for asset classes

You may be wondering why the expected returns are higher than the historic returns for bonds and lower than the historic returns for stocks. Bond prices have become more volatile since the 1950s, due to increased volatility in the inflation rate. Since we must get paid more for taking more risk, the projected return of bonds is higher than the previous 50-year average. On the other hand, the return of stocks since 1950 reflects expanding valuations in the form of higher price-to-earnings (P/E) ratios. Although the bear market of 2000-2002 has knocked down valuations some, they are still on the high side relative to historic norms. As long as inflation stays low, stocks can remain at a higher than average P/E ratio. However, if inflation increases, then I would expect the P/E of the market to fall as prices fall.

Risk premiums make sense from a practical standpoint. Greater risk should yield greater returns. In addition to forecasting individual market returns, the CAPM is useful in determining the relationship of returns that should occur *between* markets and showing how mixing asset classes together actually reduces risk and increases return. The subject of asset allocation is explored in Chapter 12.

Forecasting Returns Based on Economic Growth

Until this point we have used only past market risk and returns to create a market forecast. A second method for calculating expected market returns is through the use of economic models. For example, using economic growth assumptions, we can forecast corporate earnings growth, which can be used to forecast stock returns. The formula for expected stock market returns looks like this:

expected earnings growth + cash dividend yield ± speculative premium

To better understand this model, you need to understand each part:

1. Earnings Growth: The primary driver behind stock prices is current earnings and projected earnings growth. The more money companies make and the more they are expected to make, the higher the stock market goes. To measure earnings growth potential in the stock market, you start with the growth in the overall economic activity. Gross Domestic Product (GDP) is the single best measure of economic activity. GDP is the sum total of all goods and services produced in the U.S. during the year. There is a direct and consistent relationship between GDP growth and corporate earnings growth. Figure 11-4 illustrates that, in the very long term, corporate earnings (the jagged line) follow GDP growth (the smooth line). As you can see, the lines are almost parallel.

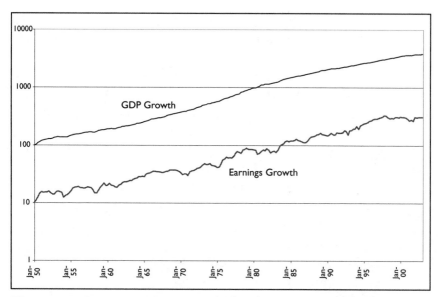

Figure 11-4. Corporate earnings growth relative to GDP growth
Source: U.S. Department of Commerce

Since it is the Federal Reserve's job to "adjust" the economy using monetary policy, it targets GDP growth. In general, the Federal Reserve would like to see the economy grow by 3% per year adjusted for inflation. Since corporate earnings growth seems to follow GDP growth closely over time, we can forecast earnings growth to be about 3% per year adjusted for inflation.

2. Cash Dividends: The second part of the formula covers the cash payment of dividends. U.S. stocks currently pay about 1.7% per year in dividend yield as measured by the S&P 500 Index. That is historically a very low number. As we learned earlier, dividend yields have dropped significantly since the 1950s, hitting a low of 1% in 1999.

3. Speculation (P/E expansion and contraction): The third driver of total return is speculation. If most investors believe that corporate earnings will increase faster and greater than the average, then the price of stock will increase in anticipation of the greater earnings forecast. This is exactly the reason Internet stocks kept going higher and higher in the late 1990s. The prices of those stocks were simply adjusting to the lofty earnings forecasts of investors. When real earnings (or no earnings, in the case of most Internet stocks) became known, value of the stocks fell.

Figure 11-5 clearly illustrates the speculative booms and busts experienced in the stock market over the years. The ratio used here is derived by dividing the price of the S&P 500 by the Gross Domestic Product per capita. The ratio is similar to the price-to-earnings (P/E) ratio, only it is more stable. Using GDP in place of earnings in the ratio eliminates a lot of noise that market P/E ratios create. In September 1981, the S&P 500 was trading at only 0.6% of GDP per capita, but by September 1999 it was trading at 3.2% of GDP per capita, over six times the 1981 level. In a good economy, with low inflation, I believe a ratio of about 1.5% to 1.7% is appropriate, which is close to the current level. You can see how speculation radically changed the value of the stock market in the late 1990s, even though the level of economic activity in the U.S. remained fairly consistent during the same period.

In the short run, speculation creates the volatility in stock price, but in the long term, economic growth proves to be the real driver of returns. It is impossible to predict what investors will think about

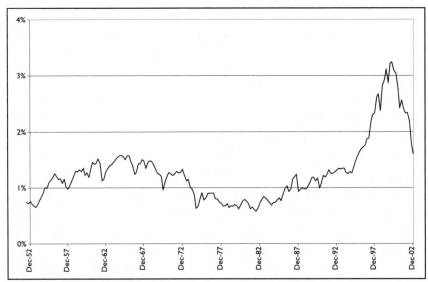

Figure 11-5. Ratio of real S&P prices to GPD per capita
Data source: Standard & Poor's, Federal Reserve

the value of the markets next week, next month, or next year, let alone 30 years from now. Speculation is not predictable, so there is no sense in trying to input that variable into a long-term forecast. For our forecasts below, we will assume the price-to-GDP and P/E ratios of the stock market are held constant at current levels, thereby eliminating most of the speculative noise.

Inflation Drives Bond Returns

In the very long run, economic growth and dividends drive stock market returns. However, the bond market is different. There is a formula for calculating the expected long-term return of bonds:

interest payments + reinvestment of interest
± change in inflation rate ± change in credit risk

In the long term, the inflation rate drives the price of Treasury bonds. The additional risk of default also changes the price of all other bonds, including corporate bonds and mortgages. There is a direct and inverse relationship between the inflation rate and the price of all bonds. When inflation is rising, bond prices are falling; when inflation is falling, bond prices are rising.

Figure 11-6 illustrates the inverse relationship between inflation and bond market returns. The chart highlights one of the most volatile periods in U.S. bond market history. From 1962 through 1980, inflation soared to 15%, creating havoc in the Lehman Brothers Long-Term Government Bond Index. By 1982, inflation dropped like a rock, setting the Lehman Index up for its best gain ever. Over the next 20 years, inflation was tame and interest rates gradually fell to their lowest level in almost 40 years.

It is impossible to forecast the movement of the inflation rate. However, you can limit your risk by purchasing short-term bond index funds. Interest rates generally follow the inflation rate. If you purchase short-term bond funds, then you will not experience the intense volatility of long-term bond funds. The bonds in short-term funds are much closer to maturity, so they exhibit less fluctuation in price. Although you earn extra interest from long-term bonds, the pickup in yield does not justify the added risk. Historically, long-

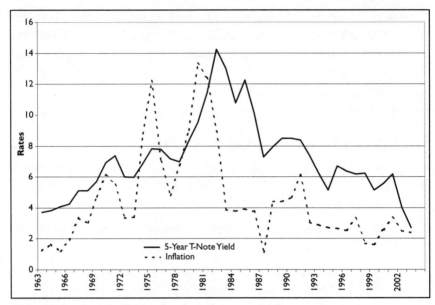

Figure 11-6. Low inflation leads to low return interest rates
Source: Federal Reserve

term bond funds have provided less than a 0.5% return advantage over short-term bond funds, while adding over 3% per year in risk. See Chapter 9, Investment Choices: Bonds, for more information on bond management and bond index funds.

Creating a Forecast

We have analyzed four primary drivers of market returns: risk, inflation, earnings growth, and cash payments from interest and dividends. These factors are part of every valuation model. It would require a book much thicker than this one to detail all the alternative models used in forecasting expected stock and bond returns.

I have drawn from a number of these models and present my best guess for the future. Table 11-3 is my median expected return for all of the major markets. These are 30-year numbers.

Chapter Summary

The market forecasts in this chapter are meant to be a guide for planning portfolios. No one knows what the returns of the markets will

Index	Nominal Forecast	Inflation Adjusted	Risk*
U.S. Treasury Bills (one-year maturity)	3.5	0.5	2.0
U.S. Treasury Notes (five-year maturity)	4.0	1.0	4.8
Government Agency Notes (five-year maturity)	4.3	1.3	5.3
Long-Term U.S. Treasury Bonds	5.0	2.0	8.0
Investment-Grade Corporate Bonds (five-year maturity)	5.0	2.0	5.5
Long-Term Investment-Grade Corporate Bonds	5.5	3.0	8.5
High-Yield Corporate Bonds (BB or less)	9.0	6.0	15.0
U.S. Large Stocks	8.0	5.0	15.0
U.S. Small Stocks	9.0	6.0	20.0
REITs (Real Estate Investment Trusts)	7.5	4.5	14.0
International Developed Country	8.0	5.0	17.0
International Small Country	9.0	6.0	22.0
International Emerging Country	10.0	7.0	25.0
Gross Domestic Product (Nominal and Real Rates)	6.0	3.0	2.0
Inflation (Consumer Price Index)	3.0	—	1.5

*Risk is the standard deviation of annual returns.

Table 11-3. 30-year estimates of bonds, stocks, REITs, GDP, and inflation

be over the next 30 years, but most people agree they will certainly be less than in the past 30 years. We know that there are consistent factors that contribute to market returns and those factors are likely to persist into the future. Most risk is reflected in price volatility, and it is clear that investments with greater price volatility demand higher returns. In addition, economic growth and inflation drive stock and bond returns. By using government and private forecasts of GDP, predicting market returns becomes more manageable, although the task is never easy and never 100% accurate.

Although the actual 30-year return of the markets cannot be known, I believe the relationships *among* the markets will be close to those predicted. In other words, small stocks should outperform large stocks, large stocks should outperform corporate bonds, and corporate bonds should outperform Treasury bills. With this information in hand, we will move on to the next step, which is to gain an understanding of asset allocation.

Since a 'close' forecast is the best it gets, always try to err on the side of a conservative approach. It is wiser to plan for lower returns and be pleasantly surprised in a bull market than to rely on a rosy forecast and possibly run out of money later in life. Simply put, it is better to be safe than sorry.

Key Points

1. Market forecasting is not easy to do. However, it is necessary to have a realistic forecast so that you can use it to plan your portfolio to fit your needs as best as possible.
2. Market history is important, but the data needs to be adjusted to compensate for changes to the speculative premium, tax code, and inflation rate.
3. One way to forecast returns is by analyzing the risk of different asset classes and assigning a higher expected premium to those asset classes with greater risk.
4. A second way of building a forecast is by anticipating the overall growth in the economy and calculating a total return model based on that expected growth.

Chapter 12

Asset Allocation Explained

To invest successfully over a lifetime does not require a stratospheric IQ, unusual business insights, or inside information. What's needed is a sound intellectual framework for making decisions and the ability to keep emotions from corroding that framework.

—Warren Buffett

"Asset allocation" is an old buzzword among large pension plans. The idea of not putting all your eggs in one basket is widely followed by those responsible for managing defined benefit pension plans for millions of workers. Unfortunately, the lesson of diversification was an expensive one for millions of individual investors who saw their retirement portfolios hammered in the last bear market. For most people under the age of 50, the recent bear market was the first taste of what can happen if you get greedy. Those over 50 were reminded of what risk is. The aggressive investments that Wall Street is typically fanatical about selling finally took a back seat to prudence, as most surviving stockbrokers switched hats and started talking about risk reduction, asset allocation, and long-term investing.

Prior to the 1970s, the mathematical models used to help

make asset allocation decisions were foreign to all but a few academic researchers and large pension fund managers. The traditional view of diversification was simply to avoid putting all your money in one place. That meant owning a few bonds in your stock portfolio. But in 1952, Harry Markowitz, a 25-year-old graduate student from the University of Chicago, wrote a revolutionary research paper titled "Portfolio Selection" that changed the way people thought about their investment portfolios.

In short, Markowitz discussed the idea that financial risk is necessary in a portfolio to achieve a higher rate of return, but that risk can be reduced through proper diversification of investments. Since this concept seemed elementary, the paper was not viewed as original research by many of his primary instructors. However, what Markowitz did was unique. For the first time, someone mathematically quantified the risk-and-return relationship among stocks in a portfolio and created formulas that predicted how these relationships work together to reduce risk in the future. He argued that the risk of an individual investment is not as important as how the entire portfolio fits together to achieve a positive result. His paper was published in the prestigious *Journal of Finance*.

Initially, "Portfolio Selection" had little following and no one at the University of Chicago anticipated that the small, 14-page paper would become the backbone of most portfolio strategies over the next 50 years. But, later in the decade, the paper started to be a reference in more financial literature. In 1959, Markowitz published a book on the subject titled *Portfolio Selection: Efficient Diversification of Investments*. The research in that book earned Markowitz wide recognition and eventually the Nobel Prize in Economics in 1990.

As computing power became less expensive, asset allocation research expanded rapidly in universities, bank trust departments, and private money management companies. Using historical data, different portfolios of stocks and bonds were tested using computer simulations. The idea was to find the best mix of each asset class that achieved the highest returns with the least risk. This strategy of portfolio management became known as *modern portfolio theory* (MPT).

Today, nearly every professional portfolio manager is trained in

MPT and uses the technique to manage money. Individual investors can also take advantage of the same risk-reduction concepts, particularly if they use index funds as a base for investment selection. (See Chapters 8 and 9.) The reason index funds work so well is because there is a lot of historical data available on most indexes and the cost of implementation is so low. Creating an asset allocation of low-cost stock and bond index funds can reduce the portfolio risk and increase the portfolio return.

MPT in Action

College professors who teach asset allocation theory start by using two asset classes, stocks and bonds. By combining stocks and bonds in one portfolio, the expected return of the portfolio is increased and risk is reduced. Figures 12-1 and 12-2 illustrate the example using two widely followed indexes, the S&P 500 Index and the Lehman Brothers Intermediate Credit/Government Bond Index. Various mixes of the two investments are combined at 10% intervals.

Figure 12-1 is the classic way of illustrating risk and return of a portfolio. The vertical axis shows the compounded annualized return of the portfolio and the horizontal axis shows the risk. Risk is meas-

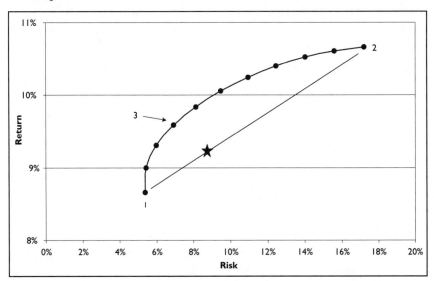

Figure 12-1. S&P 500 and LB Intermediate Bond Index, 1973-2002

ured as the average difference in annual returns. This measurement is also known as standard deviation. The more volatile a portfolio, the greater the standard deviation. Lower risk is always preferable.

Table 12-1. Data related to Figure 12-1

Based on Figure 12-1 and the data in Table 12-1, a portfolio of 100% stocks has the highest return and the highest risk and a portfolio of 100% bonds has the lowest return and the lowest risk. Now, what return and risk would be expected of a 70% bond and 30% stock mix? One would expect to have a return of 9.3% and a portfolio standard deviation of 8.9%, because these are the simple weighted averages using a 70% bond and 30% stocks. That point is marked as a star on Figure 12-1. However, the actual return of a 70% bond and 30% stock mix was better than predicted and the risk was less. The actual return was 9.6% (3 in Figure 12-1), higher than the 9.3% predicted, and the risk was only 6.9%, lower than the 8.9% predicted.

Figure 12-2 illustrates the return advantage of asset allocation in a different way. In the bottom left corner of the illustration is the risk and return of an all-bond portfolio. As we begin to add 10% positions of stock to an all-bond portfolio, there is a big jump in returns. However, after adding about 30% in stocks, the slope of the curve begins to flatten, meaning the advantage of adding more stocks to the portfolio diminishes. Does this mean that you should own only 30% in stocks? No, just that the return advantage of owning more stocks begins to diminish per extra unit of portfolio risk. Figure 12-2 also illustrated the amount of risk reduction that is gained by

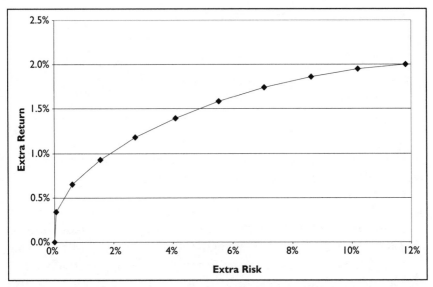

Figure 12-2. Extra portfolio gain per 10% units of equity risk

adding bonds to an all-stock portfolio. The point in the top right portion of the chart is 100% stocks. By adding 10% increments of bonds, portfolio risk falls rapidly without sacrificing much in return.

This MPT example above assumes that the portfolio is *rebalanced* every quarter to its original 70% bond and 30% stock mix. If the stock portion went down one quarter while the bond portion increased in value, the model assumes you sold bonds and bought stocks to bring the portfolio back to a 70% bond and 30% stock mix. Rebalancing sometimes feels counter-intuitive because you are selling an investment that went up to buy one that went down. However, applying a consistent rebalancing strategy over several years is why MPT increases return and reduces risk.

Table 12-2 offers an over-simplified explanation of why rebalancing works. It assumes two hypothetical investments are created and tracked over a two-year period. The risk and return of each investment are identical, but an equal weighted portfolio holding 50% of each behaves very differently than either investment.

As you see, Investment #1 and Investment #2 both individually earned 8.0% over a two-year period. However, row three shows that

	Year 1	Year 2	Total Return
Investment #1	+20%	-10%	1.20 x 0.90 = 1.08 1.08 - 1 = 8.0%
Investment #2	-10%	+20%	0.90 x 1.20 = 1.08 1.08 - 1 = 8.0%
50% / 50% mix rebalanced after 1 year	5%	5%	1.05 x 1.05 = 1.1025 1.1025 - 1 = 10.25%

Table 12-2. Example of why rebalancing works

a portfolio holding 50% in each investment, rebalanced after one year, eliminated all the volatility in the portfolio. This reduction of *portfolio* risk resulted in a 2.25% higher return than either investment measured separately. If you diversify across different investments that are not similar and rebalance at regular intervals, it increases the return of the portfolio over time. The "free lunch" from diversification and rebalancing is the essence of modern portfolio theory—and the proof of this theory earned Harry Markowitz a Nobel Prize.

Correlation Explained

The *correlation coefficient* is a mathematically derived number that measures the tendency of two investments to move in the same direction or opposite directions. If two investments tend to move in the same direction at the same time, they have *positive* correlation. If they tend to move in opposite directions, they have *negative* correlation. If the movement of each investment is totally random, then there is no correlation.

The challenge of investment management is to lower the risk in a portfolio while increasing returns, if possible. This goal can be achieved by mixing asset classes that do not have a high positive correlation with each other—for example, stocks and bonds, U.S. stocks and foreign stocks, large company stocks and small company stocks.

There is no benefit to diversifying into two investments that have a high positive correlation with each other. For example, it makes no sense to buy a mutual fund that invests in large growth stocks if you already own a mutual fund that invests in large growth stocks, even though the funds may be managed by different mutual fund companies. Many investors made this mistake in the 1990s. They thought they were diversifying their retirement portfolio by holding two or three aggressive growth funds that bought technology stocks.

Figure 12-3 illustrates a portfolio of two funds that have a high correlation with each other. Since Fund A and Fund B go up and down at the same time, there is no risk reduction in a portfolio that invests 50% in Fund A and 50% in Fund B.

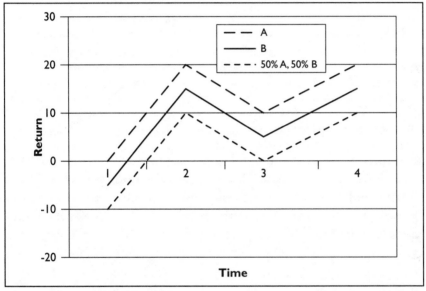

Figure 12-3. Positive correlation

Ideally, you would like to invest in two mutual funds that have negative correlation. Figure 12-4 shows that Fund C and Fund D have a negative correlation, which means they move in opposite directions. A portfolio of 50% Fund C and 50% Fund D, rebalanced after each period, will result in a return that is much smoother than either of the two investments individually. This reduction in risk will increase the portfolio return in the long run.

Unfortunately, it is very rare to find investments that are highly negatively correlated. Most portfolios are composed of several

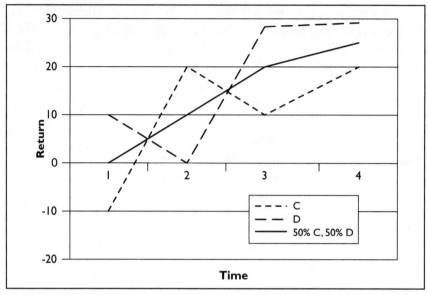

Figure 12-4. Negative correlation

investments that are non-correlated or somewhat positively correlated. You still get a diversification benefit, albeit not as strong.

A number matrix is typically used to show the correlation between investments. The matrix in Table 12-3 expresses the correlation among four asset classes from 1978 to 2002. The matrix compares large U.S. stocks (S&P 500), international stocks (EAFE Index), real estate investment trusts (Wilshire REIT), and bonds (Lehman Brothers Intermediate-Term Government/Corporate Index). The lower the number, the more diversification benefit of having that asset class in a portfolio.

Multi-Asset-Class Portfolios

So far in this chapter we have discussed an investment portfolio consisting of only two asset classes. By mixing bonds and U.S. stocks, we significantly decrease the portfolio risk without a corresponding decrease in portfolio return. We can now go a step further.

If we add positions in foreign stocks and real estate to the U.S. stock/bond mix, we further increase the portfolio return and reduce

	S&P 500 Index	EAFE Index	Wilshire REIT	LB Bond Index
S&P 500 Index	—	.53	.52	.22
EAFE Index	.53	—	.30	.15
Wilshire REIT	.52	.30	—	.21
LB Bond Index	.22	.15	.21	—

Table 12-3. Correlation, 1978-2000

the risk. An asset allocation mix using four asset classes that have low correlation with each other is more efficient than a portfolio consisting of only two. If we add a fifth low-correlation asset class, we reduce the risk even more and increase the return slightly. Figure 12-5 demonstrates how we can move the *efficient frontier* to the *northwest quadrant* of the chart by adding asset classes.

"Northwest quadrant" is a term used in investment management that describes portfolios that have theoretically high returns and low risk. "Efficient frontier" is a concept from modern portfolio theory. It refers to the curve that reflects the most efficient portfolios for all levels of risk—portfolios with the greatest return for a given level of risk. As the name suggests, the frontier marks the limit for portfolios. The asset mix that is optimal for an investor is the portfolio from the efficient frontier that maximizes the expected return for the level of risk chosen by the investor.

Multi-asset-class portfolios sound great. However, there are limits to diversification. First, it is very difficult to find major asset classes that are non-correlated or negatively correlated with each other. The best you can hope for is to find a few asset classes that have low positive correlation. Second, the correlations among asset classes can change. Investments that were once non-correlated may become more correlated in a global marketplace. Past correlations are a

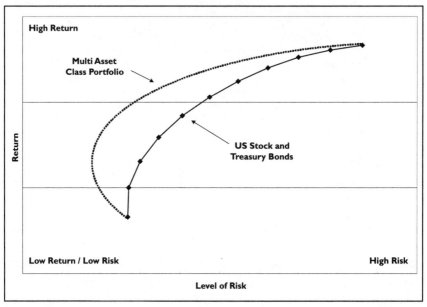

Figure 12-5. Multi-asset class portfolio versus S&P 500 and Intermediate. bond index

guide, not a guarantee. Third, during a time of extreme volatility, the correlations among some asset classes actually increase. This is the exact time when you would like to see less correlation. When the World Trade Center was destroyed in September 2001, all stock markets around the world fell by more than 5%. No amount of global stock diversification helped during that horrific period.

Asset allocation in the real world requires just as much common sense as it does quantitative number crunching. There are a number of books, Web sites, and computer programs that can help you learn about asset allocation. One of the best books on the market is *The Intelligent Asset Allocator,* by William Bernstein (McGraw Hill, 2000). Bernstein also has a great Web site where he posts free research and analysis each quarter. You can visit his site at www.efficientfrontier.com.

Chapter Summary

Asset allocation using modern portfolio theory is the science of blending investments together to create the most efficient portfolio possible given the available data. Since Harry Markowitz wrote his historic paper in 1952, asset allocation has become the cornerstone of every viable long-term investment strategy.

You do not need to be a Nobel Laureate to benefit from the reduction in risk and increase in return that proper asset allocation and rebalancing deliver. To manage a portfolio effectively, you should study how investments have acted independently over the years and how they blend together in a portfolio mix. Once you decide upon a mix based on your individual need, rebalancing the mix ensures the integrity of the strategy.

Don't be like most Wall Street brokers and wait until it is too late to diversify. Pick up a few books and start reading more about this important concept as soon as you finish reading the rest of this book.

Key Points

1. Diversify your portfolio across investments in several asset classes to reduce risk and increase return.
2. Ensure the investments you hold have a low correlation with each other.
3. Rebalance your portfolio at least once per year to create a positive effect.

Part Three

A Lifelong Saving and Investing Guide

Chapter 13

Early Savers

A person becomes an adult at the point when he produces more than he consumes and earns more than he spends.

—*Henry C. Link*

T WO KEY COMPONENTS for accumulating wealth are time and consistency. Ideally, people should start saving at the same time they land their first full-time job. The sooner we start, the better. Consistency is also important. If young people can make saving a habit from the very beginning, then they will not have to worry about financial security later in life. The amount of savings does not need to be excessive. Putting away 10% of earnings each month is ideal. This amount is less than half what most people pay in taxes.

Typically, an adult works full-time for about 40 years before retiring. During the 40-year employment period, wealth accumulation can generally be divided into two phases: Early Savers, in their 20s and 30s, and Midlife Accumulators, in their 40s and 50s. This chapter covers the first phase; the next chapter covers the second phase.

No One Said It Was Going to Be Easy

Establishing a lifelong wealth accumulation program is often difficult for people who are in their 20s and 30s. Careers can take many turns, new families require money and attention, all the while the income stream is not very high and not very certain.

After severing the umbilical cord from their parents, young adults pick up the full financial responsibility for their lives, including automobile payments, housing costs, insurance expenses, and possibly college loans. As people age, costs increase, especially housing, transportation, and insurance costs. Insurance is a growing burden: the cost of health, disability, auto, homeowner's, and possibly dental and eye-care insurance are spiraling up. In addition to individual expenses, having a family means many more expenses, including saving for a child's college education. College costs are rising faster than the general price index. (For more information on college costs, see Appendix A, Saving for Higher Education.)

Career uncertainty is another burden early in adult life. Most 20- and 30-year-olds do not know in which directions their career will take them or what their maximum earnings potential will be. At this early stage, much of a person's career control rests in the hands of his or her employer and the industry chosen. Most young adults change careers at least once during their early saving years, which typically means a temporary reduction in pay and possible relocation to another geographic area.

Career path uncertainty leads to lifestyle uncertainty. Although young people have an idea of what their ideal lifestyle should look like, few are at that point. Since the future is vague for Early Savers, it is difficult to plan for retirement, except in a very broad sense. At this stage of life, trying to put a specific price tag on the cost of retirement is an impractical exercise; younger people should not waste much time thinking about it.

Some financial advisors would argue that calculating a person's growth of savings and expenses over 30 or 40 years may yield some interesting data, but the numbers will not likely have much significance. There are too many unknown variables and uncontrollable events in life. For instance, most young people do not know if they will be working for an employer that offers a defined benefit pension plan, a stock incentive plan, or other employer-funded retirement savings enhancements. These benefits can greatly increase wealth while reducing the amount a person needs to save in a personal account.

If young adults should not be worrying about funding a specific retirement goal, what should they be doing? Early Savers need first to establish the habit of regular savings and then learn to invest those savings properly. We will discuss saving first and then investing.

Starting to Save

With growing expenses and career uncertainty to worry about, how do you as a young adult formulate a savings plan? It starts by landing a full-time job and allocating a portion of each paycheck to a savings account. The best method is to have your employer deduct the savings amount before the money reaches your check. For example, when you are doing the paperwork as a new employee, you may have the opportunity to elect to put money into the company retirement plan. This may be a 401(k), a 403(b), or a 529 plan. (See Chapter 7 for details on various employer savings plans.)

The ideal goal is to save 10% of your salary into an employer savings plan, if available. That way you never see the money. It comes out of your paycheck before federal or state taxes. That will save you money on taxes each year. If an employer savings plan is not available, then have the money automatically withdrawn from your checking account each month and deposited into a personal retirement savings account such as an Individual Retirement Account (IRA).

If you cannot afford to save 10% of your pay, then put in what you can at first, and then increase the percentage every time you get a raise. If you never see the new money coming into your wallet, then you will not miss it. Keep increasing the percentage of savings each year as you earn more, until the savings level gets to a least 10%. The more you save, the better off you will be later in life.

The Ideal Savings Plan

As mentioned earlier, refer to Chapter 7, Types of Retirement Accounts, for a summary of various employer retirement plans and information on individual savings accounts. It is also important to contact your employer for specific information about the savings plan available to you at work, including any employer match, and the cost of the plan, including the cost of the investment options in the plan. This information will have a strong impact on your decision about where to invest your money.

Designing an ideal savings plan can be complicated. Retirement savings accounts have rules, exceptions to the rules, and exceptions to the exceptions. Every employer's savings plan is a little different, the employer match may be different, and the investment options are different. The best plan for one employee may not be the best plan for the next employee, even though their earnings may be very similar. In addition, every individual has different expenses and a different tax situation. There is no "one size fits all" when it comes to designing a savings strategy. To make matters more complicated, each year the ideal strategy may change, with changes in a person's earnings and expenses and possibly also in the tax laws.

If a qualified accountant prepares your taxes, it is helpful to solicit his or her advice when designing a savings plan for yourself. Unfortunately, I must warn you that many accountants have recently teamed up with brokerage firms and insurance agencies. As a result, the accounting industry is not as clean as it once was. Many accountants are now trying to sell investment products or make referrals to brokers with whom they have a financial agreement. Pay your accountant a fair wage for his or her time, but when it comes to investing, shop around for the lowest-cost investment options.

Here are a few guidelines for a retirement savings plan, whether you are just starting to save or you are tweaking your retirement savings plan.

Save Automatically

Automate your savings with a systematic savings feature. This will ensure that money goes into your account regularly. If you save through your employer, set your account up so that the funds are automatically taken out of your paycheck each period. Your employer is required to invest that money on your behalf within seven days of withholding it from your paycheck. If you are saving in an IRA or other personal savings account outside of an employer plan, have the funds automatically withdrawn from your personal checking account each month. Periodic checking account debits can be arranged through any investment company or banking institution.

Go for the Match

If your employer has established a 401(k), a 403(b), or a SIMPLE IRA that has an employer match, take full advantage of it. This is free money that your employer gives to you just for saving! The standard plan matches 50% of the amount you save, up to 3% of salary. If you work for a company that offers this match and you are making $40,000 per year, by saving 3% ($1,200) in the plan you will net $600 in free contributions from your employer. This is the easiest money you will every make—and you do not pay income tax on the $1,800 or the growth of that money until you withdraw the funds after you retire. One word of caution: some employers have a vesting restriction on the match, so the money may not be available for several years.

Take Stock Options

If you work for a publicly traded company that offers company stock at a discount, take full advantage of that option also. Your company may allow eligible employees to buy its common stock using after-tax or pre-tax dollars at a 15% to 25% discount from market price. This is more free money, but with a hitch. You will not be allowed to sell the stock for a year or more. When the vesting period is over, sell the stock and buy more new stock at a discount.

Weigh Pre-Tax vs. Post-Tax

Savings choices can get complex after you take full advantage of free money options. For each choice, you should weigh the benefit of pre-tax savings against the future tax savings of tax-free withdrawals from a Roth IRA account. Employees can reduce their current year income tax if they save in 401(k), 403(b), 457, SIMPLE, or other salary-deferral plans. Self-employed individuals will save on current tax through a traditional IRA, a SEP IRA, a Keogh plan, or other self-employed retirement accounts. However, with pre-tax account, all savings withdrawn after retirement are taxed as ordinary income. On the other hand, money saved in a Roth IRA goes into the account after income tax has been paid on the contribution, but the savings can be taken out tax-free in retirement.

Should you save pre-tax or post-tax? The determining factors in your decision are as follows:

- Are you currently eligible for a Roth IRA?
- Do you think your income tax rate will be higher in retirement than it is now?

The first question is easy. The rules for Roth IRA eligibility are straightforward and can be obtained from any library, IRS office, tax site on the Internet, investment firm, or accountant. The second question is trickier. Will your tax rate be higher or lower in retirement? If you paid little or no federal tax last year, then your retirement rate will probably be higher. If you are eligible for a Roth IRA and think your tax rate will be higher in retirement than it is now, contribute the maximum you can to a Roth IRA before putting any more money into an employer plan or a traditional IRA. In addition, self-employed individuals can put money either into a Roth IRA or, depending on the profitability of their business, into a small business retirement plan or a traditional IRA account.

Now What?

At this point, you have invested in an employer savings plan to get the maximum match and invested the maximum in a Roth IRA, if you are eligible and if your tax rate is going to be higher in retirement than it is now. Now, you must decide either to invest more in a savings plan at work using pre-tax dollars (but no match) or to put money into a traditional IRA account if you are eligible. That decision will be based on IRA eligibility rules and the total cost of the employer savings plan, including the investment expenses.

Many small employers have savings plans with insurance companies or brokers and they are very expensive. Those plans are worth investing in to get the match, but that is about it. If the internal cost of the savings plan at work is high, then forgo the employer's plan and open an IRA account with Vanguard or some other low-cost mutual fund provider. Do not invest an IRA account with an accountant, financial planner, broker, or insurance salesperson who charges commissions and puts your money in high-fee products. That will put the cost of investing right back at the cost of the employer's plan.

After All Other Choices

The next step is to fund the remainder of the employer's savings plan. This may not be a low-cost strategy and the investment selections may stink, but it does reduce current income tax. That is worth the benefit of participation.

There is good news in Washington concerning high-cost employer savings plans. A few investor-friendly members of Congress are trying to pass legislation that will allow participants in employer savings plans to roll into an IRA account any time, rather than having to wait until retirement or termination of employment. This solution will allow people to get their money out of a high-cost, poorly run employer plan and into a lower-cost IRA Rollover account. As an extra benefit of the rollover, money can be withdrawn from IRA accounts penalty-free to help with the down payment on a first-time home and to pay college tuition expenses.

Post-Tax Savings Options

After you have taken maximum advantage of pre-tax options, the rest of the savings will take place after taxes. This means using personal accounts, trust accounts, and joint accounts as savings vehicles. The investments in taxable accounts should be low-cost, tax-efficient, and liquid. Younger people need liquidity, especially if they are considering buying a home or they are between jobs and careers. Avoid all investments that have a sales charge, high fees, or a back-end sales load.

Finally, a house can be a home and also a wonderful storage of wealth. Early Savers who buy a house are making a wise investment. A single-family home has some incredible tax benefits. Not only are mortgage interest and property tax a tax deduction, but also the gain from the sale of a primary residence is tax-free, up to $500,000. If the house is in a good location and properly maintained, it should appreciate in value over the years.

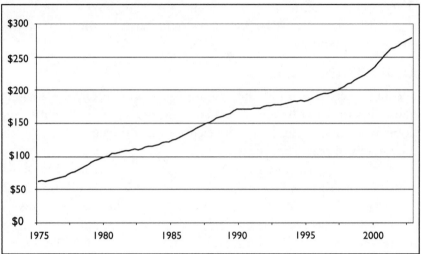

Figure 13-1. Housing price index (in thousands of dollars)
Data Source: National Association of Realtors

The equity buildup in a house can someday be turned into extra retirement income by refinancing or downsizing to a smaller home. I highly encourage young people to buy their own home as soon as they have a stable job and can afford the monthly mortgage payments.

Saving Is More Important than Investing ... at First

To a young adult, consistent savings is more important than the rate of return on those savings. This concept is illustrated in Figures 13-2 and 13-3. Consider two people who both started working at age 22 for $24,000. Both received a 3% pay raise each year. One saved 5% and made a 10% return on investments; the other saved 10%

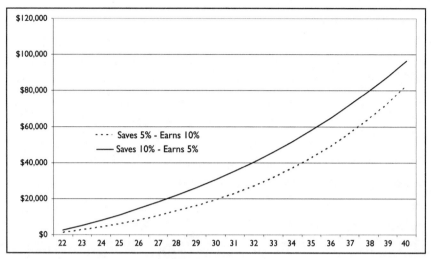

Figure 13-2. Saving rate is most important early

and earned a 5% return. Who has the most money saved by the time they are both 40 years old?

The person who saves 10% per year and earns 5% on those savings accumulates about $13,600 more than the person who saves 5% and earns 10%. Clearly, it is the savings rate that is most important early in life.

However, the chart takes a different course when the scenario is extended into the second half of the accumulation years. From the early 40s on, a high rate of return becomes much more influential than the savings rate, as Figure 13-3 illustrates for the 5% difference in return on the two accounts. By age 60, the person who saved 5% and earned 10% has accumulated nearly $324,000 more than the person who saved 10% and earned 5%.

The figures illustrate an interesting fact. Early in the accumulation years, it is a person's savings rate that is important, second only to the age at which the person starts to save. Sometime early in midlife, when an account reaches $70,000 or more, the rate of return becomes most important.

When a young adult first begins to accumulate wealth, the act of saving matters more than the rate of return on those savings. While it helps to invest wisely at a young age, it is not necessary. Most

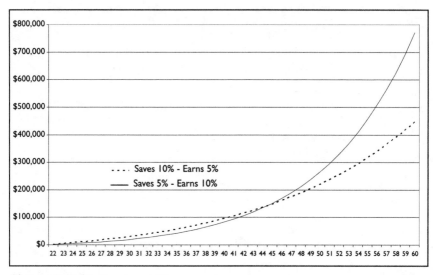

Figure 13-3. Parity at age 45

young people think they have a special skill that allows them to defy the odds and pick winning investments that the rest of us have overlooked. I had that misconception when I was young and many college students I instruct have it today. Young adults who think they are blessed with market smarts are lucky if they lose money early in life. That makes them humble and respectful of market forces. Young people who learn to invest properly in their 20s and 30s will be better prepared to invest during midlife, when they have accumulated enough money to make a difference.

Investment Considerations

Money in a savings plan must be invested. Figures 13-2 and 13-3 use examples of 5% and 10% rates of return, but they are for illustration purposes only. While it is possible to get a fairly consistent 5% return in today's investment environment, earning 10% or more per year requires a significant amount of risk—more than most people can handle. Using the forecasts from Chapter 12, a well-diversified portfolio of stocks, bonds, and real estate can be expected to earn between 6.5% and 7.5% over the long term, depending on how aggressive the portfolio is.

Throughout Part Three of this book, I will make reference to accumulating wealth as though it were a mysterious ocean voyage. For Early Savers, the ship is at the dock. Navigational aids help guide the ship out of the harbor and into open water. Early Savers need to follow navigational aids to get their ship on its way, even though they do not know yet where it is heading. The rest of this chapter discusses those navigational aids that Early Savers should use.

Risk Tolerance

People in their 20s and 30s are just beginning to raise families and develop a lifestyle, so it is difficult to make decisions concerning the amount of wealth they need to accumulate to attain financial security and ultimately retirement. Coming out of the harbor, it does not make much sense for an Early Saver to try and turn the ship toward a destination too early, because the ship will end up on the rocks. It is better for young people to work toward understanding their personal tolerance for investment risk and developing a portfolio that fits their personality.

Contrary to popular belief, one does not need to take a lot of risk while young to attain wealth later in life. Most of the problems in wealth accumulation occur because people take too much risk at some time in their lives—and that leads to the behavioral mistakes discussed in Chapter 3, Bear Markets and Bad Investor Behavior, and Chapter 4, Getting Trampled by the Herd. If an Early Saver can understand his or her fears and greed, personal preferences and sensitivities, he or she will be far ahead of most other young investors. Risk preference is the beacon that guides a young saver.

There is a safe harbor out there waiting for the Early Saver, but it is much too early to pick a specific retirement date or to set a specific dollar amount for a retirement nest egg. Later in the journey, after 15 or 20 years of work experience, it will be time to think about a retirement time clock and establish a specific dollar and goal to complete the voyage. Those ideas will be developed and discussed in Chapter 14, Midlife Accumulators. Early Savers need not worry about those technicalities yet.

Understanding Risk

The beacon that should guide investment decisions for Early Savers is known in financial industry as *risk tolerance*. Risk tolerance is a measure of how rough the financial markets can get before you get seasick and abandon ship. The ideal portfolio has only enough risk in it to make you queasy during stormy market conditions, but not so much up-and-down movement that you make an wild decision to abandon your investment strategy. If a portfolio has a lot of stock exposure, then it will be volatile in bear markets. Before investing in stocks, you need to know how much volatility you can handle or you will make emotional mistakes. Know yourself before investing.

It is interesting that many Early Savers do not take enough risk and, as a result, give up the potential for higher returns. This is evident by the large number of young people who invest in the safe, low-interest fixed income option in their employers' saving plans. (See Chapter 2, Investment Return Shortfalls.) As Early Savers begin to understand their tolerance for risk, they increase the amount of riskier assets in their portfolio, which is very likely to result in a larger nest egg at retirement.

Finding one's personal risk tolerance can be a tricky business. Most people understand that successful investing requires some risk; however, a large number of people overestimate the amount of risk they can handle, especially when the stock market has been going up for a long time. (As you may remember from Part One of this book, overconfidence is particularly prevalent for men who work in a professional occupation like medicine and law.)

When a person overestimates his or her tolerance for risk, a bear market can cause subconscious fears to emerge and change investing behavior. At that point, the investor clears out of most risky investments and many times will swing in the opposite direction and become overly conservative. The recent bear market has brought a moment of truth for many overconfident investors. These wild swings between fear and greed need to be understood and controlled before an investor can truly create a portfolio that fits his or her personality.

Risk tolerance questionnaires are designed to measure an investor's reaction to investment loss and suggest an appropriate stock-and-bond mix that might be right for a his or her psychological makeup. These questionnaires are available through all mutual fund companies and brokerage firms. A sample of a better than average risk tolerance questionnaire is provided at the end of this chapter. It is fashioned from the questionnaire found on the Vanguard Group Web site.

The intent of most risk tolerance questionnaires is noble, but most do not achieve the desired goal of finding an investor's ideal portfolio. One problem is that most questions are too vague and they can be interpreted in different ways by the people answering them. Another problem is that the questions tend to be biased toward taking risks rather than finding a balance. Most questionnaires tend to suit the person asking the questions; for example, brokerage firms and mutual fund companies tend to ask questions that guide people into riskier investments, because those investment choices generate higher commissions and management fees than less risky investments.

Although there are many flaws, risk tolerance questionnaires do shed some light on how a person should structure his or her first investment portfolio. However, before embracing any particular stock-and-bond portfolio, the investor should take another important test.

The *stress test* is a simple form of market simulation that will help you understand how you may react during the next bear market with the suggested portfolio. Instead of investing real money in a mix and going through the gut-wrenching bear market experience of discovering that you have taken on too much risk, a better way to assess your reactions to loss is by simulating a bear market on paper first. This technique is nothing more than asking a series of "what if" questions and taking time to ponder your answers.

Here is an example of a stress test. Assume that you have invested half of your life savings in a stock market index fund, such as the Vanguard U.S. Total Stock Market Index Fund (VTSMX), and the other half in a bond market index fund, such as the Vanguard Total Bond Market Index Fund (VBMFX). The stock market collapses by 30% right after you make your investments. That means your account is down 15%. What action would you take? Would you be concerned about losing more money and sell part of the stock index fund? Would you sell part of the bond index fund to buy more of the stock index fund? Or would you do nothing?

The correct answer is to sell part of the bond fund index fund and buy more of the stock index fund to get back to a 50% stock and 50% bond mix. Rebalancing is the driver behind portfolio management theory as discussed in Chapter 12, Asset Allocation Explained.

If you are inclined to sell stocks to reduce risk further or let the portfolio remain out of balance, then a 50% stocks and 50% bond mix is beyond your tolerance for risk. If that is the case, adjust the starting mix. For example, try the simulation again, starting with 60% bonds and 40% stocks. If you still do not feel comfortable rebalancing back to a 50/50 mix after a 30% market decline, keep reducing your starting stock exposure until you reach a level low enough so that you will always rebalance, an asset allocation point at which you will look at the stock market loss as an opportunity to buy rather than a money eater. This level is that mix of stocks and bonds for your portfolio. This asset allocation represents your true tolerance for risk.

It is very important to know your riskiest stock-and-bond mix and not to invest beyond it. It does not matter how low you go in stocks, finding the right level is the key. I do recommend trying to maintain at least 20% in stocks, because that percentage has historically resulted in higher portfolio returns than 10% or 15% in stocks, without adding any more risk (see Chapter 12). In practice, I find that most people have a true risk tolerance that is lower than they are first willing to admit. They need to correct that perception before it is too late—and the bear market of 2000-2002 proved it.

I have used the stress test with many clients over the years and have written about it many times. This little simulation saved a lot of people a lot of money during the last bear market, because they realized beforehand they had taken on too much risk during the 1990s. Knowing your true tolerance for risk is the most important investment discovery you will make in your life. If you know the level of risk you can handle, whatever it may be, you significantly improve your odds of managing your wealth successfully.

An Example of the Stress Test

The next section is a detailed example of a stress test. It gives you insight into how an imaginary person reacts to shocks in his or her portfolio and the changes that need to be made to bring the risk down to a level that person finds tolerable.

Suppose you are a young professional in your late 20s and you are about to transfer $30,000 from a former employer's 401(k) plan into an IRA rollover. You meet with a financial advisor to ask for investment advice. The advisor asks you to complete the firm's risk tolerance questionnaire, which consists of 10 questions. After you complete the questionnaire, the advisor tallies the points and informs you that your "proprietary risk profile" suggests an allocation of 80% in stocks and 20% in bonds. You acknowledge this information.

At that point, the advisor starts selling an assortment of loaded mutual funds or possibly a wrap-fee mutual fund managed account targeted to an 80% stock and 20% bond mix. For illustration purposes, we will assume that the advisor recommends placing 80% of your money in a no-load, low-cost total stock market index fund and 20% in a no-load, low-cost total bond market index fund. You agree and $24,000 of your money goes into VTSMX and $6,000 goes into VBMFX. (Note: most advisors who are paid by commissions would never select these excellent investment choices because they would not get paid enough for recommending low-cost index funds.)

Theoretically, a person with a high tolerance for risk will keep a high percentage of his or her assets in stocks year after year, regardless of the losses. In reality, most investors who picked an 80% stock and 20% bond portfolio based on a risk tolerance questionnaire would have been starting to look for a new investment strategy by the third quarter of 2001—and certainly by the third quarter of 2002.

If you feel the inclination to pick up the phone and ask your investment advisor for a more conservative strategy after losing over 20% over two and one half years, then an 80% stock portfolio is too aggressive for your personality. I do not mean the 80% stock is too aggressive for you in a bear market; I mean 80% in stock is too aggressive for you during your lifetime.

	Stock Fund Return	Bond Fund Return	80/20 Portfolio Return	Account Value
2000			Starting Value:	**$30,000**
1st Q	3.8%	2.4%	3.5%	$31,056
2nd Q	4.4%	1.5%	(3.2%)	$30,056
3rd Q	0.3%	3.1%	0.9%	$30,314
4th Q	(10.2%)	4.0%	(7.4%)	$28,083
2001				
1st Q	(12.3%)	3.2%	(9.2%)	$25,500
2nd Q	7.5%	0.8%	6.2%	$27,070
3rd Q	(16.0%)	4.3%	(11.9%)	$23,838
4th Q	12.3%	(0.1%)	9.8%	$26,179
2002				
1st Q	0.1%	0.1%	0.1%	$26,205
2nd Q	(11.5%)	1.6%	(8.9%)	$23,878
3rd Q	(16.8%)	3.7%	(12.7%)	$20,837

Table 13-1. Stress Test #1—80% stocks and 20% bonds

The stock market is never the problem. It has always been volatile and always will be volatile. The problem is that people do not understand their true tolerance for risk and are constantly swinging their portfolio between too much risk and too little risk. These inadvertent market-timing actions cause portfolios to earn less than optimal returns. (See Chapter 3, Bear Markets and Bad Investor Behavior.)

Let's repeat the stress test, this time using a 50% stock and 50% bond portfolio. After reviewing this portfolio, you may be disappointed with the results, but you are not disgusted enough with the portfolio to change the asset allocation. In that case, a 50% stock and 50% bond portfolio is closer to your risk tolerance level.

Investing effectively means holding realistic expectations about market returns and having a solid understanding about the amount

	Stock Fund Return	Bond Fund Return	50/50 Portfolio Return	Account Value
2000			Starting Value:	**$30,000**
1st Q	3.8%	2.4%	3.1%	$30,930
2nd Q	4.4%	1.5%	(1.5%)	$30,482
3rd Q	0.3%	3.1%	1.7%	$31,000
4th Q	(10.2%)	4.0%	(3.1%)	$30,039
2001				
1st Q	(12.3%)	3.2%	4.6%	$28,672
2nd Q	7.5%	0.8%	4.2%	$29,862
3rd Q	(16.0%)	4.3%	(5.9%)	$28,115
4th Q	12.3%	(0.1%)	6.1%	$29,830
2002				
1st Q	0.1%	0.1%	0.1%	$29,860
2nd Q	(11.5%)	1.6%	(5.0%)	$28,382
3rd Q	(16.8%)	3.7%	(6.6%)	$24,650

Table 13-2. Stress Test #2—50% stocks and 50% bonds

of risk you can personally handle. If you assume too much risk in a portfolio, then it is highly probable that you will abandon your investment strategy during severe market downturns. Investors who are not emotionally prepared for the risk they have elected to take will not be able to keep that risk level for a long period of time.

Reducing risk in a bear market cripples the long-term performance. As a result, it is always better to have a lower amount of risk in a portfolio than too much risk. If you have less risk, then there is a very strong likelihood that you will hold onto your stock allocation during a severe downturn. By investing in a well-balanced portfolio and maintaining a level of risk at or below your pain threshold, you can ensure that your portfolio will be well prepared to face the uncertainties of the markets.

Simple Portfolios Are Best

Now that you have discovered an approximation of your tolerance for risk using a stock-and-bond mix, it is time to pick individual stocks, bonds, and mutual funds that will go into your portfolio. So, you visit a friendly broker and ask his or her advice on which investments to buy.

No! Don't waste your time or money. Stockbrokers are salespeople who are compensated based on the investment products they sell. That means you will be paying commissions or high fees. Relying on a commission-oriented broker or financial planner for investment advice is not in your best interest. (See Chapter 6, Advice About Investment Advice.)

This book was written for people who are inclined to do it themselves. That means designing and following appropriate portfolio management techniques, including the use of low-cost investments such as stock and bond index funds. This is not difficult. Early Savers need only two or three no-load mutual funds to fill an investment portfolio. Start with a total U.S. stock market index fund and add a total bond market index fund. A third choice would be a low-cost foreign stock market index fund. Any shares of restricted company stock that you get in a 401(k) or other employer incentives should be considered part of an equity portfolio for asset allocation.

If you invest through your employer, you may not be able to choose a total stock market index fund or a total bond market index fund. If that is the case, look for substitutes among the other mutual fund options. Perhaps there is an S&P 500 index fund that can be used instead of the total U.S. stocks index. A guaranteed fixed income investment fund can be used in place of a bond market index fund. Look for a low-cost international mutual fund in place of a foreign market index fund. The trick is to find low-cost substitutes.

If there are neither index funds nor low-cost substitutes, you may need to speak to your employer. Many smaller plans are very bad. The investment choices include only high-cost mutual funds or high-cost variable annuities offered through an insurance company. If this sounds like your plan, file a request with your employer to

add low-cost, no-load index fund options to the investment choices. If those funds cannot be added, request that your employer find
a new provider for the entire plan. Caution against switching to an
insurance company or brokerage firm plan that pushes high-cost
investments. If your employer brushes off your written request, the
next step is to file a complaint with the Department of Labor claiming that the trustees of your employer's plan are not upholding their
fiduciary responsibility. Granted, this act may cause some unintended consequences for you, so you may not want to go that far, but the
threat of filing a complaint will get management's attention.

If you are saving for retirement in a taxable account in addition
to or instead of a tax-sheltered retirement account, tax-free municipal bonds may play a role in your portfolio. The investment choice
is more appropriate for people in high tax brackets, because the low
level of interest from tax-free bonds is free from federal income tax.
Before investing, you would have to measure whether the tax-free
return from municipals would be higher or lower than the after-tax
return of taxable fixed income investments. The Vanguard Group
offers the lowest-cost municipal bond funds on the market. The
company also offers municipal bond funds that are specific to certain states, so there is no state income tax on the interest in the fund
for residents of those states.

Rebalancing

Once you have established a long-term investment plan, write it
down, so you will not forget. It is amazing much time you can spend
coming up with the right investment mix and then, six months later,
forget how you want to allocate the account. When it is time to
make contributions to a plan or when the account is out of whack
and needs rebalancing, always check your written asset allocation.
That makes life much simpler.

Since you will be contributing to your retirement savings account
systematically, the money should be spread across your mutual funds
according to your set asset allocation. Most employer plans will automatically allocate across investments for you, but the programs do
not distinguish which investments need it most. Naturally, the ebbs

and flows of the market action will cause the portfolio mix to shift from its original asset allocation. Therefore, you will be making manual adjustments and need a written plan to follow.

Rebalancing gets the portfolio back in line with the original target mix. Doing this annually works fine. Just remember to reposition your portfolio once per year, at approximately the same time in the year. Use January 1—the traditional date for making improvements in our lives. Some professionals may argue that rebalancing annually is not enough, while others argue that it may be too much. In my opinion, annual rebalancing will achieve the objective.

Rebalancing is also a test of risk tolerance. If your portfolio is within your risk tolerance, then you will reposition the portfolio at the same time each year without hesitation. If you hesitate in rebalancing, then your portfolio allocation may be too aggressive for you. Hesitation normally occurs after a couple of bad years in the market. If you are hesitant about rebalancing your portfolio after a couple of bad years, perhaps it is time to take the stress test again and then make a permanent adjustment in your asset allocation.

A Final Word on Stock Investing

Contrary to the hype on Wall Street, if you believe that you are going to beat the market and become rich by being a savvy stock picker or mutual fund investor, you are mistaken. The fact is, individual investors have no control over the stock market, and neither does your financial advisor. Believing that you are different will only lead to a costly and humbling experience.

I encourage young people to experiment and pick a few individual stocks, but realize that any gains above the market are a result of luck and not skill. It takes superior information and superior trading skill to earn a superior return in the stock market. You do not have those necessities.

Every wealthy client with whom I work is a multimillionaire as a result of his or her professional occupation, not through picking the right stocks or the right mutual funds. Good businessmen and businesswomen realize early in life that trying to outsmart the stock market is a loser's game. As a result, they invest their excess capital in a diversified portfolio of conservative stock and bond investments that include many index funds. If you are a young adult who is just starting to accumulate wealth, follow the smart money.

Chapter Summary

Early Savers have a long future ahead of them. Life is full of uncertainties. Nevertheless, a young person will benefit greatly from starting to save for retirement as soon as possible and as consistently as possible. This money should go into a tax-efficient, cost-effective savings plan and be invested at or below the individual's tolerance for risk. Shares of restricted company stock are considered part of the overall equity allocation. Annual rebalancing of the investments will keep the portfolio at or below the investor's tolerance for risk. In addition, when children arrive, a small amount of money should automatically put aside each month for private school and/or college. (See Appendix A.)

Key Points

1. Early Savers should start a systematic retirement savings program as soon as they land a full-time job. If they increase the amount of savings each time they get a raise, they will not miss the extra money.
2. Take full advantage of the free money from an employer match in a 401(k), a 403(b), a SIMPLE plan, or a subsidized stock savings program.
3. Compare retirement account options to get the best tax advantage and lowest fees by considering a Roth IRA or traditional IRA in lieu of a high-cost employer plan (after the match is exceeded).
4. Establish the investments in a proper mix of low-cost stock and bond index funds where available. Write the mix down so that you can refer to it later. Rebalance the mix annually and when contributions are made, in order to keep it in line with the plan.

Sample Risk Tolerance Questions

Note: This is not a complete questionnaire.

1 When making a long-term investment, I plan to hold the investment for:
   - ❏ 1-2 years
   - ❏ 3-4 years
   - ❏ 5-6 years
   - ❏ 7-8 years
   - ❏ 9-10+ years

2. In October 1987, stocks fell more than 20% in one day. If I owned an investment that fell by 20% over a short period, I would:
   - ❏ Sell all of the remaining investment.
   - ❏ Sell a portion of the remaining investment.
   - ❏ Hold onto the investment and sell nothing.
   - ❏ Buy more of the investment.

   (If you owned stock in 1987, check the answer that corresponds to your actual behavior.)

3. My previous investment experience in asset classes is (check all that apply):
   - ❏ Short-term assets (cash, money markets)
   - ❏ U.S. government/corporate bonds or bond mutual funds
   - ❏ Large stocks and stock funds
   - ❏ Small company stocks and funds
   - ❏ International stocks and funds

4. Generally, I prefer investments with little or no fluctuation in value and I'm willing to accept the lower return associated with these investments.
   - ❏ Strongly disagree
   - ❏ Disagree
   - ❏ Somewhat agree
   - ❏ Agree
   - ❏ Strongly agree

5. During market declines, I tend to sell portions of my riskier assets and invest the money in safer assets.
   - ❏ Strongly disagree
   - ❏ Disagree
   - ❏ Somewhat agree
   - ❏ Agree
   - ❏ Strongly agree

6. I would invest in a mutual fund based solely on a brief conversation with a friend, a co-worker, or a relative.
   - ❏ Strongly disagree
   - ❏ Disagree
   - ❏ Somewhat agree
   - ❏ Agree
   - ❏ Strongly agree

7. During the first half of 1994, some bond investments fell by more than 10%. If I owned an investment that fell by 10% over a short period, I would:
   - ❏ Sell all of the remaining investment.
   - ❏ Sell a portion of the remaining investment.
   - ❏ Hold onto the investment and sell nothing.
   - ❏ Buy more of the investment.

   (If you owned bonds in 1994, check the answer that corresponds to your actual behavior.)

8. My current and future income sources (for example, salary, Social Security, pension) are:
   - ❏ Very unstable
   - ❏ Unstable
   - ❏ Somewhat stable
   - ❏ Stable
   - ❏ Very stable

The answers to these questions and more will help develop a general asset allocation based on your tolerance for risk. However, more work will be required to develop an appropriate portfolio for your needs.

Chapter 14

Midlife
Accumulators

*One of the many things that nobody ever tells you about middle
age is that it's such a nice change from being young.*
— *Dorothy Canfield Fisher*

P EOPLE MATURE in several ways, including physically, emotionally, professionally, and financially. Accumulating and maintaining wealth during our 40s and 50s requires a different attitude and
a different set of financial tools than it did during our 20s and 30s.
Sometime in midlife we realize that we are mortal and that there
are limits to our abilities. We become more conservative and set
in our ways. We also change the way we manage our wealth as
retirement draws closer.

As we learned in Chapter 13, Early Savers are busy establishing
careers and forming families. Reaching permanent financial security is only a vague image in the distant future. As a result, the planning aids that guide wealth accumulation center around learning
to save on a regular basis and investing that money at an acceptable level of risk.

By midlife, managing wealth takes a new direction. By this
time, retirement accounts should have adequate assets in them

and savings habits should be well refined. Careers and family life are generally well established at this point and we have formed a lifestyle that is comfortable and affordable. It is now time to refine our ideas of a secure retirement. Armed with genuine content about our lifestyle, we begin to envision what retirement will be like and where the money must come from to fund that vision.

By midlife, saving for retirement is no longer an option; it is a necessity. If you have not started a regular saving program, procrastination is no longer a luxury that you can afford. The realization that you must save in midlife is coupled with the realization that investment returns are also becoming increasingly important. As the assets in retirement accounts grow, the investment returns on those savings will have a much greater impact on your lifestyle in retirement than the investment return during your Early Saver years. Midlife Accumulators must understand and apply sound investment principles. These principles include a proper asset allocation and the use of low-cost investment products, such as index mutual funds.

In addition to saving regularly and understanding personal risk tolerance, Midlife Accumulators should form a detailed investment plan. This chapter introduces a method for creating a detailed plan that uses a six-step approach. This program estimates the amount of wealth you will need at retirement to sustain your standard of living and establishes guidelines for creating an appropriate investment portfolio that has the best chance of reaching your wealth accumulation goal.

Where Does All the Money Go?

Over 80% of midlife adults have children. As families mature, they tend to accumulate a lot of stuff, like automobiles, appliances, electronic gadgets, closets and boxes full of clothes, tools, and possibly a vacation home, a boat, a recreational vehicle, or all three. Of course, raising children is extremely expensive, including increased insurance costs, medical costs, and dental costs. The older they get, the more they cost. Demand for space usually leads to a larger house, which means larger bills, including higher mortgage payments, utilities, and taxes. Having children also creates a need to save for their education so that some day they will leave the nest and be self-sufficient.

At least that is the plan. There are other reasons midlife can be very costly. By that time, many people are on their second or third marriage and are supporting two families and two homes.

The Art of Budgeting

Managing household budgets becomes a fine art form in midlife. We earn more, we spend more, and, at the same time, we need to save more. Regardless of how difficult it sounds, saving for retirement and saving for the children's education has to take priority over all the other bills.

The most successful savers in history have a mantra—"Pay yourself first." How do you do that? The way to do it is through payroll deduction. As we covered in Chapter 13, have the money for retirement and education automatically deducted from your paycheck so it does not get spent someplace else. Don't let the house bills overpower your need to save. Granted, this is not easy. A successful saving plan requires you to take a good look at exactly how much you earn and how much you spend and then form a workable budget around those numbers.

There are plenty of good financial planning books at your local bookstore and library to help with budgeting. I highly encourage you to pick up one or two of these books and read them. In addition, the Internet is full of family budgeting tips that are absolutely free. Simply type the phrase "family budgeting" in a search engine like Google.com and you will get a list of dozens of sites offering free software and planning.

If you are having trouble saving because you have lost track of your expenses, get back on track. Keep a list of your expenses for at least three months. There are some fabulous software packages that can help you track household inflows and outflows. Try Microsoft Money® or Quicken®.

Redefining Retirement Savings

Sometime during our 40s, we wonder if and when we will ever have enough money to retire with security. Financial independence seems so far away. Being financially independent means having enough accumulated wealth so that you can quit working for pay any time you want and not change your lifestyle. Thoughts about financial independence naturally lead people to inquire about the amount of savings needed to sustain a certain standard of living and how to get to that point from where they are currently.

This chapter helps you develop a plan for achieving financial independence over a period of time, although the methodology assumes that you have not set a firm date for retirement. A firm retirement date will be introduced in Chapter 15, Pre-Retirees and Retirees.

Accumulating Wealth for Retirement

As we cruise through midlife, with the joys, trials, and tribulations of managing a career, and raising a family, we begin to think more about other goals we want to pursue while we are on this great Earth. Many people envision retirement as a time of pursuing hobbies, learning new and interesting things, traveling, making new friends, and possibly starting a small business or doing volunteer work while maintaining a comfortable standard of living.

Whether or not our vision of retirement actually becomes a reality depends on several factors. The most important factor is our health. Without good health, retirement will not be the joy we envision it to be. The second factor is the wealth that we accumulate prior to retirement. Over-funding a retirement plan is better than under-funding one. The third factor is how much we will spend in retirement. Overspending and outliving our money is not much fun either. We will start an analysis of retirement needs with the third factor.

If you are like most people, your expenses will go down after retirement. There are three reasons for this decrease: taxes are lower, a high savings rate is no longer required, and usually there are fewer mouths to feed at home. On the other hand, a few expenses may be higher, such as travel expenses and health care costs. A good rule of thumb is that 80% of your current *pre-tax* income should sustain the moderate lifestyle you envision in retirement.

One piece of good news for retirees is that taxes will be lower. Once you stop drawing a paycheck, federal and state income taxes are significantly reduced. In addition, there are no Social Security or

Medicare taxes unless you work part-time. The government also gives retirees several tax breaks. Everyone over the age of 65 gets an extra exemption on Form 1040. Several states give retirees an assortment of tax breaks. Many states allow retirees to draw tax-free retirement income from their pensions and IRA accounts. Since state governments get federal money based on the number of residents, the state governments give retirees tax breaks so they will not change their residency to non-taxing states like Florida, Texas, or Nevada. Retirees can also control the remaining income taxes by juggling the way distributions are made from various retirement accounts. For more information on controlling taxes on investments and pensions, see Chapter 15, Pre-Retirees and Retirees.

The second reason people do not need as much income in retirement as they did while working is that they no longer need to save for retirement, although many people continue to put some savings away each year as a hedge against inflation. In addition, retirees seem to find many unique ways to cut costs and save money. For example, retirees may take on the smaller home repair jobs themselves rather than calling on a professional. In addition, if an adult child is still hanging around the house, that resident should be encouraged start paying his or her full share of expenses. As a result of lower taxes, less savings, and some cost reductions, 80% of your current income is a good goal when planning for retirement.

After establishing the amount of after-tax income needed in retirement to sustain your lifestyle, start piecing together a retirement plan, which concludes with an investment strategy. One way to do this is to look at your savings in the same way as a corporation would look at a defined benefit pension plan.

When a large corporation manages a defined benefit pension plan, the trustees estimate that future retirement checks will be based on some percentage of employees' current compensation. The company then manages the retirement account to best match those future liabilities. The idea is to match the expected annual cash inflows of plan assets with the expected annual cash outflows to retirees. If the inflows equal outflows, then the plan is fully funded.

Individuals can manage their retirement savings the same way.

They simply match expected annual cash inflows from pensions, Social Security, and investment income during retirement with expected annual living expenses. Granted, there will be many uncertainties to this approach, such as the rate of inflation, so you will need to adjust your plan as time goes by. Nonetheless, if expected cash inflows from all sources of income equal or exceed the expected cash outflows, then your personal liabilities are matched and you have attained financial independence.

The Six-Step Retirement Saving and Investing Program

The six-step retirement saving and investing program should help set the course for your savings plan over the midlife accumulation phase and into the pre-retirement period, which starts about five years prior to retirement. First, I will outline the six steps; then I will explain each step in more detail.

One important note before we begin: all the lessons we learned in Chapter 13, Early Savers, still apply. When the plan is complete, make sure you save automatically and the asset mix is within your tolerance for risk. Here are the steps:

1. Calculate your current living expenses using the *direct* or *indirect* method (explained below). Make adjustments as necessary to estimate expenses in retirement.

2. Estimate your known sources of income at retirement, not including savings.
   a. The difference between the figure from Step 1 and the figure from Step 2 is your income gap.
   b. Multiply your income gap by 22.5 to determine your required nest egg if you were to retire today. (Why 22.5? That is the inverse of a 4.5% withdrawal rate, a figure that will be discussed in detail in Chapter 15.)
   c. Figure the number of years you have until retirement and adjust this amount upward by 3% per year to cover inflation.

3. List your current and future savings.
   a. Inventory the assets you own that may be converted to income-producing investments at retirement.

    b. Estimate the amount you will save each year, starting this year and for every year until you retire at age 65 (or age 62 if you want to retire earlier).

4. Compute—using a spreadsheet or a financial calculator—the required rate of return on your current retirement assets and future savings that you need to reach your required nest egg goal (Step 2b).

    a. Do not adjust any numbers for inflation before the calculation.

    b. Any required return over 8% is too aggressive at this stage. If the required return is over 8%, you will have to recalculate the numbers so that you work longer, save more, or spend less in retirement.

5. Using the market forecasting tools in Chapter 11 and asset allocation tools in Chapter 12, design a diversified portfolio that has the least amount of risk needed to achieve your required rate of return on investments. Shares of restricted company stock are considered part of the equity allocation.

6. Ensure that your asset allocation is at or below your tolerance for risk by stress-testing the stock-and-bond mix as outlined in Chapter 13. Write down the asset allocation and then rebalance your portfolio to the allocation periodically.

If you design an investment strategy to achieve your objectives while not exceeding your tolerance for risk, it is very likely that you will be able to meet income liabilities when they come due. The trick is to set a course and follow it, without being swayed by the irrational investment behavior that surrounds us. The remainder of this chapter explains each of the six steps in detail, complete with examples of portfolios that may be used as a guide.

1. Estimate Your Annual Expenses in Retirement

By midlife, we have a good idea of the standard of living that makes us comfortable and how much that lifestyle costs. Most people desire to maintain their standard of living after retirement, which is what this program assumes. It is fairly easy to anticipate your income needs in retirement: simply figure out how much you are spending now and make a few adjustments.

There are two methods for determining your annual expenses— direct and indirect. The direct method means tracking every dollar of household income and recording where it is spent or saved. The indirect method takes the gross pre-tax earnings and subtracts taxes and savings to arrive at annual spending.

The *direct* method is the most accurate, because it itemizes each expense, but it is also the most time-consuming. It is a tedious task to keep track of all your cash outflows, including taxes and savings. For a helpful list, see the income and expense guide at the end of Chapter 15. Once you have created a list of expenses and categorized them, it is easy to derive an annual budget from the data and to adjust specific line items in the budget that will likely be different when you retire.

For example, many people have paid off their mortgage by the time they retire, which is a big cash savings each month. In addition, life insurance is generally not needed after you have accumulated enough to retire, so that expense should go away. Automobile costs will be lower, since you will not commuting to work each day and your children will be off your auto insurance policy. Speaking of the children, you should be done paying for their educational costs by the time you retire or you should hand over the remaining bills to the newly well-educated and hopefully employed adult children.

Some costs may increase in retirement. Health insurance may rise, especially if you retire before Medicare begins at age 65. Also, prescription drug costs are not currently covered under Medicare. In addition, it is a good idea for most people over age 60 to purchase a long-term care insurance policy that covers home care, assisted living, and nursing home costs not covered by Medicare.

If keeping detailed records of all household expenses sounds too tedious, there is an *indirect* method to approximate your annual expenses. The indirect method is quick, but not as accurate or detailed and not very useful for budgeting. To find your annual living expenses, your will need last year's tax returns and W-2 form and the annual statements on all savings accounts.

Go to the bottom of your IRS Form 1040 and find your adjusted gross income (AGI). According to the government, this is how much you made last year. First, if you moved to a new location, add back the cost of moving that was deducted to get the AGI. Second, subtract from the AGI any taxable interest, dividends, and capital gains (losses) from your taxable savings account. In addition, net out new *after-tax* savings and withdrawals for the year for all taxable investment and savings accounts. This will tell you your savings-adjusted AGI. Third, subtract all federal and state income tax from the savings-adjusted AGI. What you are left with is a close approximation of the amount of money you spent last year.

Here is an example of the indirect method for the past year. Assume you had an AGI of $75,000 last year and did not move to a new location. Of that amount, $5,000 was earned in capital gains, interest, and dividend income from taxable investments. In addition, you added $6,000 to personal savings in taxable accounts, including college funds. That equals a savings adjusted AGI of $64,000. Next, subtract $20,000 in income taxes paid to the federal and state governments. What you are left with is a close approximation of the amount that you spent—$44,000. Once you know this amount, it helps to go a bit further and take out major items like the mortgage, health and auto insurance, other auto costs, utilities, and other items you can identify. The remaining money was spent on food, clothing, travel, gifts, etc. Finally, make any adjustments that you think will be more or less in retirement, e.g., mortgage, college costs, insurance. The entire process is listed in Table 14-1. The indirect method of estimating expenses is not perfect, but it gets you in the ballpark.

2. List Known Sources of Pension Income, Including Social Security

In Step 2, add your known pension income, including Social Security. This does *not* include employee savings plan assets such as a 401(k). Most workers in America pay into the Social Security system and, depending on your age and the amount you paid in, you should get something out of it starting at age 62. In addition, many large employers still offer a defined benefit pension plan. (See

Item	Amount	Cumulative
Earned income	$70,000	$70,000
Taxable interest and dividends	$5,000	$75,000
All savings and reinvestment	($11,000)	$64,000
Federal/state income taxes	($20,000)	$44,000
Adjustment for retirement*	($2,000)	$42,000

*Known additions or reductions in retirement living expenses.

Table 14-1. Indirect method to calculate living expenses

Chapter 10, Other Sources of Retirement Income.)

The Social Security Administration sends you a statement each year that you can use in the exercise; however, I would use a lower amount than given in the statement because the amount is destined to change as the trust fund runs out of money. A reduction of perhaps 15% is appropriate for someone in their early 50s and maybe 25% for some in their early 40s. So, for example, if you are 45 years old and the Social Security statement says you are entitled to $20,000 per year starting at age 65, I recommend using $15,000.

Employer defined benefit plans fall into two groups: those whose benefits adjust for inflation each year and those that pay a flat amount. Each year your employer will provide a statement of projected pension benefits if you continue to work for the company until retirement. While the future benefits statement may be interesting, you need to calculate what your pension benefit would be worth today if you stopped working for that employer. The value of the pension today is the important number. In addition, is that benefit adjusted for inflation each year or does it stay a flat amount? A flat monthly payout is not worth as much as inflation-adjusted benefits.

For our example, we will assume you have a vested pension from a former employer that is worth $500 per month at age 65. Add this known employer pension benefit of $6,000 per year to an adjusted Social Security income of $15,000 per year to equal an expected total income of $21,000 per year. Assume that you will be paying some taxes on the income; since income tax on Social Security is significantly reduced after age 65, use $20,000 after tax.

In Step 1, we calculated an after-tax income need of $42,000 in retirement. Since $20,000 of this amount is covered by pension and Social Security benefits, your income gap is $22,000. This is the amount of annual income that you will need to withdraw from your savings to live the lifestyle to which you have grown accustomed.

In order to calculate the minimum size of the nest egg that you will need at retirement at age 65, multiply $22,000 by 22.5. The answer is $495,000. (For simplicity, we will round up to $500,000.) So, if you were to retire today and were eligible for Social Security and pension benefits, you would need $500,000 to maintain your lifestyle. Table 14-2 sums up this calculation.

Item	Expenses	Income
Estimated living expenses in retirement	$42,000	
Social Security benefit		$15,000
Pension income		$5,000
$500,000 savings @ 4.5% withdrawal		$22,500
Total Income		$42,500

Table 14-2. Calculating a minimum nest egg at age 65

We are almost done with this step, but we need to adjust the numbers for the effects of inflation. If you are 45, then you have 20 years until retirement; $500,000 will not provide enough inflation-adjusted income. That means we need to increase the $500,000 by some inflation rate to calculate the inflation-adjusted amount of savings needed. I use 3% because it has been the historic average for the past 75 years and is a conservative forecast. However, inflation rate forecasts are subjective, so you may want to use a lower or higher number.

You can calculate the inflation-adjusted nest egg using the future value function of a financial calculator or a spreadsheet program. Several financial Web sites have future value calculators that you can use free. A simple way to calculate the inflation-adjusted nest egg is to add 80% to your nest egg goal; that comes close to 3% inflation compounded for the 20 years. In our example, that means adding $400,000 to the nest egg of $500,000, for a target of $900,000 in savings and investments. If you have only 10 years before retirement, increase the nest egg by 35% to adjust for inflation, for $675,000.

3. Figure Your Current Wealth and Plan Your Future Savings

Now that you have a general idea of how much liquid wealth you need at retirement, how do you get there?

First, develop a net worth statement. That means adding up the value of everything you own and subtracting what you don't own. Don't forget the cash value of life insurance policies and the equity in your home. Although you may not use all of these assets to produce income in retirement, the equity is there if you need it.

The assets of greatest interest at this point are your savings accounts, i.e. personal savings accounts, joint accounts, IRAs, Keogh plans, and employee savings plan assets such as 401(k), 403(b), or 457 plans. I do not recommend counting the money saved for a child's education as part of your overall wealth, because you are likely to be spending it in the near future, although that can change. In our example, we will assume that you have saved $170,000 in various accounts that are intended for retirement.

Now that you have a net worth statement, the second part of Step 3 is to develop a savings plan. Hopefully, you are already saving on a regular basis and have been increasing those savings as you earn more. At a minimum, your savings should increase at the rate of inflation. For example, if you saved $5,000 last year, next year it will be $5,150 at a 3% inflation rate. If you save a certain percent of income through a 401(k) or other work-related plan, then you already have a method that automatically increases savings as you earn more through annual raises and regular promotions.

4. Calculate Your Required Return

The next step is to calculate a rate of return on the retirement savings needed to reach the retirement goal of $900,000 in our example.

Here is what we know so far in our example:

- You are 45 years old and plan to retire in 20 years.
- Your income needs in retirement will be covered approximately 50% by withdrawals from savings and 50% by Social Security benefits and pension income.
- You have $170,000 in savings today.
- You saved $5,000 last year and will increase your annual savings by an average of 3% per year until retirement.
- You will need $900,000 in savings to retire in 20 years based on a 3% inflation rate.

Now comes the interesting part. One important question that can be answered by the data is:

What rate of return is needed to achieve your objective of having $900,000 in 20 years, given the above parameters?

This is a straight mathematical question. You already have $170,000 saved. You will add $5,150 this year and will increase that amount by 3% per year for the next 20 years. At retirement, you need at least $900,000. That set of numbers will occur only if the rate of return on the savings is at or above a certain minimum rate.

Using a spreadsheet program, like Microsoft Excel®, the *Rate* function will calculate the minimum rate of return needed to achieve the desired goal. Enter a starting value of $170,000 and an ending value of $900,000, plus a series of 20 yearly contributions starting at $5,150 and increasing at 3% annually. The spreadsheet calculates a minimum rate of 6.75% for this problem. That means if you save according to the parameters above and earn a 6.75% return on your money over the next 20 years, you will have very close to the $900,000 needed at age 65. A required rate of return of 6.75% gives you enough money to match your future cash inflows with your future cash outflows.

Sometimes a required return analysis yields a return that is so high it is not attainable in the market or that implies an investment mix that is too risky. Most people cannot handle a high-risk portfolio and will not stick to the investment strategy in poor market conditions. (See Chapter 3, Bear Markets and Bad Investor Behavior.) It is my belief that any investment goal that requires a rate of return over 8% is too aggressive. If your required return is over 8%, do not pray for a bull market and hope for the best. Instead, adjust something to lower the required rate of return. This means working a couple more years, saving more money each year, or cutting costs in retirement. None of these are easy options, but they are better than taking too much risk with your retirement savings and risking making emotional mistakes in the future.

It is important to know the rate of return needed on your investments to make a plan work. This is not an easy calculation because of all the variables. If you are not familiar with spreadsheets, find someone who is familiar with them and is able to help you. Perhaps you can go to your local library, college, or even a high school to see if someone will teach you. Your CPA may also be a good person to ask. If you are still stumped, there are alternatives to using a spreadsheet program. Try one of the many financial planning Web sites or purchase a computer program such as Quicken.

5. Find the Optimal Investment Mix

So far our model is based on simple mathematics using known expenses, current savings, anticipated savings, and a reasonable inflation forecast. Now it is time to take a leap of faith into the financial markets. In Step 5, you develop an investment portfolio that you expect to meet your required return objective by using the market forecasts from Table 14-3, which is a reprint from Chapter 11, Realistic Market Expectations. Since no one knows what the returns of the stock and bond markets will be, our portfolio will reflect a conservative allocation, meaning the one that has the best chance for achieving a 6.75% return with the least amount of risk.

Chapter 13, Early Savers, introduced a simple portfolio using a combination of the Total Stock Market Index Fund and the Total Bond Market Index Fund. Those funds are still perfectly acceptable for Midlife Accumulators. In fact, the portfolio is preferred for most investors because of its simplicity. Using the data in Table 14-2, I calculate that, in order to achieve an *expected* rate of return of 6.75% using the two funds, you would need to invest 50% in the Total Stock Market Index Fund for an 8.0% expected return and mix 40%

Asset Class	Expected Return
Stocks	
Total U.S. Stock Market Index Fund	8.0%
U.S. Large Stocks	8.0%
U.S. Value Stocks	8.5%
U.S. Small Stocks	9.0%
Foreign Stocks, Developed Markets	8.0%
Foreign Value Stocks	8.5%
Foreign Stocks, Emerging Markets	9.0%
Real Estate (REIT)	7.5%
Bonds	
Total U.S. Bond Market Index Fund	5.0%
Short-Term Government Bonds	3.8%
Short-Term Corporate Bonds	4.0%
Intermediate-Term Government Bonds	4.2%
Intermediate Corporate Bonds	5.0%
GNMA Mortgages	5.5%
High-Yield Corporate	9.0%
Emerging Market Debt	9.0%

Table 14-3. Long-term asset class forecasts

of the Total Bond Market Index Fund with 10% of a high-yield corporate bond fund for a 5.5% expected return. If the funds achieve their expected results or higher, then an asset mix of 50% stocks and 50% bonds will earn at least the 6.75% needed to achieve your investment objective. Granted, there is a lot of subjectivity involved in any forecast of investment return, but we have to start with something, and this method is better than no method at all.

You can extend your investments of stock and bond funds by adding international stocks, value stocks, REITs, emerging market bonds, and other asset classes discussed in Chapter 8, Investment Choices: Stocks, and Chapter 9, Investment Choices: Bonds. Theoretically, wide diversification of a portfolio of stock and bond funds will lower the volatility of the account and increase the return.

The theory of asset class diversification is outlined in Chapter 12, Asset Allocation Explained. In addition, there are several fine books on the subject of asset allocation on the shelves of your local bookstore and library, such as *The Intelligent Asset Allocator: How to Build Your Portfolio to Maximize Returns and Minimize Risk* by William Bernstein (McGraw-Hill, 2000) and *Asset Allocation: Balancing Financial Risk* by Roger C. Gibson (McGraw-Hill, 2000).

There is no guarantee that adding various asset classes and asset class styles will generate higher, but chances are very good that it will yield no less. So, why not try?

Listed in Table 14-4 are a couple of examples of diversified portfolios that maintain a 50% stock and 50% bond mix, but spread the asset classes across several styles. Portfolio #1 includes foreign stocks, REITs, extra small U.S. stock exposure, and corporate bonds. Portfolio #2 expands into U.S. value stocks, foreign value stocks, foreign small stocks, and high-yield corporate bonds.

Based on the expected return of these asset classes and asset class styles, both portfolios are expected to earn a higher rate of return than a 50% total stock and 50% total bond portfolio. Therefore, investors may be able to hedge their bets a little by adding more diversification within the stock and bond asset classes. To repeat, our forecast returns on asset classes and asset class styles are subjective enough already. I would not rely on premiums from small stocks, value stocks, emerging markets, or high-yield bonds to generate a higher return in your retirement account. For all you football fans, forecasting market returns is about at easy as predicting the winner of the Super Bowl in August.

There are two disadvantages to wide diversification of mutual fund styles.

First, you must maintain the asset mix for a number of years to get the diversification benefit. That means each year you must rebalance the portfolio to get it back to its original mix. As more asset classes and styles are added, more maintenance is required and more trading needs to be done in your account. This could become costly, depending on your custodian and how much the custodian charges to buy or sell a fund. In addition, you may be locked into a

Portfolio #1: Moderate Diversification	
Stocks	**50%**
U.S. Large Stocks	20%
U.S. Small Stocks	10%
Foreign Stocks, Developed Markets	15%
REITs	5%
Bonds	**50%**
Total Bond Market	30%
Short-Term Corporate	10%
Intermediate Corporate	10%
Portfolio #2: Heavy Diversification	
Stocks	**50%**
U.S. Large Stocks	10%
U.S. Small Stocks	10%
U.S. Value Stocks	10%
Foreign Stocks, Developed Markets	5%
Foreign Stocks, Emerging Markets	5%
Foreign Value Stocks	5%
REITs	5%
Bonds	**50%**
Total Bond Market	20%
Short-Term Corporate	15%
High-Yield Corporate	10%
Emerging Market Debt	5%

Table 14-4. Two portfolios, one with moderate diversification and one with heavy diversification

poorly created employer savings plan that offers only expensive, actively managed mutual funds or expensive variable annuities. The high cost of some investments in the plan may restrict you from adding particular funds to your mix.

The second disadvantage of a widely diversified portfolio is called *tracking error risk*. The more you chop up the stock portion of your account into pieces, the less it follows the performance of the broad U.S. stock market. One day the Dow Jones Industrial Average may go up 5%, but you are very disappointed that the widely diversified portfolio went up only 1% or not at all. Since only a small portion of Portfolio #2 in Table 14-5 is tied directly to the large U.S. stocks in the Dow, it will not track the Dow in performance.

Many people are at a psychological disadvantage if their stock portfolio does not follow the broad market. In 1998 and 1999, the only stocks that did very well were large U.S. growth stocks. There are not many large growth stocks in Portfolio #2. As a result, investors who held Portfolio #2 had mediocre performance, while their friends and neighbors bragged about great gains in large growth stocks. As a result, many abandoned the strategy for more mainstream stock funds—right in time for the bear market to begin. This is tracking error risk.

6. Ensure the Asset Allocation Does Not Exceed Your Risk Tolerance

Recall the tools that we introduced in Chapter 13, Early Savers, to find a risk tolerance level. These tools are useful also in midlife. Once you find an asset mix that meets your required return, you must decide if you have the personality to handle the risk inherent in the investment mix. Markets can become extremely volatile: you could lose a substantial amount of money under various conditions. If you are not able to maintain the same asset mix under all market conditions, than the asset mix is not right for you and you must rework the six-step program.

Finishing Touches

Probably the most important thing you can do to help yourself grow wealth is to create a plan and follow it. The problem is, most people forget what their plan is and why they set it up this way. Write the plan down, including your reasons for selecting an asset allocation and what you expect going forward. Portfolio design is a lot of work; your thought process should be reflected in your investment policy statement. Reread your notes on occasion to ensure that the portfolio is being managed according to the plan. This document should prevent your ship from running aground on your journey to financial success.

After following a portfolio strategy for a few years, you may decide it is time to change course by changing the asset mix. This is fine as long as you do it for the right reasons. If the markets have been kind and you are ahead of schedule toward your wealth accumulation goal, then it is a good idea to reduce the percentage of risky assets in the portfolio. This will lock in your gains. On the other hand, if the markets fall on hard times, I do not recommend becoming more aggressive in an allocation and trying to catch up. That might place your portfolio outside your tolerance for risk, which would reduce your chance for success.

Chapter Summary

As the years race by, Midlife Accumulators realize retirement is no longer a distant dream. They must address accumulating and maintaining wealth—and do so correctly. They must save continuously and they must adhere to proper investment principles.

Investing during our 40s and 50s requires a different attitude and a different set of financial tools than earlier in life. You must assess where you are and how you are going to build the nest egg you need for retirement. The six-step retirement saving and investing program will help guide you in the right direction. A savings discipline and a sensible investment philosophy are critical to success. Your future depends on it.

Key Points

1. Estimate the retirement income needed from investments by using the six-step method.
2. Take an inventory of your current retirement investments and savings plan. Then, calculate the return needed to achieve your goal.
3. Develop a long-term investment strategy that has the highest chance of reaching your required return with the lowest risk. Ensure the strategy is at or below your tolerance for risk.
4. Write down the strategy—and stay the course.

Chapter 15

Pre-Retirees and Retirees

We grow neither better nor worse as we get old, but more like ourselves.

—*May Lamberton Becker*

Y OU HAVE BEEN WORKING for many years and it is almost time to do something different. Most people enter retirement joyfully, looking forward to it like a permanent vacation. Others will be forced into retirement due to corporate cutbacks or other unanticipated events. Regardless of the circumstances, as retirement draws near, you must address many issues. One issue is the way you manage your wealth. Common wisdom suggests that it would be appropriate to lower the level of risk in your investment portfolio. This will prepare your accounts to make monthly distributions during retirement without the threat of a large loss in market value. In addition, you may want to keep extra cash on hand in your checking account to cover unexpected expenses in the first few years.

This chapter actually covers two periods. The first period is a pre-retirement phase, which starts about five years prior to your anticipated retirement date. The main concern most people have in the pre-retirement stage is whether or not they will have enough money to retire. That issue is covered in detail in this chapter. The second phase covered in this chapter is actual retirement, including IRA rollover considerations, distributing from retirement accounts (including the best tax strategy), and investing in retirement. For the purposes of organizing this book, the retirement period starts on retirement day and goes for many years until health reasons cause you to slow down dramatically. The crest life is covered in Chapter 16, Experienced Retirees.

The Pre-Retirement Period

Sometime during our late 50s or early 60s, most people enter the pre-retirement stage. This period begins when we have about five years of full-time work left before retiring or transitioning to part-time work.

By the time most people reach the pre-retirement period, they are at peak career earnings. In addition, their children are generally out of the house and self-sufficient or only a few years away from becoming fully self-sufficient. (Of course, there may be an adult child who does not want to leave home, but in that case he or she should be required to pay for room and board.) This means that monthly living expenses should be falling. As a result of increased earnings and lower expenses, the last few years of full-time work should also be a person's peak savings years.

When people enter the pre-retirement period, their first question is "Do I have enough money to retire?" To find the answer, we need to review the six-step program described in Chapter 14 and modify the results. The modified program consists of the following steps:

1. Project your living expenses in retirement.
2. Estimate your known sources of retirement income, excluding savings. Subtract income from expenses to find the income gap.
3. Update your net worth statement. In the process, inventory your current retirement savings and estimate future contributions.
4. Update the required rate of return needed to reach financial security and fill the income gap.
5. Update your investment strategy and asset allocation to match

your goal. (Shares of restricted company stock are considered part of the equity allocation.)

6. Reduce portfolio risk as soon as practical.

By the time you reach the pre-retirement period, you have likely grown accustomed to a certain standard of living. At this point in life, you are no longer trying to climb the social ladder, stretching for a bigger house in a classier neighborhood, looking to buy a fancier car, or interested in most other expensive trappings of life. You are realistic about getting down to the business of planning a comfortable retirement that you can afford. This generally leads to two important questions. First, how much can you afford to spend each year in retirement without outliving your money? Second, where you will live?

Reviewing your current situation using the modified six-step program is an important step toward determining how much you can spend each year without risking running out of cash. Each step is essentially the same as Chapter 14, only with more detail and with some modifications.

Step 1: Estimate Your Living Expenses in Retirement

In Chapter 14, we discussed two ways of estimating living expenses in retirement. One approach is the *direct* method: you create an ongoing list of current expenses for as long as it takes to paint an accurate picture of annual costs, then adjust the list for changes that you anticipate in retirement. The second and much faster technique is the *indirect* method: you start with pre-tax income and subtract all taxes and savings from that amount to arrive at your spending level. Technically, both direct and indirect methods should yield the same result.

In the pre-retirement period, only the direct method should be used to determine expenses. You need to know exactly where your money is going and how much is going to each expense. The direct method will also allow you to make adjustments to certain expenses that will change once you are retired. If you do not know how expenses may change, such as the cost of health insurance and prescription drugs, it is the time to find out. Go to the benefits department of your employer or contact your service representatives.

Another source of information is friends who have recently retired from the same employer.

Sometimes there are large, one-time expenses that need to be budgeted. About 50% of adult children get married in their mid- to late 20s. That may be an added one-time expense depending on who pays for weddings in your family. Another expense may be a son or daughter who is involved in a divorce. Parents seem to help with the finances during these periods, especially if there are grandchildren involved.

Speaking of grandchildren, one expense that many retirees do not anticipate is the cost of caring for grandchildren. Visiting the grandchildren and giving then gifts is a joy and easily worked into an annual budget. But for 2.4 million grandparents who care for their grandchildren full-time, the expense can put a deep hole in a retirement fund.

According to the 2000 census, over 6.3% of children under the age of 18 were living in a household headed by a grandparent. That compares with 5.5% in 1990, 3.6% in 1980, and 3.2% in 1970. Many grandparents assume responsibility when the parents separate, divorce, die, run into trouble with the law, or have severe financial problems. Caring for your grandchildren is naturally the first priority, but it can be a tremendous financial burden, not to mention the stress. If you are in this situation, your expenses may be about 25% higher than you anticipated.

Step 2: Estimate Your Sources of Retirement Income

What income can you expect in retirement from Social Security, pensions, part-time work, and installment sales of a business?

Reduced Social Security benefits can begin at age 62. However, the longer you wait to collect, the more you will receive each month. If you wait, the amount of the benefit increases from 3% to 8% per year, topping out at age 70. Each year the Social Security Administration sends you a benefits update that lists how much you can expect to receive monthly, depending on your age when you start to collect. Medicare begins at age 65, regardless of the year you start collecting Social Security, and is a big cost savings.

If your spouse has paid into the Social Security system for the required 40 quarters, then he or she is also entitled to reduced benefits beginning at age 62. If your spouse has not paid in 40 quarters, then he or she is still entitled to a monthly benefit, equal to 37.5% of your Social Security benefit, if you are collecting. If your spouse waits until "full retirement age" (between 65 and 67, depending on year of birth), he or she is entitled to 50% of your benefit. This information is also contained in your annual benefits update.

For some people, employer defined benefit pension plans will provide a second income at retirement. If you are eligible for a defined benefit pension plan, you may receive an annual benefits update from your employer or former employer. The report should detail the amount of monthly income you can expect to receive at a certain age, depending on the plan. If your current employer or a former employer does not send annual updates, then you can request one through the Human Resources office.

A pension payout that provides a monthly check to you alone is called a *single-life annuity*. This option will provide the biggest benefit, because it is based on your life expectancy alone. When you die, the benefit ends. If you opt to have your spouse receive a pension in the event you die first, this is called a *joint and survivor annuity*. The payout to you will be lower because of the cost of insurance, and sometimes the benefit to a surviving spouse is lower still.

Some pension plans provide for a cost-of-living adjustment (COLA) in benefits. Most government-managed plans have a COLA; most corporate plans do not. Social Security has a built-in COLA. A plan with a COLA is worth far more than a plan without any adjustment for inflation. You need to know if your pension plan has COLA and how adjustments are made.

If you have a *cash balance* pension plan that is funded by your employer, the amount of your retirement payout will not be known while you are working. That is because your retirement benefit is based on the final value of your account at retirement rather than a guaranteed amount based on pay. Check with your employer to see what amount they anticipate your retirement pay to be, subject to change with market conditions.

Other items to include in expected payments at retirement are personal annuities for which you decide to *annuitize* the contract. This process will convert the investment from a floating rate of return to a fixed rate payout over your life and possibly the life of your spouse. Annuity payments vary based on the number of options built into the contract. A contract that covers two lives and pays an estate for a minimum number for years in the event that both die will pay a much lower monthly rate than a contract that covers one person until death.

Many retirees will work part-time and supplement their income. Typically, these jobs bring in an extra $4,000 to $10,000 per year, depending on where you work and how much. In addition, a business owner may sell his or her business and receive multi-year payouts. This practice is common, because it allows the buyer to earn revenue from the business and use it to make installment payments. Occasionally, the sale of a business dovetails into a part-time consulting job, which adds to retirement income.

Once you have made a complete list of all income sources, *not* including investments, compare the annual income amount against your estimated annual retirement expenses determined in Step 1. The shortfall between projected income and projected expenses is your income gap. This is the amount that you need to make up by withdrawing from retirement savings accounts. The income gap can vary from year to year, depending on many factors, including the age at which you retire, the age at which your spouse retires, when Social Security and Medicare kicks in, and if your pension income has COLA. If you have a defined benefit plan that does not have a COLA, the income gap will widen each year by the amount that inflation reduces the real pension benefit.

Once you have collected all income and expense data, set up a cash flow summary for the first few years. Include all expected retirement living expenses, including taxes, and all known income including Social Security, pension, and part-time work. Be sure to increase expenses and Social Security benefits by about 3% per year to account for inflation. Any pension plan with COLA should also increase.

Table 15-1 shows an example of a 60-year-old male pre-retiree who will retire in about five years. His non-working spouse is 57.

Years in Retirement	Estimate of Expenses	Social Security	Fixed Pension	Part-Time Work	Income Gap
1	$50,000	$15,000	$12,000	$6,000	$17,000
2	$51,500	$15,450	$12,000	$5,000	$19,050
3	$53,045	$15,914	$12,000	$4,000	$21,132
4	$54,636	$22,537	$12,000	$0	$20,099
5	$56,275	$23,214	$12,000	$0	$21,062
6	$57,964	$23,910	$12,000	$0	$22,054
7	$59,703	$24,627	$12,000	$0	$23,075
8	$61,494	$25,366	$12,000	$0	$24,128
9	$63,339	$26,127	$12,000	$0	$25,211

Table 15-1. Determining the income gap during retirement at 3% inflation

The table lists estimated retirement expenses, known retirement income, and the income gap to be made up by investments.

The retiree in this example expects to work part-time until his spouse is eligible to collect Social Security benefits at age 62, which is Year 4. The income gap in the example averages about $22,000 for this couple during the 10-year period, with a little less income needed in the early retirement years. Filling that income gap is the job of their retirement savings.

Step 3: Create a Net Worth Statement

The next step in the process is to inventory your assets. Make a detailed list of all assets, including everything you own that can be turned into income-producing investments if needed. These items include retirement savings, personal savings, the cash value of life insurance, home equity, land, vacation properties, antiques, fine art, and other collectibles. Create a separate section on your net worth statement for investments intended to produce income in retirement and a section for assets that can be converted to cash if needed. Ideally, you will be drawing income only from retirement accounts and investments whose purpose is to provide income in retirement. See the end of the chapter for a guide.

Many people look at retirement as an opportunity to downsize their living space by moving to a smaller residence. The sale of a larger home turns equity into cash that can be invested to produce additional retirement income or used to pay down a large percentage of the cost of a smaller home, thus reducing monthly bills. Sometimes the smaller home was family vacation property that was acquired several years earlier and is nearly paid for. If that is the case, all the equity from the sale of a primary residence can be placed into an income-producing investment for retirement.

If you do not intend to downsize your home at retirement, then list the equity in your home as a potential source of emergency capital. If need be, you could take out a home equity loan, refinance and take equity out, or do a reverse mortgage. (A reverse mortgage is a form of home equity loan that allows you to convert some of the equity in your home into cash while you continue to own it. You take a regular check out of home equity and pay the bank back when the home is sold or your estate is settled.)

Other potential sources of capital are passive ownership in private businesses, land, an extra car that will no longer be needed, boats, tools, artwork, antiques, and other collectibles. It may not be your intent to sell any of these assets at first, but these items can be converted to cash if needed.

Finally, inheritances from parents and relatives are playing an increasing role in many retirement plans. While it may not feel right to count known inheritances as part of retirement assets, they will come into play at some time.

The last part of Step 3 is forecasting the amount of new savings you will be able to put into a retirement account prior to retirement. This amount will typically be larger than in recent years, because you are in your peak earning years and the expense of raising children should be close to over. Of course, once your children are on their own, an unexpected wedding or two may jump up. If you plan on paying for a child's wedding, then your savings forecast may be temporarily restrained.

In this running example, we will say our 60-year-old pre-retiree and his wife have $450,000 saved for retirement savings, in addition to $15,000 in a checking account for emergency money. The couple will also save $6,000 per year over the next five years before retirement.

Step 4: Update the Rate of Return Needed for Financial Security

Based on the income gap estimates in Step 2, our pre-retiree couple needs $22,000 per year based on current dollars. The table lists a smaller gap in the early years, but unexpected expenses have a habit of popping up in the early retirement years. To find their nest-egg goal, multiply $22,000 by 22.5 and then add 15% to cover potential inflation during the five years before retirement. In this example, $22,000 x 22.5 x 1.15 = $570,000 nest egg goal. (Why use 22.5 as a factor? That is the inverse of a 4.5% withdrawal rate, which is a figure that will be discussed in more detail later in this chapter.)

Next, we revisit the couple's list of retirement assets, from Step 3. We see that they have $450,000 in current savings and will add $6,000 per year in contributions over the next five years. The $15,000 emergency money is not included in this calculation. Using the *rate* function on a financial calculator or a spreadsheet, it is easy to find the required rate of return in this problem. Using an Excel spreadsheet:

1. Enter 5 in the number of payment periods [Nper = 5].
2. Enter negative $6,000 in the payment window [Pmt = - 6,000].
3. Enter negative $450,000 in the present value window [Pv = - 450,000].
4. Enter positive $570,000 in the future value window [Fv = 570,000].
5. Hit Enter.

The result is 3.63%. This is the rate of return required on invested assets of $450,000 plus contributions of $6,000 per year to reach $570,000 in five years. The couple is in a good position to reach their retirement goal.

Step 5: Update Your Investment Strategy to Achieve the Required Return

Let's assume that, until this point in their lives, our couple has been investing about 60% of their retirement assets in stock funds and 40% in bond funds. Now that they require only a 3.6% return over the next five years to make it to nirvana, there is no reason to take that much risk. The couple should reduce their exposure to stocks from the current 60% position. The right amount of stock exposure for the couple is somewhere between 20% and 40%, with the rest of the portfolio in fixed income.

Our couple needs only a 3.6% rate of return over the next five years. They can coast into retirement using an investment mix that is very conservative. A decision to sell stocks at this point in the couples life has *nothing* to do with the current state of the stock market or any forecast about the direction of the stock market. The decision to reduce risk is based on the fact that the couple's $570,000 retirement goal is virtually guaranteed if they do not assume a lot of financial risk. If the couple ignores this advice and maintains a high level of stocks, there is a chance that a bad stock market will wipe out their retirement dreams, or at least put them on hold.

The biggest mistake most pre-retirees make in their investment portfolio is that they do not reduce their exposure to risky investments when they no longer need to take a lot of risk to meet their retirement goals.

When your retirement goal is within reach, reduce risk. Let me say that again a bit louder:

**WHEN YOUR RETIREMENT GOAL IS
WITHIN REACH, REDUCE RISK!**

Step 6: Ensure the New Asset Allocation Is Within Your Risk Tolerance

If they have done a good job of saving money and not squandering their wealth on poor investments, most pre-retirees will be able to invest their assets well below their tolerance for risk. Again, the decision to reduce risk in a portfolio has nothing to do with the opinions about the stock market or the future of the economy. It is based on reaching a financial goal. Your assets and liabilities in life are now matched. Don't risk going back into the red due to an unexpected poor market. You have done well thus far to build and maintain wealth; don't risk losing it. Remember: a ship slows down as it approaches harbor.

One of the unfortunate occurrences during the recent bull-and-bear market cycle was that many pre-retirees increased their risk at the peak of market prices in 1999. As the stock prices went up, many people invested more at higher prices. Some even mortgaged their homes to invest in technology stocks. A couple of years later, those people found themselves with far less money in their retirement accounts and several more working years ahead. In Chapter 3, Bear Markets and Bad Investor Behavior, we learned that a large percentage of 50-somethings who increased stock exposure in their TIAA-CREF account as the stock market went up. These people were sorry for that mistake a few years later.

Some of the more familiar cases of taking big risks prior to retirement were documented by media coverage of the Enron and WorldCom bankruptcies. Thousands of older employees lost hundreds of thousands of dollars in their company stock and were now out of work. It does not matter who is to blame for those business disasters. The fact is that the older employees did not take the opportunity to lock in gains from company stock when many clearly had enough money to retire and live happily ever after.

Pre-Retirement Planning Issues

This book is not designed as an all-inclusive retirement planning guide. Its intent was to help you think about important savings and investment issues surrounding the growth and management of your wealth through life. There are a couple of issues mentioned in this chapter that may greatly affect your income and expenses in retirement, issues that I consider important enough to merit greater discussion. The first is the way Social Security benefits are taxed and the second is your insurance needs.

The Taxation of Social Security Benefits

Social Security payments are subject to taxation depending on how old you are and how much other income you make. There are two levels of taxation. One is a straight income tax on benefits based solely on your income; the other is a benefit reduction tax based on your age and the amount of money you earn working part-time. Together, the dual tax on Social Security can wipe out your entire benefit.

The percent of your Social Security benefit that is subject to ordinary income tax depends on the amount of your *provisional* income, which includes tax-free municipal bond interest, and your filing status. In 2003, Social Security benefits are subject to federal taxes based on the grid in Table 15-2. In addition, at present 15 states tax Social Security benefits as ordinary taxable income. Check with your tax advisor or state tax department to determine if your benefit will be subject to state income tax.

	Provisional Income, Including Social Security	
Tax on Benefits	**Single**	**Married**
Social Security not taxed	Up to $25,000	Up to $32,000
50% of Social Security taxed	$25,000 to $34,000	$32,000 to $44,000
85% of Social Security taxed	Over $34,000	Over $44,000

Table 15-2. Estimated federal tax on Social Securty benefits for 2003

Is the government being fair by taxing benefits? Since 50% of payments into Social Security come from your employer, so you have never paid tax on that money, taxing 50% of the benefits would seem fair. But that is not the final answer. In addition, the rate of growth on the money in the Social Security system has never been taxed either, so it is probably fair to tax something over 50% of Social Security benefits. However, 85% still sounds too high. Nevertheless, don't wait for Table 15-2 to change anytime soon.

In addition to taxing more of your Social Security benefit as you earn more, if you retire before age 65 the federal government will reduce your benefit by $1 for every $2 of earned income from employment over $11,520 in 2003. The penalty is lowered to $1 for every $3 earned over $30,720 if you turn 65 in 2003; starting the month you turn 65, the exempt amount is unlimited. That means you can earn as much as you want by working without losing benefits. The exempt income amounts change each year based on a formula provided by the Social Security Act.

The annual exempt amount formula makes it irrational for a vibrant 62- to 64-year-old retiree to continue working part-time. As a result, many experienced professionals opt out of productive employment. I understand the reasoning behind the government discouraging people from retiring before reaching their full retirement age; it saves money in the short term. But this onerous tax makes productive part-time work unaffordable for millions of bright citizens. That hurts the competitiveness of our nation in the long term.

Insurance Expense Issues

Most people carry several forms of insurance during their working years. These insurance costs can be divided into three basic types:

- auto, home, and liability, which insures our possessions
- life and disability, which insures earned income
- healthcare, which insures our bodies and minds.

In retirement, insurance needs change. Auto, home, and liability insurance is still needed, although maybe in lesser amounts if you don't have children on your auto policy or downsize your home in retirement. Life and disability insurance is no longer needed in most cases, since you no longer have earned income. On the other hand, the cost of health insurance may increase significantly, especially if you have pre-existing conditions and retire before Medicare begins at age 65.

Clearly, disability insurance is no longer needed at retirement, because its purpose is to directly insure your earned income. Since most retirees have little or no earned income, there is no reason to continue paying a monthly premium after the paychecks stop.

Life insurance is a different. When you were young, insurance salespeople told you that life insurance was designed to replace the wealth that you have not yet earned; thus, in the event of a tragedy, insurance money would provide your spouse and family with enough income to live adequately. (As my wife is fond of saying, at age 45, I am worth more dead than alive.) Now that you have wealth, is life insurance really needed? Insurance salespeople will come up with a dozen reasons why life insurance is still needed later in life, but in truth, most people can drop the coverage and cash in the value of their policies. The house may already be paid off, the children are self-sufficient, and your spouse has a nest egg to provide retirement income in addition to Social Security and other sources. So, I recommend canceling the term policy and cashing in the whole life policy. At the very least, reduce the amount of term insurance and convert the cash value of a whole life policy to a paid-up life-time level term policy.

Healthcare is probably the most over-regulated industry in our country. The system is complex and the administrative process is frustrating at best. The more the government regulates, the worse it gets, and every year the government becomes more and more involved. As a result, more than 50 cents of every healthcare dollar is tied up in administrative costs.

The largest healthcare insurer in the county is a government-run program called Medicare. Currently, there are close to 40 million people age 65 and older enrolled in the Medicare system. That number is expected to double in the next 30 years. Unfortunately, according the latest budget estimates, Medicare will be out of money by 2012. That will be a big problem. Medicare is funded mostly through a special 1.5% unlimited income tax placed on all working Americans. That means the system is funded by people who are not eligible to use the services because they are too young.

There are two parts to Medicare. Part A is hospitalization; Part B is medical insurance. If you are directed by a physician to go to a hospital, you pay a deductible and Medicare picks up the rest. There is no premium for this part of the coverage. Part B is medical insurance. This covers 80% of most doctor's fees, supplies, medical equipment, X-rays, and other services not covered under Part A. You pay $50 per month and a small annual deductible.

The most important items not covered by Medicare are prescription drugs, routine physical exams, eyeglasses, dental, foot care, custodial care, hearing aids, or any healthcare while traveling outside the U.S. For this and more you will need supplemental private insurance, appropriately called Medigap. These plans offer a smorgasbord of options based on the amount you want to pay. There are 10 basic types of Medigap plans that are standard in all states, regulated by federal and state rules. The plans run from A to J, with A being the most basic policy, offering less at a lower price, and J being the most comprehensive.

Pre-retirement is also a time to consider long-term care insurance. The harsh realities of aging in America are coming into sharp focus. A 95-year-old baby boomer without long-term care insurance may have to rely on a 90-year-old spouse or a 70-year-old son or daughter for day-to-day personal care. Consumers cannot rely on Medicare, Medicare supplemental insurance, or health insurance, because they do not cover most long-term care expenses.

For people who have considerable wealth, there is no need to buy long-term care insurance. They can fund their health care needs. If one spouse goes into a facility, the other spouse has adequate income to cover the cost of two residences. In addition, a person who is living alone and is financially secure may not need the coverage either; if that person goes into a facility, there is no need to keep a residence. In my view, the idea of long-term care insurance is to be able to fund two residences at the same time, one in a medical setting and the other for the healthy spouse. Even if a person chooses home care, the cost can run nearly as much as having two residences. Therefore, long-term care fits well in a situation where a couple has enough wealth to live out their life comfortably, but not much over that.

When buying long-term care insurance, age is the primary factor in determining cost. The younger you are when you get the policy, the lower the premiums. Of course, if you buy the insurance at a younger age, you will be paying those premiums for a longer time before taking any benefits, so the cost advantage is relative.

A good time to shop for long-term care insurance is around age 55, according to the American Health Care Association (AHCA), a federation of 50 state health organizations representing assisted living, nursing facility, long-term care, and sub-acute care providers. A policy that costs $800 annually when you're 55 will cost nearly twice as much if you wait until age 65.

There is an exception, however. You might want to purchase a long-term care policy before age 55 if your employer sponsors an attractive group plan at an affordable price.

If you buy a long-term care policy, make sure it has an inflation-protection option. This will give you some protection against price increases. No one can predict what the cost of medical care will be in the future and you do not want tour coverage to be inadequate.

Many aspects of financial and insurance planning require professional expertise, so you may want to talk to a knowledgeable person before making any major decisions. Be careful to screen the people you are seeking advice from. Many advice givers have ulterior motives, such as insurance salespeople posing as financial planners. To avoid a conflict of interest, I recommend seeking the advice of an hourly, fee-only financial planner, not a commission-based advisor. Hourly, fee-only financial planners are paid by the hour, the same way as most accountants and attorneys. They can help you make the right choices and can save you money by searching out the lowest-cost products. To locate an affiliated planner in your area, call The Garrett Planning Network, Inc. at 866 260-8440 or visit www.garrettplanningnetwork.com.

Retirement Day

You made it! You are finally retiring. Your ship is now safe in the harbor. Your employer has congratulated you, handed you a memento, taken your security badge, and shut the door behind you. But the work is not over yet. There are still many decisions to make concerning your money in the pension plan. Should you roll it into an IRA? Should you leave it in the plan?

Once the rollover question is answered, you will have other questions. How much can you safely withdraw from savings each month and which account that money should come from? How do you pay income tax now that you are no longer pay through employer withholding? The following section helps answer some of those questions—and more.

Rollovers

If your employer has a 401(k), 403(b), 457, or other type of defined contribution plan, upon retirement you will either be instructed to roll your portion of the plan into an IRA rollover account (see

Chapter 6) or be given the option to leave your assets in the plan. A third option is to cash in the plan and take the money out. But cashing in the plan means paying income tax on the distribution and a penalty if you are below age 59½. Cashing in is the least desirable option.

In general, most people are better off doing a transfer directly into an IRA rollover. Employee plans tend to be high in administrative costs and the investment options tend to have high expense ratios. That makes the choice simple. As long as you are confident in your ability to select the best investments, do a rollover.

Rolling over an account into an IRA is easy. Simply open an account with a low-cost custodian such as Vanguard or TIAA-CREF and fill out a transfer form. Then, your former employer transfers the assets directly into the account. You never touch the money, nor do you want to. If you ask that the check be made out to you instead of transferring it directly to another firm, there will be a mandatory federal tax withholding of 20%.

Some of the employer plan money may not be eligible to roll over or it may be too costly to do a rollover. If your employer has a match, a portion of the contribution may not have vested in the plan and you will not be eligible to roll it over. Check with your employer to see when that portion is eligible to be rolled over, if at all.

Many employers use an insurance company plan. That means your money may be tied up in a back-end-loaded variable annuity. This is a bad deal, but there is nothing you can do about it except pay the fine or leave that portion of the money in the employer plan until the back-end fee period expires. You may get a call from the insurance rep that sold your employer the plan, asking you to do a rollover with him or her. That would be a good time to express your discontent about the high fees and commissions of the insurance-related product in which you have been stuck all those years.

Whether you roll your plan assets into an IRA rollover account or not, you can start taking penalty-free taxable distributions from the account at age 59½ and you must start taking distributions at age 70½. The minimum distribution is based on age. The younger you start taking money, the lower the minimum distribution amount will be later on. At age 70½, the distribution is about 4% of the account assets. Note: there is one way to take a penalty-free distribution before age 59½, but it is restrictive. Talk to your tax advisor.

If you are eligible for a defined benefit plan, some employers offer a lump sum pension payout into an IRA rollover instead of a monthly check. Normally, companies do this because it is cost-effective to them, which generally means it is not a good deal for you. However, you need to look at all aspects. Do you know if the plan is fully funded and the employer is sound or if the plan has a deficit and the employer is in financial trouble? If the plan is funded and the employer is sound, figure out the rate of return you are being asked to give up and whether you can realistically earn that rate of return in an IRA rollover account. On the other hand, if the plan is not funded and the employer's fate is unknown, you may want to consider a rollover. Realize that most defined benefit plans pay into a government insurance program called the Pension Benefit Guaranty Corporation (PBGC). If the plan is insured and your former employer goes under, then PGBC will pay your benefits up to certain limits. Your former employer is legally obligated to provide you with all the information necessary to make an informed decision.

Investing During Retirement

You should invest your current savings and any lump sum payments according to the stock-and-bond asset allocation that you decided upon using the six-step program. Lump sum payments are large cash distributions that can come from employee savings plans, employer pension plans, the cash value of whole life insurance, the sale of property or businesses, an inheritance, or other sources. There is no reason to treat lump sum payments any differently than current retirement savings.

The type of mutual fund to purchase in each account depends on whether the account in question is taxable, tax-deferred, or tax-free (Roth IRA). For information on stock and bond investing, see Chapter 8, Investment Choices: Stocks, and Chapter 9, Investment Choices: Bonds. In addition, read good investing books on the subject. Appendix B has a partial list of some of my favorites. Don't forget to read my other two books, *All About Index Funds* (McGraw-Hill, 2002) and *Serious Money: Straight Talk About Investing for Retirement* (Portfolio Solutions, 2000), a free on-line book found at www.PSinvest.com.

Safe Withdrawal Rates

What is the optimal rate for withdrawing from savings? Several independent academic studies have concluded that 4.5% is a reasonable number. If you take out 4.5% or less, there is very good chance your money will last longer than you do.

There are some problems with those academic studies. For example, they assume you will be spending the same amount at age 90 that you will at age 65, even after adjusting for inflation. That is highly unlikely. In my opinion, a withdrawal rate of 5% is fine for most people and can even be temporarily higher at times during retirement if needed.

There are a lot of variables involved in the withdrawal rate that is right for you. In Step 4 of the six-step program, we calculated the savings goal for retirement for the couple in our example by multiplying their income gap of $22,000 by 22.5. Why 22.5? That is the inverse of 4.5%, the academically approved safe rate for withdrawals during retirement. If you have a well-balanced, diversified portfolio with about 30% in stocks and 70% in bonds, then 4.5% almost guarantees that you will not outlive your money. As stated earlier, I believe a 5% withdrawal rate is also OK, but there is a slight chance that you may outlive your money. This assumes you do not have any equity in a home, cash value of insurance, or collectibles that can be sold and do not expect to get any financial help from children and relatives who care about you.

One thing is certain; if at age 75 or so, you will realize that you are spending less than anticipated and are accumulating more wealth, withdraw more each year and *spend it!* A withdrawal rate of 6% is fine at that point (even more, according to Jack Bogle, the 70-something founder of the Vanguard Group).

I have seen many older retirees reluctant to spend their money because they want to pass it on to the children and grandchildren. This is done through a combination of frugal living, estate planning, and life insurance. All I will tell you is enjoy your money while you can. For years I tried to talk a 70-something widow into taking her family on a nice Caribbean cruise. She thought it was a great idea, but did not do it because she did not want to spend her grandchildren's inherence. When she died, the government picked up $2 million in estate taxes.

Enjoy your money. Some estate planning is fine if it avoids taxes, but do not buy life insurance to pay those taxes unless your assets are illiquid, like a business or commercial real estate. You will have to trust me when I say that I have seen the other side of these good intentions. Inherited wealth does not last. Most of it is squandered away in two generations. Enjoy your money while you can.

How to Take Distributions from Savings

Taking annual distributions from savings accounts is all about taxes, or rather, the best way to avoid paying unnecessary taxes. The "science of taking distributions" is two parts math, one part art, and one part humor. You need a good sense of humor, because the tax laws are so complicated in places that the only thing you can do is laugh. Nevertheless, we will persevere.

Formulating a tax-effective series of distributions from taxable and non-taxable accounts requires a careful analysis, including the effects on the taxation of Social Security benefits. If you do a poor job of paying yourself, you tax bill can quickly double. For example, the rate on a taxable portion of a Social Security benefit can quickly jump from 0% to 85% (see Table 15-2). As a result, you need to spend time understanding the tax code and finding the best mix of distributions.

The first step in this process is dividing your retirement savings accounts into three tax categories:

- **Category 1.** Accounts from which distributions are 100% taxable, such as an IRA rollover, a 401(k), or a Keogh plan. You did not pay income taxes on the principal going into the accounts or on the gains, so it is all fully taxable as ordinary income when any comes out. The IRS mandates taking a minimum distribution out of these plans at age 70½.

- **Category 2.** Accounts from which distributions are not taxable, such as personal accounts, trust accounts, joint accounts, and Roth IRA accounts. You have already paid taxes on the principal in these accounts. Income and realized capital gains are taxed each year on a separate line item on IRS Form 1040 (except for gains in a Roth IRA, which are tax-free).
- **Category 3.** Accounts from which distributions may be either taxable or not, such as a personal annuity and after-tax IRA contributions (not Roth IRAs). The money going into these accounts was taxed, but the earnings in the accounts were not. In these accounts, the earnings come out before principal and are taxed as ordinary income. The principal is not subject to tax.

Now that you know the rules, let's do an analysis. In the example we used earlier in this chapter, our couple needs $50,000 in pre-tax income to meet expenses. Of that amount, $18,000 is coming from a pension and part-time work and $15,000 is coming from Social Security. They need to get the remaining $17,000 from other savings, but from which account? Let's assume that taxable interest and dividend income on taxable investments is $4,000. So, now they are up to an income of $37,000, which leaves $13,000 to come from retirement savings.

When taking money from a savings account, many issues have to be considered. Social Security becomes taxable for a married couple filing a joint return when their adjusted gross income (AGI) is over $32,000, including one-half of Social Security benefits and any tax-exempt interest income. If their AGI is between $32,000 and $44,000, 50% of Social Security benefits are taxed. Above $44,000, 85% is taxed. Naturally, the trick is to take money from savings in a way that keeps your AGI income below $32,000, while still getting the income you need to sustain your lifestyle.

Currently, the couple has $29,500 in gross income for Social Security tax purposes ($18,000 from pensions and work, $4,000 in interest, and $7,500 as one-half of Social Security). To keep Social Security taxes at $0, the couple can take only $2,500 from Category 1 accounts (IRA rollover, Keogh, etc.); the remaining $10,500 must come from Category 3 accounts (personal savings, Roth IRA). This is the best tax strategy in Year 1 of retirement. Next year things might be different, so a different dance will be formed.

If your income from sources other than Social Security is above $30,000, then 85% of your benefit will be subject to taxation and there is not much you can do about it. So, the next level of analysis is based on tax brackets. Tax brackets are coming down due to the Tax Reduction Act of 2001. Therefore, it benefits you to defer as much taxable income as possible into the future, so it will be taxed at a lower level. That typically means paying yourself from Category 3 personal accounts first, because the principal taken from personal accounts is not taxable. In addition, a reduction in principal also lowers the amount of taxable or tax-free interest you will receive in the following years, which may help reduce the tax you pay on Social Security benefits.

After age 70½, distributions from Category 1 accounts are mandatory. The IRS wants its money. At that point, you need to start taking about 4% out of those accounts each year. There is a big penalty imposed if you do not take the money, so don't miss the December 31 deadline. The rules on minimum distributions are always changing, so check with your tax advisor. In addition, there may be occasions where your CPA or tax advisor recommends taking some money out of IRA rollovers and other Category 1 accounts before age 70½. These decisions need to be discussed in conjunction with tax bracket changes and potential tax law changes.

As you can see, the IRS does not make it easy for retirees. There are so many income variables, age variables, and exceptions to the rule that it is nearly impossible for the average retired person to figure out the tax strategy that is best for him or her. In many ways, I think the tax code was designed by a group of CPAs who wanted to create job security. They did a fine job.

Special Considerations for Early Retirees

If you retire before you are eligible for Social Security benefits at age 62, it will mean funding more living expenses out of your pocket.

Depending on how much you have saved, making up the difference may or may not be a problem. If you are very close to the minimum amount needed to make ends meet, then I offer these suggestions:

1. In the years prior to collecting Social Security, it is OK to withdraw up to 6% per year from your retirement funds. Understand there will not be much growth, if any, in the portfolio.
2. Be much more conservative in your investments than you would otherwise. You cannot afford to withdraw up to 6% of an investment portfolio and have a bear market in stocks. That would significantly impair your lifestyle. An allocation of 25% to 35% in stocks is the maximum recommended.
3. If you retire before age 59½, there is a way to get a distribution from your IRA account penalty-free, but the rules are strict and a multi-year commitment is required. See your tax advisor.
4. When you reach age 62 and start collecting Social Security benefits, reduce your withdrawal rate to between 4% and 4½%.

Having an aggressive investment account can be very risky if you do not have sizable wealth. If you are aggressive and get trapped in a bear market while taking out 5% or more from savings, your account could go down very fast. Million-dollar portfolios were reduced to a few hundred thousand dollars in 2000-2002, as early retirees made large withdrawals and tried to make up for it by being aggressive in the stock market. If you have a high withdrawal rate, do not be aggressive. If you retire with more wealth than you need, you can be more aggressive because you can afford to lose it.

There is one more important item about early retirement worth discussing. Early retirees need to purchase full health care coverage, because Medicare does not start until age 65. Federal law allows you to stay with your former employer's plan for several months, if it is a group plan with 20 or more participants. Some large employers provide retirees affordable group medical care coverage. Those early retirees not covered under a previous employer will need to seek their own coverage through a private health insurance policy, which can be very costly.

Chapter Summary

Retirement is a critical time for people. Nearly everything changes, including the way you manage your wealth. There are many factors to consider, and much work needs to be done. This chapter is a brief overview of the investment considerations and focuses mainly on reducing risk.

When you near retirement, take an inventory of everything you own, your expenses, and sources of known retirement income. If you have achieved financial independence or it is just a short distance away, then reduce your investment risk. It is only logical to lock in a secure retirement when you have the opportunity, rather than remaining in a riskier portfolio and possibly losing your secure nest egg to the markets.

Taxes play a major role in the way you pay yourself. Learn the rules and exceptions to the rules about the taxation of Social Security benefits. Taxes will affect your decision to collect or delay Social Security, your decision to get a part-time job or not, and your decisions about which accounts offer the best after-tax withdrawal rate. The more time you spend reading and learning about these issues, the better prepared you will be for retirement.

Key Points

1. About five years from retirement, spend as much time as needed to understand where you are and what you need to do to lock in financial security.
2. Study your expected retirement income and expenses and make decisions on insurance, Social Security, and part-time work (see Table 15-3 for help in doing this).
3. Reduce investment risk in your retirement accounts as soon as possible.
4. Enjoy retirement. You deserve it!

Income Guide
Sources of Fixed Income
Social Security Benefits
Pensions
Part-Time Work
Interest Income
Dividend Income
Annuity Income
Installment Sale of Business
Rental Income
Retirement Account Assets
401(k), 403(b), 457
IRA Accounts
SEPs or Keoghs
Annuity Contract Value
Employer Stock Plans and ESOPS
Employer Stock Options
Other Assets
Savings Accounts
Certificates of Deposit
Direct Holdings of Stocks
Direct Holdings of Bonds
Mutual Funds
Cash Value of Life Insurance
Business Ownership
Home/Condo
Vacation Property
Rental Property
Other Property
Cars
Collectibles
Jewelry and Furs
Known Inheritance
Other Assets

Table 15-3. Sample income and expense guide (continued on pages 264 and 265)

Expense Guide
Nondiscretionary Expenses
Home Mortgage Payments Insurance Maintenance Property Tax Homeowners Association Dues
Auto Payments or Lease Fuel Insurance Service and Repair Tax and License
Food Groceries Medical Dental Insurance Doctors' Visits Prescriptions and Other Items
Taxes State Income Federal Income City Income
Utilities Electricity Heating (Gas and Oil) Water Telephone Garbage Removal
Investment Bank Fees Investment Management

Table 15-3. Sample income and expense guide (continued)

Expense Guide
Discretionary Expenses
Retail
Clothing
Cards and Gifts
Hobby
Leisure
Dining
Lodging
Travel
Sports
Entertainment
Movies
Subscriptions
Cable TV
Internet Access
Clubs
Miscellaneous Expense
Savings
Everything Else

Table 15-3. Sample income and expense guide (continued)

Chapter 16

Experienced Retirees

Sure, I'm for helping the elderly. I'm going to be old myself some day.

—Lillian Carter (at age 85)

T HE GOOD NEWS is that Americans are living longer. But the Fountain of Youth has not yet been discovered, so we are not going to live forever. At some point, retirees need to have their financial house in order for that inevitable time when someone else will be handling their affairs, either while they are still around or after they leave this great Earth.

According to the Department of the Treasury, the average life expectancy of a 65-year-old is 86, which is about 10 years more than in 1940. Many diseases are being diagnosed earlier and treated more effectively. In addition, today's seniors are more health-conscious. They eat better, get more exercise, and smoke less than prior generations. The longevity trend is so strong that the new life insurance tables proposed by the Society of Actuaries go out to 120 years.

This chapter focuses on two critical actions that need to be taken sometime during retirement. First, retirees need to make sure all of their financial paperwork is in order. Increased longevity is great news, but it is not an excuse to put off the task of preparing a will, writing and funding trusts, ensuring the correct beneficiaries are listed on insurance policies and retirement accounts, and, most important, making a list of where everything is and important people to contact in the event of an emergency. The second critical issue is to appoint a personal helper. This is the family member or friend who will take over the responsibilities of your financial life in the event you become incapacitated and will act as the executor of your estate at death. Chose a competent, level-headed, financially responsible adult. This can be a sibling, a close relative, a trusted friend, or a professional trustee who is hired to assist you and your family in these financial affairs. Do not delay the selection until the last moment. It cannot be emphasized enough how important it is to have a competent person become knowledgeable about your financial affairs before a serious health problem develops.

Putting Your Affairs in Order

Do you and your spouse have trust and a will? Do you have a limited power of attorney signed in case someone needs to act on your behalf? If you have these documents, do you know where they are? Do you remember what they say? When was the last time you read them? Are the documents updated regularly to reflect changes in estate law? Are you sure that your assets are titled correctly and beneficiaries of your retirement accounts and insurance policies are on file with the financial institutions? If the answer to any of these questions is "No" or "I don't know," then you may have serious deficiencies in your estate plan.

I strongly recommend reviewing your documents once per year and, if needed, having an estate-planning attorney review them with you. Procrastinating could cost your estate a lot of money. Not only does the government get more of your money when you die, but the rest of your assets may go to someone you never intended. Below are a few estate-planning documents and their intended uses, but this list is far from all-inclusive. You should seek the help of an hourly-fee financial planner or an estate-planning attorney.

List Your Assets and Liabilities

Create a detailed list of everything you own and everyone you owe. How detailed? It should be detailed enough so that someone can pick it up and find everything. The list should include the locations of physical assets such as homes, other real estate, hard assets such as coins and jewelry, and account information on intangible assets including statements, contact addresses, and phone numbers (bank accounts, investment accounts, insurance policies).

I have witnessed several households where the husbands are the sole managers of the family wealth, including all investing decisions and tax payments. The wives are left out of nearly all the financial matters. Needless to say, when the husband passes away, the wife is left with piles of paper she knows nothing about. Most of the time the husband does not leave a list of assets and liabilities or any recognizable accounting system for paying taxes. Many times, life insurance policies and privately held investments are not discovered until months later when a statement for renewal comes in the mail.

Make a list of assets and liabilities now. It is a good way to greatly reduce the time and expense of settling an estate—and reduce stress for the surviving spouse and other family members.

After you list what you own, you need to identify who rightfully owns it, title the asset correctly, and decide to whom it will go after you die. Who or where assets go upon the death of the owner depends on how they are titled and what the will or trust document directs.

Assets Titled in Joint Tenancy

Assets titled in *joint tenancy with right of survivorship* (JTWROS) will go directly to the surviving owner, such as a home titled jointly between husband and wife or between father and daughter. If one dies, the property goes to the other.

This is different from *tenancy in common* (TIC), in which each joint tenant owns an undivided equal interest in the property. That means each tenant's interest in a TIC asset is subject to the wishes of his or her will or trust.

JTWROS property can have some interesting consequences, because it supersedes the direction of a will or a trust document. For example, if a father intends to give his three children equal shares in a vacation property that he owns, but the property is titled in JTWROS with only one of those children, when the father dies the other two children are out of luck, regardless of what the father's will directs. In a more serious case, children can easily get cut out of an estate in the event their mother or father remarries.

Here's an example. A man and a woman marry, each for the second time. They each have children from their first marriages but no children together. Assume the woman owns a home from her first marriage and intends to pass that property on to her children. She writes her wish into her will. Unfortunately, the property was retitled in JTWROS with her second husband. That means that if she dies before her second husband, the property transfers to the second husband and not to her children. There is nothing they can do about it, because property titled as JTWROS supersedes wills and trusts.

Wills and Trusts

If assets are not titled, such as artwork, or if they are titled in just one name, then a *will* decides where those assets will go upon death. In most states, these assets pass to a surviving spouse first, and then to the children. However, a will can direct that assets are to go to another relative or to charity when the second spouse dies, as long as the assets were not retitled jointly with another person after the first spouse died. The direction to move assets is written into the will and those wishes are carried out during the probate process. A person in his or her second marriage who wants assets to go to children from the first marriage can indicate that wish in a will, as long as the asset is not titled in joint tenancy with the new spouse. The surviving spouse usually has the right to live in the house until he or she dies or move out; it then goes to the heirs.

Another way to title assets is in the form of a trust. In the event of the owner's death, assets titled and held in the trust go directly to the beneficiary listed in the trust document, without the expense of probate. This is an efficient and affordable method for the settlement of an estate and can reduce the amount of estate tax.

The most common type of trust is called a *living trust*. In a living trust, you grant money to a trust, manage the trust assets as the trustee, and are the beneficiary of the trust while you are alive. Upon your death, the assets pass directly to the beneficiaries named in the trust document, less any estate taxes due. Sometimes, as a matter of convenience, two or more people are named as co-trustees. If you are no longer able to manage the trust or you pass away, the co-trustee can step in and ensure that the trust is managed properly.

There are three big mistakes people make with trusts. First, many trust documents are poorly written and, as a result, it is hard to discern what the owner of the assets really wanted. Second, trust laws and family situations change frequently, but trust documents are not kept up to date. Third, many people spend thousands of dollars getting trust documents written, but they never title assets in the name of the trust or direct assets to the trust upon death. This renders a trust document useless. You have to title assets in the name of the trust for it to be an effective estate-planning tool.

Just as with assets in JTWROS, assets in retirement accounts and life insurance policies pass directly to the beneficiaries named on the account contract, regardless of what a will or trust document says. It is very important to know who is the beneficiary listed on your accounts. Most people make their spouses the beneficiary of retirement accounts and insurance policies. However, do not take these issues lightly. There are tax benefits to naming children as the beneficiaries of a retirement account and a trust as the beneficiary of insurance policies. Check with your estate-planning attorney to ensure you are optimizing your beneficiary designations.

Giving Money Away

If you are lucky, at some point in life you may realize that you have accumulated more wealth than you or your spouse will ever need. At that point, you may start putting money into a separate account that you know will be passed on to someone else or to charity. I highly recommend separating this excess capital from your other assets by placing it in a separate account. That keeps your money organized in different pots for different purposes.

This extra money can be invested based on the risk and return

requirements of your heirs, rather than your risk and return requirements at the time of the gift. For example, many grandparents set up
a Uniform Gifts to Minors Act (UGMA) account (known in some
states as a Uniform Transfers to Minors Act [UTMA] account) or a 529
plan to help fund a grandchild's education. In both cases, the grandparent retains control over the investments in the account. The risk
and return of the account should be based on the child's need, not the
grandparent's need. (See Appendix A, Saving for Higher Education.)

At some point in life, you may decide to donate excess capital to
charity. There are several ways to do this, all of which will increase
your charitable tax deduction and decrease your taxes. A greater tax
deduction benefits you by increasing your after-tax income without
increasing distributions from tax-sheltered accounts like IRAs.
Depending on how you structure the gift, the money may go to charity directly or upon your death.

To donate money after you die, you can place it in a *charitable
remainder trust* (CRT). A CRT is an irrevocable trust with two sets of
beneficiaries. The first are the income beneficiaries—you and, if
married, your spouse. The income beneficiaries receive a set percentage of income from the trust as long as they live. The second beneficiaries are the charities that will receive the principal of the trust
after the income beneficiaries die. A partial tax deduction is taken
the year assets are placed in a CRT; that deduction is based on the
IRS actuarial tables and has certain limitations. The CRT assets
would be invested in part based on the risk and return needs of the
charity and in part based on your income needs.

There are lots of options for gifting. I recommend consulting an
estate attorney for complete details.

Another way to reduce taxes is through a *generation-skipping trust*
(GST) set up for grandchildren. When your parents pass away, you
may decide to decline some of your inheritance and send it on to
your children in the form of a GST. Simply set up a GST for your
children as a group, place the assets in it, and name yourself as the
trustee. Since this account is for the benefit of your children, the
assets are not included in your estate, which lowers any estate tax
due when you die. Since you are the trustee, you retain full control.

The assets in the trust should be invested based on the needs of your children, since the money will eventually go to them. Usually, that means being more aggressive. Once again, before declining an inheritance and placing the assets in a GST, be absolutely sure that you do not need the money for your own retirement. Take care of yourself and your spouse first and worry about the children's inheritance later.

Prepare the People Around You

At some point late in life, someone else will need to help you manage your affairs. That means paying your bills, making investment decisions on your behalf, and ultimately settling your estate. If you are married, your spouse would normally assume this responsibility. If not, it would be handled by a sibling, another relative, or a hired professional. I highly recommend that you choose the person far in advance, while you are still capable of managing your own affairs. Once you have chose a helper, he or she will need to become fully aware of your financial situation as early as possible, including having an understanding of your estate plan, net worth, and where everything is.

Many seniors keep important financial information secret from their children because they do not want them to know how much of the estate they will be getting or how they will get it. This creates a major obstacle for the executor, especially if that person is a surviving spouse who is not knowledgeable about finances. Also, many couples have several children and do not want to hide from one what they tell the other. I do not think it is prudent to tell all your children everything, but it is prudent to disclose everything to at least one or two children whom you choose to assist with your finances and ultimately execute your will. On the other hand, do not get more than two children deeply involved. The children who are not involved will just have to accept that what is being done is best for the family. Having dealt with trusts that have named five children as co-trustees, I can tell you that the situation quickly becomes unworkable. There can be too many opinions, too many meetings, and too many attorney hours billed.

Power of Attorney

A *power of attorney* (POA) is the legal document used to turn over control of financial accounts and other property. One should be on file in case you suddenly become incapacitated and cannot handle your affairs. Normally, a husband and wife name each other in one POA. In other cases, a responsible adult child or close friend is named. There are two types of POAs: one for property and the other for health issues. A *general* POA will allow the person named to handle financial matters. A *medical* POA will allow the person named to make medical decisions and sign medical documents. Many people have four sets of POAs on file: one for each spouse covering each other and two more naming an adult child or other person who will act as co-trustee of their property and executor of their estate.

All of these documents probably sound expensive. To save money, you can use a do-it-yourself legal program to create many documents listed in the chapter, but I do not recommend that. Don't be too naive about the computer programs. If you do decide to do it yourself, pay a qualified professional to check your documents. Legal documents are not a good place to cut corners when doing estate planning.

Investment Considerations

You have been a good manager of your wealth over the years. Your current investments are conservative, since it is not prudent to take a lot of risk in retirement. The distributions you are taking from your retirement accounts have been appropriate for your needs and tax situation. After these annual distributions, the value of your estate has kept pace with inflation and them some. Everything is working out fine.

However, everyone eventually needs help managing his or her financial affairs. That means someone else will become involved in helping you make investment decisions. Do you have a written investment policy that this person can read and follow? Nine times out of 10 there is no written investment plan, so the accounts are vulnerable to mismanagement.

When seniors invest their money, there are two types of people that they should avoid.

One type of person is obvious. These are investment con artists who push outlandish investment deals and insurance products. They invite people to "senior seminars" to explain new and unique ways in which to earn 20% interest a year with no risk. Pure logic should tell you to keep you away from these sharks. Unfortunately, many seniors do not—and every year thousands of retirees lose their life savings.

The second type of people senior investors should avoid is not nearly as obvious. These are the sons and the daughters who think they are better investors than is actually the case. These children believe they have found superior ways to manage money and convince their parents to let them have discretion over the investment decisions.

I have witnessed siblings destroy their parents' portfolios in a few years. One daughter took $100,000 in equity from the sale of her mother's home and bought a WorldCom bond. This was the only money the mother had to her name. The WorldCom bond became worthless within 12 months. In another case, a son invested 50% of his parents' wealth in one speculative biotech stock. He was a medical doctor and was convinced this particular company was going to make it big. Within a year the company was in bankruptcy and the family lost over $1,000,000.

On the other side of the coin, I have seen the transition of investment responsibility from parents to children work out very well. These children spent time to understand and follow the sound investment principles of diversification, risk avoidance, tax management, and low fees.

To help prepare your children to manage your money, prepare them for the task. Here are three steps to a successful transition:

1. Consolidate all of your investment accounts with one or two custodians, such as Charles Schwab, Vanguard, or Fidelity. This will make the transition easy and will help settle the estate when you pass away.

2. Write a detailed *investment policy statement* in your own words, describing how the money has been managed in the past and how you expect it to be managed in the future. This document should include a general asset allocation between stocks and bonds; it may get as detailed as naming specific low-cost mutual funds.

3. Insist that the person you have chosen to help manage the family money understand basic investment principles, including asset allocation and the use of index mutual funds. The best place to learn about the basics is from books. For starters, have your children read *this book!*

Hiring an Advisor

One solution to the problem of managing an investment portfolio in retirement is to hire a professional investment advisor. They exist to help you formulate an investment plan, implement it, monitor the results, and modify the portfolio when needed.

When you find a good advisor, he or she will not only ensure that the account is managed according to your specifications, but also talk with your children and educate them about proper investment principles. There is no guarantee that an advisor will get superior investment returns, but that should not be the only consideration.

Here is a partial list of the benefits of employing an advisor:

1. **An advisor helps tailor an investment plan.** Many people need help formulating an investment plan and developing the correct asset allocation for their needs. They may already have a general idea of where they want to go financially, but not the tools or expertise to put a complete plan together. A competent advisor will help clients understand how to meet their needs through index fund investing and help them implement and manage the complete investment plan.

2. **An advisor provides consistency of strategy.** On average, people switch investment strategies about every three years (as measured by Investment Company Institute mutual fund turnover statistics). Three years ago people could not buy enough growth stocks, now everyone is moving to bonds, and three years from now it will be something else. Advisors are (or

should be) more consistent. This consistency of management style will help achieve higher lifetime returns.

3. **An advisor serves as a circuit breaker.** Sometimes, when an investor wakes up in the middle of the night because of a nightmare about the markets collapsing, the advisor is there to act as a psychologist. This usually means calming the investor and talking him or her out of making an emotional investment decision.

4. **An advisor is on duty 24/7/365.** Believe it or not, there will come a time in your life when you just do not want to deal with this investment stuff anymore or can't deal with it for health reasons. Advisors are there to do the investment chores for you, day in and day out.

Investment advisors are paid an annual fee for designing, implementing, and managing a portfolio. These fees vary between 0.2% and 2.0% per year, depending on the firm you choose and the size of your portfolio.

The problem with hiring an investment advisor is that they come in all shapes, sizes, and levels of competence. You will definitely need to do some homework. I suggest checking the Vanguard Web site, where you can get information from the company on selecting a financial advisor (http://flagship2.vanguard.com/web/planret/AdvicePTHWTSeekFinancialAdvice.html).

Chapter Summary

This chapter discussed two critical issues that you must address sometime during retirement. First, make sure your financial paperwork is in order and up to date, including correct titles on accounts and correct beneficiaries. Second, appoint somebody to act as a fiduciary on your accounts in the event you become incapacitated.

The financial paperwork should include an inventory of assets, correct titling of accounts, preparing a will, creating and funding trusts, and preparing for multiple contingencies using a power of attorney when needed. Don't forget to fund the trusts. A trust that does not have assets titled in it or receives assets at your death is a useless document.

Managing a retirement portfolio gets more complicated later in life, particularly when other people get involved in your affairs. Insist that whoever helps you with your accounts be educated on the matters at hand. The best place to start is by having them read good books, such as those recommended in Appendix C.

Key Points

1. Make a list of everything you own, how it is titled, and who to contact.
2. Ensure that all legal documents are in order, including the correct beneficiaries on retirement accounts and insurance papers.
3. Select the most suitable son or daughter to assist you with your finances and disclose to that person all your financial information.
4. When you are done reading this book, pass it on to a friend.

Saving for Higher Education

Give a man a fish and you have fed him for today. Teach a man to fish and you have fed him for a lifetime.

—Chinese proverb

Money is nice, but wisdom lasts forever. A good education is the greatest gift you can give a child.

But there is one problem. Higher education is becoming prohibitively expensive. In June 2002, the Advisory Committee on Student Financial Assistance reported that 400,000 qualified high school students were unable to attend a four-year college because they could not afford it and that 170,000 of those young adults did not have enough financial aid to take classes at a community college. It is estimated that by the end of the decade, nearly two million people will be academically ready for higher education, but financially unable.

Clearly, students need their parents' support to pay college bills. That means parents must save for their children's education. That is a difficult task for middle-aged workers who pay increasingly high living expenses, a growing assortment of taxes, and the need to save for retirement. The good news is that parents have more choices than ever when it comes to saving for college. However, figuring out the best way to do it can be daunting.

Savings Habits

The best way to put money away for higher education is by starting with a small, fixed monthly allotment. Then increase that amount as a child grows. If you start putting aside just $50 per month when a child is born and then increase that amount to $100 per month when he or she reaches age 9, the account will grow to $29,000 by the time the child is 18 years old, assuming a 7% rate of return. While that amount will not put a child through Harvard, it will likely be a good start toward tuition at a state college, even adjusting for inflation.

Savings Programs

One piece of good news that came out of Washington recently was about liberal tax-free and tax-advantaged educational savings accounts. Thanks to a new generous tax law and a change in policy, there is no reason for you or your child to pay income taxes on the growth of his or her higher education fund, as long as the money is used for education. Let the buyer beware. Anything tax-free is going to be complicated. For example, if you put the wrong person's name on an account, it could have a significant impact on tax status of the account. There is much to learn and think about.

To tackle the area of saving plans, the first order of business is to understand the types of accounts that are available. Then you can decide which makes the most sense for your situation. Although all plans are designed for college expenses, some of the plans can be used for trade and professional schools. If you are looking into trade schools, it is best to contact a school to see if the program you are interested in qualifies as an institution of higher education. There are lots of ready-made savings vehicles, but some are better than others, depending on your situation. Here are a few of the popular choices.

State 529 College Savings Programs

These programs allow you to save money for higher education through state-sponsored investment accounts. The highlights of these plans are:

- Earnings and withdrawals are free from federal tax.
- You can use the funds at any college or university, in any state.
- Funds are treated as parental assets: current financial aid formulas count only 5% of parental assets when calculating a family's need figure.
- Since the account is legally in the name of the parent or guardian, the money can be transferred from one child's 529 plan to another's without a tax consequence.

529 plans are a good deal. The account can grow tax-free and you can contribute up to $250,000 in most states, regardless of income. Withdrawals to cover college expenses are never federally taxed and in many cases you can receive a state tax deduction on your contributions and still do not have to pay state taxes on the withdrawals.

What's the catch? If you want control over how the account is invested, you might find a 529 plan limited. Most college savings plans give you only a handful of mutual funds to choose from. Two low-cost plan options are sponsored by Iowa and Utah; contributions are invested in Vanguard mutual funds. For information, visit www.collegesavingsiowa.com or www.uesp.org. Another low-cost plan is in Michigan; contributions are invested in TIAA-CREF funds. For information, visit www.michigan.gov/treasury (MESP).

Improved Education IRAs

Education IRAs (EIRAs) have been around for a while and are now officially titled Coverdell Education Savings Accounts. Originally, you could contribute only a paltry $500 annually, but in 2002 the maximum jumped to $2,000 per year. Annual contributions are allowed until the college-bound child turns 18. That makes EIRAs attractive and gives you quite a nice little tax break.

Like contributions to Roth IRAs, EIRA contributions are nondeductible. EIRA earnings build up tax-free and then money can be withdrawn tax-free to pay the beneficiary's college expenses. If the beneficiary doesn't attend college or doesn't incur enough expenses to exhaust his or her account, the balance can be rolled over tax-free into another family member's EIRA. Here are the highlights of EIRAs:

- Earnings and withdrawals are federally tax-free if used to pay for college or other higher education expenses.
- You can use the funds at any college or university, in any state.
- Funds that are not used can be rolled into another child's EIRA penalty-free.

Your contributions are further limited if your adjusted gross income (AGI) is higher than the specified levels. If you are unmarried, your ability to make EIRA contributions is phased out if your AGI is between $95,000 and $110,000. If you file jointly, the phase-out range is now between $190,000 and $220,000. You cannot contribute if your AGI for the year is above $110,000 (individual) or $160,000 (joint).

Uniform Gifts to Minors Act (UGMA)

UGMAs are custodial accounts that parents can establish for a minor. (These are known in some states, with some differences, as Uniform Transfers to Minors Act [UTMA] accounts.) The account is not an educational savings account, but is often used as one. The parent gifts money to a child when placing money in a UGMA account. The parent or other person then manages the investments in the account for the benefit of the child.

There is no limit on the amount of money that can be placed in a UGMA account, but the strategy has lost favor with investors. The major reason that parents do not utilize this form more often is the fact that the child has the right to the assets at the age of majority, which varies from state to state from age 18 to 21. (Delaware and New York allow the custodianship to last to age 21.)

For children under the age of 14, another drawback is that unearned income is subject to the "kiddie tax rules." The first $750 earned will be tax-free and the second $750 will be taxed at the child's rate of 15%. All income over $1,500 is taxable at the parents' tax rate. From age 14 up, gains are taxed the same as any adult. So from a pure tax perspective, less will go to taxes if you save in your child's name.

Financial Aid

Any type of account you set up—529 plan, EIRA, or UGMA—could affect your child's eligibility for financial aid. Just how much it affects aid depends, in part, on the type of account and whether it is titled in your name, a child's name, or someone else's name. Before you begin any investment strategy, you should understand the potential financial implications of different savings and account titling options. In addition, keep in mind that schools are constantly changing how they assess financial aid, so what is true today may not be true by the time your son or daughter heads off to school.

Each year, every student applying for financial aid has to complete the U.S. Department of Education Free Application for Federal Student Aid (FAFSA). The form has the look and feel of an IRS Form 1040. You will be required to disclose everything: parent earnings, parent savings, student earnings, student savings, etc. The idea is to rate the student's need for financial aid based on the cost of the school and your ability to pay. A working mockup of this form can be found at www.finaid.org.

Generally speaking, when applying or filling out the FAFSA form, the idea is to look as poor as possible on paper, even if you are not that way in real life. That means hiding money—legally, of course. For example, you may be better off not holding assets in the student's name. That's because under the federal financial aid methodology (the criterion used by most public institutions) a student is expected to contribute just as much of his or her assets as the parents are expected to contribute.

A little-known fact is that the financial aid form does not ask for what grandparents are contributing to college costs. So, if your child is close to being entitled to financial aid, but the money you have saved is putting you out of parameters, you could consider gifting that money to your parents. Then, when the time comes, let them pay for a child's education. This reduces your net worth and may make your student eligible for financial aid. Just keep in mind, should something happen to your parents while they are in possession of the money, it goes into their estate, which may be divided up equally among heirs.

Saving While Spending? A New Gimmick

In addition to cash savings, modern technology has brought a new way to help you save a little money for college. Two companies—Upromise.com and BabyMint.com—have entered into arrangements with local and national merchants to automatically rebate a percentage of what you spend into a special savings account for college. You can let the cash account accumulate over time or you can invest it in a 529 plan for tax-free growth.

Here is how it works. Every week buy products from hundreds of companies. Those companies will rebate 1% to 5% of the amount you spend into a central college savings account set up for your family. The primary way to get this rebate is to buy those products through a credit card or grocery shopper card. Just register your cards with Upromise.com or BabyMint.com and the money flows into the account. It is not a lot of money, maybe $50 per year, unless you buy something big, like a car from General Motors. Nonetheless, the signup procedure is painless and you are going to buy from these companies anyway, so take the money!

Final Piece of Advice About Educational Savings

Here is one last piece of advice about saving for higher education. Parents should not tell children they intend to pay for school and grandparents should not tell parents they intend to pick up the cost of their grandchildren's education. Parents and grandparents can hint that they have put some money away to help students, but do not divulge the fact that you intend to pay the entire cost.

It has been my experience that a child who knows his or her parents will pay for their child's higher education makes for a lazy student. In addition, grandparents who say they will pay for their grandchild's higher education makes for a lazy student and lazy parents. It is important that both students and their parents be involved in financing higher education. Students are much more apt to seek out scholarships, fill in financial aid forms, and find a good-paying summer job if their own money is at stake. I made the mistake of telling my oldest son that I would pay for his college. He got so lazy, I had to tell him that he could keep 50% of any scholarship money he found. That made him very eager to find several scholarships— and he got a few! But of course, I never gave him a dime.

Appendix B

Web Sites for Saving and Investing

AARP (formerly American Association of Retired Persons)
www.aarp.org
AARP is a nonprofit membership organization dedicated to addressing the needs and interests of persons 50 and older.

American Savings Education Council
www.asec.org
There is a wealth of information on saving and investing here, including a great list of financial tools that complements this book very well.

Garrett Financial Planning, Inc.
www.gfponline.com
The firm specializes in providing fee-only financial planning services and investment advice to individuals and families, on an hourly, as-needed basis.

Internal Revenue Service
www.irs.gov
Tax forms, publications, and information.

Marketguide.com (Multex.com)
www.marketguide.com
The "benchmark for quality financial education"—investment information, research, and screening tools.

Morningstar, Inc.
www.morningstar.com
This company provides news and analyses on markets, stocks, and mutual funds for the individual investor. The conversation boards are a great place to find information and ask questions.

Portfolio Solutions, LLC
www.psinvest.com
The author's Web site. Portfolio Solutions, LLC, is a leading investment advisor firm specializing in low-cost passive management.

Quicken (Intuit, Inc.)
www.qfn.com
Investment, mortgage, insurance, tax, banking, and retirement information, plus quotes.

Social Security Administration
www.ssa.gov
News and information on tax withholding, obtaining a replacement card or a statement of earnings and benefits, etc.

The Vanguard Group
www.vanguard.com
One of the best places to shop for index funds, Vanguard also offers a "Planning & Advice" section that is one of the best on the Web. There is a lot of good information in the Plain Talk® investment guides.

Books About Saving and Investing

The Four Pillars of Investing: Lessons for Building a Winning Portfolio
William J. Bernstein
McGraw-Hill, 2002
An easy-to-read guide that walks you through the steps needed for investment success.

Common Sense on Mutual Funds: New Imperatives for the Intelligent Investor
John C. Bogle
John Wiley & Sons, 2000
Index fund icon shares his views in this must-read book for any index investor.

The Richest Man in Babylon
George S. Clason
Bantam Books, 1982; Signet, reissue edition, 2002
This thrift-and-savings classic is one of my favorite books for sound principles.

I'm Retiring, Now What?!
Hope Egan and Barbara Wagner
Marboro Books, 2001
An easy-to-read, smart guide to an enjoyable retirement.

All About Index Funds
Richard A. Ferri
McGraw-Hill, 2002
Soup-to-nuts guide to low-cost index investing. This book is a must!

The Millionaire in You
Michael LeBoeuf
Crown Publishing Group, 2002
The subtitle says it all: "Ten things you need to do *now* to have money and the time to enjoy it."

A Random Walk Down Wall Street
Burton G. Malkiel
W.W. Norton & Company, 7th edition, 2000
A comprehensive look at today's market and what is driving it.

Retirement Bible
Lynn O'Shaughnessy
John Wiley & Sons, 2001
A detailed guide to the ins and outs of planning a successful retirement.

The Coffeehouse Investor: How to Build Wealth, Ignore Wall Street, and Get on with Your Life
Bill Schultheis
Longstreet Press, 1998
Wonderful reading in this little classic for those who don't have time to waste.

Stocks for the Long Run
Jeremy J. Siegel
McGraw-Hill, 2002
This is another classic book, with market data going back 200 years.

Rational Investing in Irrational Times
Larry E. Swedroe
Truman Talley Books, 2002
An excellent summary of 52 investment mistakes we all make.

Appendix D

Glossary of Terms

active management An investment strategy that seeks to outperform the average returns of the financial markets. Active managers rely on research, market forecasts, and their own judgment and experience in selecting securities to buy and sell.

adjusted gross income (AGI) This is a tax term for all your income, including salary, interest, dividends, and retirement income. It is adjusted for Social Security, IRA contributions, and other items.

advisory fee The amount a mutual fund pays to its investment adviser for the work of overseeing the fund's holdings. Also called a *management fee*.

alternative minimum tax (AMT) A separate tax system designed to ensure that wealthy individuals and organizations pay at least a minimum amount of federal income taxes. Certain securities used to fund private, for-profit activities are subject to the AMT.

annualize To make a period of less than a year apply to a full year, usually for purposes of comparison. For instance, a portfolio turnover rate of 36% over a six-month period could be annualized to 72%.

annuity An investment that guarantees income payments to its owner for the owner's lifetime. When an investor buys an annuity, the growth is tax-deferred until payments begin.

asked price The price at which a security is offered for sale. For a no-load mutual fund, the asked price is the same as the fund's net asset value (NAV) per share. Also called *offering price*.

automatic reinvestment An arrangement by which the dividends or other earnings from an investment are used to buy additional shares in the investment vehicle.

average coupon The average interest rate (coupon rate) of all bonds in a portfolio.

average effective maturity A weighted average of the maturity dates for all securities in a money market or bond fund. (The maturity date is the date that a money market instrument or bond buyer will be repaid by the security's issuer.) The longer the average maturity, the more a fund's share price will move up or down in response to changes in interest rates.

back-end load A sales fee charged by some mutual funds when an investor sells fund shares. Also called a *contingent deferred sales charge*.

benchmark index An index that correlates with a fund, used to measure a fund manager's performance.

beneficiary The person named to receive the life insurance settlement or the remaining portion of a retirement account, such as an IRA, at the time of your death.

beta (β) A measure of the magnitude of a portfolio's past share-price fluctuations in relation to the ups and downs of the overall market (or appropriate market index). The market (or index) is assigned a beta of 1.00, so a portfolio with a beta of 1.20 would have seen its share price rise or fall by 12% when the overall market rose or fell by 10%.

bid-ask spread The difference between what a buyer is willing to bid (pay) for a security and the seller's ask (offer) price.

blue-chip stocks Common stock of well-known companies with a history of growth and dividend payments.

book value A company's assets, minus any liabilities and intangible assets.

broker/broker-dealer An individual or firm that buys or sells mutual funds or other securities for the public.

capital gain/loss The difference between the sale price of an asset—such as a mutual fund, stock, or bond—and the original cost of the asset.

capital gains distributions Payments to mutual fund shareholders of gains realized during the year on securities that the fund has sold at a profit, minus any losses realized.

capitalization See *market capitalization*.

cash investments Short-term debt instruments—such as commercial paper, banker's acceptances, and Treasury bills—that mature in less than one year. Also known as *money market instruments* or *cash reserves*.

Certified Financial Planner® (CFP®) An investment professional who has passed exams administered by the CFP Board of Standards on subjects such as taxes, securities, insurance, and estate planning.

Certified Public Accountant (CPA) An investment professional who is state licensed to practice public accounting.

Chartered Financial Analyst (CFA) An investment professional who has met competency standards in economics, securities, portfolio management, and financial accounting as determined by the Institute of Chartered Financial Analysts.

closed-end fund A mutual fund that has a fixed number of shares, usually listed on a major stock exchange.

Cloverdell Education Savings Account An Individual Retirement Account formerly called an *education IRA (EIRA)*, created by the Taxpayer Relief Act of 1997.

Consumer Price Index (CPI) A measure of the price change in consumer goods and services. The CPI is used to track the pace of inflation.

contingent deferred sales charge See *back-end load*.

contributory IRA An Individual Retirement Account into which an investor makes yearly contributions.

cost basis The original cost of an investment. For tax purposes, the cost basis is subtracted from the sales price to determine any capital gain or loss.

cost of living adjustment (COLA) An annual, predetermined increase in retirement benefits from a defined contribution plan or Social Security increase, usually based on the Consumer Price Index (CPI).

country risk The possibility that political events (a war, national elections), financial problems (rising inflation, government default), or natural disasters (an earthquake, a poor harvest) will weaken a country's economy and cause investments in that country to decline.

coupon/coupon rate The interest rate that a bond issuer promises to pay the bondholder until the bond matures.

credit rating A published ranking, based on a careful financial analysis, of a creditor's ability to pay interest or principal owed on a debt.

credit risk The possibility that a bond issuer will fail to repay interest and principal in a timely manner. Also called *default risk*.

currency risk The possibility that returns could be reduced for Americans investing in foreign securities, because of a rise in the value of the U.S. dollar against foreign currencies. Also called *exchange rate risk*.

custodian A bank, agent, trust company, or other organization responsible for safeguarding financial assets or the individual who oversees the mutual fund assets of a minor's custodial account.

declaration date The date on which the board of directors of a company or mutual fund announces the amount and date of its next dividend payment.

default Failure to pay principal or interest when due.

default risk See *credit risk.*

defined benefit plan A retirement plan that pays employees an annuity each month after they retire, for life. The annuity may or may not have a cost of living adjustment (COLA).

depreciation A decrease in the value of an investment.

derivative A financial contract whose value is based on ("derived" from) a traditional security (such as a stock or bond), an asset (such as a commodity), or a market index (such as the S&P 500 Index).

discount broker A brokerage that executes orders to buy and sell securities at commission rates lower than a full-service brokerage.

distributions Withdrawals made by the owner from an Individual Retirement Account (IRA) or payments of dividends and/or capital gains by a mutual fund.

dividend reinvestment plan (DRIP) The automatic reinvestment of shareholder dividends in more shares of the company's stock.

dividend yield The annual rate of return on a share of stock, determined by dividing the annual dividend by its current share price. In a stock mutual fund, this figure represents the average dividend yield of the stocks held by the fund.

dollar-cost averaging Investing equal amounts of money at regular intervals on an ongoing basis. This technique ensures that an investor buys fewer shares when prices are high and more shares when prices are low.

early retirement Retirement prior to age 62, when a person is eligible for Social Security benefits.

earnings per share A company's earnings divided by the number of common shares outstanding.

education IRA (EIRA) An Individual Retirement Account, now called a *Cloverdell Education Savings Account,* created by the Taxpayer Relief Act of 1997.

efficient market The theory—disputed by some experts—that stock prices reflect all market information that is known by all investors. Also states that investors cannot beat the market because it is impossible to determine future stock prices.

equivalent taxable yield The yield needed from a taxable bond to give the same after-tax yield as a tax-exempt issue.

exchange privilege The shareholder's ability to move money from one mutual fund to another within the same fund family, often without additional charge.

exchange rate risk See *currency risk.*

exchange-traded fund An index fund that trades on the stock market. Some common ETFs are the NASDAQ-100 Index Tracking Stock (QQQ), which tracks the NASDAQ-100, and Standard & Poor's Depositary Receipts (SPY), which tracks the S&P 500.

ex-dividend date The date on which a distribution of dividends and/or capital gains is deducted from a mutual fund's assets or set aside for payment to shareholders. On the ex-dividend date, the fund's share price drops by the amount of the distribution (plus or minus any market activity). Also known as the *reinvestment date.*

executor The person responsible for settling an estate.

expense ratio The percentage of a portfolio's average net assets used to pay its annual expenses. The expense ratio—which includes management fees, administrative fees, and any 12b-1 fees—directly reduces returns to investors.

Federal Reserve System The central bank that regulates the supply of money and credit throughout the United States. The Fed's seven-member board of governors, nominated by the President and confirmed by the Senate, has significant influence on U.S. monetary and economic policy.

fee-only advisor An arrangement in which a financial advisor charges a set hourly rate or a percentage of assets under management for a financial plan.

first in, first out (FIFO) A method for calculating taxable gain or loss when mutual fund shares are sold. The FIFO method assumes that the first shares sold were the first shares purchased.

front-end load A sales commission charged at the time of purchase by some mutual funds and other investment vehicles.

full faith and credit A pledge to pay interest and principal on a bond issued by the government.

full retirement age The age at which a person is entitled receive full Social Security benefits, between 65 and 67, according to year of birth.

fundamental analysis A method of examining a company's financial statements and operations as a means of forecasting stock price movements.

fund family A group of mutual funds sponsored by the same organization, often offering exchange privileges between funds and combined account statements for multiple funds.

global fund A mutual fund that invests in stocks of companies in the U.S. and foreign countries.

Gross Domestic Product (GDP) The value of all goods and services provided by U.S. labor in a given year, formerly known as the Gross National Product (GNP). One of the primary measures of the U.S. economy, the GDP is issued quarterly by the Department of Commerce.

hedge A strategy in which one investment is used to offset the risk of another investment.

high-yield fund A mutual fund that invests primarily in bonds with a credit rating of BB or lower. Because of the speculative nature of high-yield bonds, high-yield funds are subject to greater share price volatility and greater credit risk than other types of bond funds.

indexing An investment strategy to match the average performance of a market or group of stocks. Usually this is accomplished by buying a small amount of each stock in a market.

index provider A company that constructs and maintains stock and bond indexes. The main providers are Standard & Poor's, Dow Jones, Lehman Brothers, Morgan Stanley, Russell, and Wilshire.

inflation risk The possibility that increases in the cost of living will reduce or eliminate the returns on a particular investment.

interest rate risk The possibility that a security or mutual fund will decline in value because of an increase in interest rates.

international fund A mutual fund that invests in securities traded in markets outside of the U.S. Foreign markets present additional risks, including currency fluctuation and political instability. In the past, these risks have made prices of foreign stocks more volatile than those of U.S. stocks.

investment advisor A person or organization that makes the day-to-day decisions regarding a portfolio's investments. Also called a *portfolio manager*.

investment grade The rating of a bond whose credit quality is considered to be among the highest by independent bond-rating agencies.

junk bond A bond with a credit rating of BB or lower. Also known as *high-yield* because of the rewards offered to those willing to take the additional risk of a lower-quality bond.

large-cap A company whose stock market value is generally in excess of $10 billion, although the range varies according to the index provider.

liquidity The degree of a security's marketability, how quickly the security can be sold at a fair price and converted to cash.

living trust A legal arrangement that allows assets to pass directly to heirs without going through the probate process. Assets in a living trust are subject to estate tax.

load fund A mutual fund that levies a sales charge, either when shares are bought (a *front-end load*) or when shares are sold (a *back-end load*).

long-term capital gain A profit on the sale of a security or mutual fund share that has been held for more than one year.

long-term care insurance A health insurance policy that covers the costs that traditional health insurance and Medicare do not, such as an extended stay in a nursing home and home care assistance.

management fee The amount a mutual fund pays to its investment adviser for the work of overseeing the fund's holdings. Also called an *advisory fee*.

market capitalization A determination of a company's value, calculated by multiplying the total number of company stock shares outstanding by the price per share. Also called *capitalization*.

maturity/maturity date The date on which the issuer of a money market instrument or bond has agreed to repay the principal, or face value, to the buyer.

median market cap The midpoint of market capitalization (market price multiplied by the number of shares outstanding) of the stocks in a portfolio. Half the stocks in the portfolio will have a higher market capitalization and half will have lower.

Medicaid Government health insurance that provides free coverage for low-income people of any age.

Medicare Government health insurance program for people age 65 and over at little or no cost. It does not include prescription drugs or routine doctor visits.

Medigap insurance A supplemental insurance policy that provides health care services not covered by Medicare.

mid-cap A company whose stock market value is between $2 billion and $10 billion, although the range varies according to the index provider.

money market instruments Short-term debt instruments—such as commercial paper, banker's acceptances, and Treasury bills—that mature in less than one year. Also known as *cash investments* or *cash reserves*.

municipal bond fund A mutual fund that invests in tax-exempt bonds issued by state, city, and/or local governments. The interest obtained from these bonds is passed through to shareholders and is generally free of federal (and sometimes state and local) income taxes.

NASD An organization of brokers and dealers designed to protect the investing public against fraudulent acts, formerly known as *National Association of Securities Dealers*.

net asset value (NAV) The market value of a mutual fund's total assets, minus liabilities, divided by the number of shares outstanding. The value of a single share is called its *share value* or *share price*.

no-load fund A mutual fund that charges no sales commission (load).

nominal return The return on an investment before adjustment for inflation.

offering price The price at which a security is offered for sale. For a no-load mutual fund, the offering price is the same as the fund's net asset value (NAV) per share. Also called *asked price.*

open-end fund An investment entity that has the ability to issue or redeem the number of share outstanding on a daily basis. Prices are quoted once per day, at the end of the day, at the net asset value (NAV) of the fund.

operating expenses The amount paid for asset maintenance or the cost of doing business. Earnings are distributed after operating expenses are deducted.

option A contract in which a seller gives a buyer the right, but not the obligation, to buy or sell securities at a specified price on or before a given date.

payable date The date on which dividends or capital gains are paid to shareholders. For mutual funds, the payable date is usually within two to four days of the record date. The payable date also refers to the date on which a declared stock dividend or bond interest payment is scheduled to be paid.

portfolio manager A person or organization that makes the day-to-day decisions regarding a portfolio's investments. Also called an *investment advisor.*

portfolio transaction costs The expenses associated with buying and selling securities, including commissions, purchase and redemption fees, exchange fees, and miscellaneous costs, but not the bid/ask spread. In a mutual fund prospectus, these expenses would be listed separately from the fund's expense ratio.

power of attorney A written, legally binding document that gives a person the right to make financial or health care decisions for a specified person.

premium An amount that exceeds the face value or redemption value of a security or of a comparable security or group of investments. It may indicate that a security is favored highly by investors. Also, a fee for obtaining insurance coverage.

price/book ratio The price per share of a stock divided by its book value (i.e., net worth) per share. For a portfolio, the ratio is the weighted average price/book ratio of the stocks it holds.

price/earnings (P/E) ratio The share price of a stock divided by its per-share earnings over the past year. For a portfolio, the weighted average P/E ratio of the stocks in the portfolio. The P/E is a good indicator of market expectations about a company's prospects: the higher the P/E, the greater the expectations for a company's future growth in earnings.

prospectus A legal document that gives prospective investors information about a mutual fund, including discussions of its investment objectives and policies, risks, costs, and past performance. A prospectus must be provided to a potential investor before he or she can establish an account and must also be filed with the Securities and Exchange Commission.

proxy Written authorization by a shareholder giving a person or an entity (such as fund or company management) authority to represent his or her vote at a shareholder meeting.

real estate investment trust (REIT) A company that manages a group of real estate investments and distributes to its shareholders at least 95% of its net earnings annually. REITs often specialize in a particular kind of property or transaction. They may, for example, invest in real estate (such as office buildings, shopping centers, or hotels), purchase real estate (an equity REIT), or provide loans to building developers (a mortgage REIT).

real return The actual return received on an investment after factoring in inflation. For example, if the nominal investment return was 8% and inflation was 3%, the real return would be 5%.

record date The date used to determine who is eligible to receive a company's or fund's next distribution of dividends or capital gains.

redemption The return of an investor's principal in a security. Bonds can be redeemed at or before maturity; mutual fund shares are redeemed at net asset value when an investor's holdings are liquidated.

redemption fee A fee charged by some mutual funds when an investor sells shares within a short period of time.

registered investment advisor (RIA) An investment professional who is registered—but not endorsed—by the Securities and Exchange Commission (SEC) and who may recommend certain types of investment products.

reinvestment Use of investment income to buy additional securities. Many mutual fund companies and investment services offer the automatic reinvestment of dividends and capital gains distributions as an option to investors.

reinvestment date The date on which a distribution of dividends and/or capital gains is deducted from a mutual fund's assets or set aside for payment to shareholders. On the reinvestment date, the fund's share price drops by the amount of the distribution (plus or minus any market activity). Also known as the *ex-dividend date*.

REIT See *real estate investment trust*.

required minimum distribution The minimum amount the IRS mandates that you withdraw from IRAs and other tax-deferred retirement funds once you reach age 70½.

required rate of return The minimum return needed on an investment portfolio to achieve a financial goal within a stated amount of time.

return of capital A distribution that is not paid out of earnings and profits.

risk tolerance An investor's ability or willingness to endure declines in the prices of investments while waiting for them to increase in value.

rollover Transaction by which an employee at retirement or end of service may move his or her portion of a pension account into an IRA without paying current income taxes or penalty.

rollover IRA An IRA created by rolling over funds from your company's tax-deferred retirement plan when you leave your job. It's the only time you can put more than the annual limit into an IRA.

Roth IRA An individual retirement account that is funded with after-tax dollars that grow tax-free until money is withdrawn tax-free after age 59½.

R-squared A measure of how much of a portfolio's performance can be explained by the returns from the overall market (or a benchmark index). If a portfolio's total return precisely matched that of the overall market or benchmark, its R-squared would be 1.00. If a portfolio's return bore no relationship to the market's returns, its R-squared would be 0.

sector fund A mutual fund that concentrates on a relatively narrow market sector. These funds can experience higher share-price volatility than some diversified funds, because sector funds are subject to issues specific to a given sector.

Securities and Exchange Commission (SEC) The agency of the federal government that regulates mutual funds, registered investment advisors, the stock and bond markets, and broker-dealers.

Sharpe ratio A measure of risk-adjusted return. To calculate a Sharpe ratio, an asset's excess return (its return in excess of the return generated by risk-free assets such as Treasury bills) is divided by the asset's standard deviation. A Sharpe ratio can be calculated in terms of a benchmark or an index.

short-term capital gain A profit on the sale of a security or mutual fund share that has been held for one year or less. A short-term capital gain is taxed as ordinary income.

small-cap A company whose stock market value is less than $2 billion, although the range varies according to the index provider.

spread For stocks and bonds, the difference between the bid price and the asked price.

standard deviation (σ) A measure of the degree to which a fund's return varies from its previous returns or from the average of all similar funds. The larger the standard deviation, the greater the likelihood (and risk) that a security's performance will fluctuate from the average return.

survivor rights The rights of a surviving beneficiary to receive benefits or the rights of a joint tenant with right of survivorship to take possession of the jointly titled asset.

taxable account An account subject to ordinary income tax each year, such as personal accounts, joint accounts, trusts, and custodial accounts.

taxable equivalent yield The return from a higher-paying but taxable investment that would equal the return from a tax-free investment, depending on the investor's tax bracket.

tax credit An expense incurred that allows you to reduce your tax bill by the same amount, such as a $600 tax credit for each child under the age of 17.

tax-deferred account An account for which payment of income taxes is delayed. For example, owners of traditional IRAs do not pay income taxes on the interest, dividends, or capital gains accumulating in their accounts until they begin withdrawing.

tax-exempt bond A bond, usually issued by municipal, county, or state governments, whose interest payments are not subject to federal and, in some cases, state and local income tax.

tax-free account An account from which all interest, dividends, and capital gains are not subject to income tax now or in the future. An example is a Roth IRA.

tax swapping Creating a tax loss by the simultaneous sale of one index fund and purchase of a similar fund.

total return A percentage change, over a specified period, in a mutual fund's net asset value, with the ending net asset value adjusted to account for the reinvestment of all distributions of dividends and capital gains.

transaction fee/commission A charge assessed by an intermediary, such as a broker-dealer or a bank, for assisting in the sale or purchase of a security.

Treasury security A negotiable debt obligation issued by the U.S. government for a specific amount and maturity. Treasury securities include bills (one year or less), notes (one to 10 years), and bonds (over 10 years).

trust A term used to describe a wide range of vehicles used to own property. A trust can be used when a person wants to put restrictions or controls on property during and after death. Trusts do not reduce income taxes, but can reduce estate taxes.

turnover rate An indication of trading activity during the past year. Portfolios with high turnover rates incur higher transaction costs and are more likely to distribute capital gains (which are taxable to non-retirement accounts).

12b-1 fee An annual fee charged by some mutual funds to pay for marketing and distribution activities. The fee is taken directly from fund assets, which reduces a shareholder's return.

unit investment trust (UIT) An SEC-registered investment company that purchases a fixed, unmanaged portfolio of income-producing securities and then sells shares in the trust to investors, usually through intermediaries such as brokers and usually in units of at least $1,000.

unrealized capital gain/loss An increase/decrease in the value of a security that is not "real" because the security has not been sold. When the portfolio manager sells the security, the fund "realizes" the capital gain/loss and any payment to the shareholder is taxable during the tax year in which the security was sold.

volatility The degree of fluctuation in the value of a security, a mutual fund, or an index. Volatility is often expressed as a mathematical measure such as a standard deviation or beta. The greater a fund's volatility, the wider the fluctuations between its high and low prices.

wash sale rule The IRS regulation that prohibits a taxpayer from claiming a loss on the sale of an investment if the taxpayer purchases that investment or a substantially identical investment within 30 days before or after the sale.

will The basic estate planning document for controlling the distribution of various assets after death.

Yankee dollars/bonds Debt obligations, such as bonds or certificates of deposit bearing U.S. dollar denominations, issued in the U.S. by foreign banks and corporations.

yield curve A line plotted on a graph that depicts the yields of bonds of varying maturities, from short term to long term. The line (curve) shows the relationship between short- and long-term interest rates.

yield to maturity The rate of return an investor would receive if the securities held by a portfolio were held to their maturity dates.

Index

Personal liability of stockholders, 119
Personal savings accounts, 116
Pooled investment accounts, 19
Poor performance, evaluating,
 20–26. *See also* Rate of return
"Portable" retirement plans, 6
"Portfolio Selection," 186
*Portfolio Selection: Efficient
 Diversification of Investments*
 (Markowitz, Harry), 186
Positive correlation, 190–191
Power of attorney, 275
Precious metals, 46. *See also* Gold
Predictions. *See* Forecasting markets
Pre-retirement period
 planning issues, 251–256
 six-step program, 242–251
Pre-tax savings
 defined, 105
 recommended rates, 12–14
 weighing benefits of, 203–204
Price volatility, 43, 175–176. *See
 also* Risk
Priming the pump, 95–96
Principia database, 91
Prospectuses, 123
Provisional income, 252
Public employee plans, 108–109
Pure no-load funds, 75–76
Putnam fund closures/mergers, 95

Q
Questionnaires, risk tolerance, 211,
 220–221
Quill, Gavin, 50–51

R
Random results, false patterns in, 25
Random Walk Down Wall Street, A
 (Malkiel, Burton G.), 291
Rate of return. *See also* Forecasting
 markets
 actively managed versus index
 funds, 125–130
 adjusting for inflation, 174

computing for retirement planning, 228, 233–235, 249
evaluating poor performance,
 20–26
impact of fees on, 21, 27, 71–76,
 80
importance, 16–17
overall performance record, 17–20
quantifying with risk, 186–190
reasonable expectations, 14,
 234–235
reporting methods, 62–63
savings rate versus, 206–208
Rational Investing in Irrational Times
 (Swedroe, Larry E.), 26, 291
Real estate investment trust (REIT)
 funds, 134
Rebalancing
 benefits of, 189–190, 217–218
 in stress test, 212
Rebates, 286
Recessions, relation to bear markets,
 31
*Reinventing Retirement Income in
 America* (Hamilton, Brooks, and
 Burns, Scott), 18
Rental income, 163–164
Reporting techniques for mutual
 funds, 92–97
Research analysts, 83
Restricted stock awards, 161–162
Retirement
 beginning, 256–258
 benefits of, 3–4
 estate planning, 269–274
 investment during, 258–263,
 275–278
 late-life assistance, 274–278
 questions to guide planning,
 13–15
Retirement accounts. *See also*
 Retirement plans
 basic types, 7–9

"Turmoil 2001" report, 45–46
Turnover of funds
    as disadvantage of active management, 129–130
    excessive, 20, 51–53, 59

U

Uniform Gifts to Minors Act accounts, 273, 284–285
Unit benefit plans, 156
Upromise.com, 286

V

Vacation property, 166
Value stocks
    growth stock performance versus, 57–60, 64–65
    selected mutual funds, 134
Vanguard 500 Index Fund
    defined, 125
    investor returns versus, 50, 51
    performance data, 127–129
Vanguard Group
    bond index funds, 148–149
    foreign stock index funds, 133
    low expenses, 73, 77
    municipal bond funds, 217
    total market fund, 132

Variable annuities
    fees and expenses with, 78, 115
    when to invest in, 115–116, 118
Variable benefit plans, 156
Vesting restrictions, 160, 161, 202
Vice presidents, 84–85
Vietnam War, and stock market, 37
Volatility, 43, 175–176, 188

W

Wade Cook Financial Corporation, 89–90
Wagner, Barbara, 290
Weitz, Roy, 126
Wills, 271
Wilshire 5000 index, 131
Withdrawal rate, recommended, 14, 259–260
Written investment policies
    for early savers, 217
    for midlife savers, 239
    for retirees, 275, 277
Wu, Joanna Shuang, 92

Y

Yankee bonds, 142
Yield to maturity, of bonds, 137

Z

Zweig, Jason, 51

About the Author

Richard A. Ferri earned a bachelor of science degree in business administration from the University of Rhode Island in 1980. Following college, he served for eight years as a U.S. Marine Corps officer and fighter pilot and retired from the military reserves in 2001. In 1988, Ferri entered the investment field as a stockbroker with a major Wall Street firm. After battling in the trenches of commission sales for 10 years, Ferri founded Portfolio Solutions, LLC, a fee-only investment advisor firm. His company manages several hundred million dollars for individuals, high-net-worth families, foundations, and corporate pension plans. Ferri has earned the designation of Chartered Financial Analyst (CFA) offered through the Association of Investment Management and Research (AIMR) and also holds a master of science degree in finance from Walsh College in Troy, Michigan. Ferri also serves as an adjunct professor of finance at Walsh.

In March 2000, Ferri self-published his first book, *Serious Money: Straight Talk About Investing for Retirement*. His second popular book, *All About Index Funds* (McGraw-Hill, 2002), is essential reading for all mutual fund investors. Ferri also writes for several investment magazines, industry journals, and investment Web sites. He has been quoted in several major financial publications, including *The Wall Street Journal*, *Money*, *Barron's*, *Investor's Business Daily*, Reuters News Service, and *Kiplinger's*.